THE BATTLE
WITH
THE SLUM

Jacob A. Riis

With Photographs by the Author

DOVER PUBLICATIONS, INC.
Mineola, New York

363.5
Rii

1/00

Copyright

Bibliographical Note

This Dover edition, first published in 1998, is an unabridged republication of the work published by The Macmillan Company, New York and London, 1902. A new introduction and new footnotes are included.

Library of Congress Cataloging-in-Publication Data

Riis, Jacob A. (Jacob August), 1849–1914.
    The battle with the slum / Jacob A. Riis ; illustrated with photographs by the author.
        p.   cm.
    Originally published: New York : Macmillan, 1902. With new introd.
    Includes index.
    ISBN 0-486-40196-0 (pbk.)
    1. Poor.   2. Poor—New York (State)—New York.   3. Tenement houses—New York (State)—New York.   I. Title. ② Landlord and tenant
HV4046.N6R5   1998
305.569'09747'1—dc21   98-10020
                                                         CIP
③ Discrimination in housing
④ City planning ⑤ Labor—housing

PREFACE

Three years ago I published under the title *A Ten Years' War* a series of papers intended to account for the battle with the slum since I wrote *How the Other Half Lives*. A good many things can happen in three years. So many things have happened in these three, the fighting has been so general all along the line and has so held public attention, that this seems the proper time to pass it all in review once more. That I have tried to do in this book, retaining all that still applied of the old volume and adding as much more. The "stories"† were printed in the *Century Magazine*. They are fact, not fiction. If the latter, they would have no place here.

The Battle With the Slum is properly the sequel to *How the Other Half Lives*, and tells how far we have come and how. "With his usual hopefulness," I read in the annals of the American Academy of Political and Social Science of my book three years ago, "the author is still looking forward to better things in the future." I was not deceived then. Not in the thirty years before did we advance as in these three, though Tammany blocked the way most of the time. It is great to have lived in a day that sees such things done.

J. A. R.

Richmond Hill,
August 27, 1902

†The chapters "Jim" and "The Passing of Cat Alley."

iii

Theodore Roosevelt
a valiant battler with the slum

CONTENTS

LIST OF ILLUSTRATIONS

INTRODUCTION

Jacob A. Riis (1849–1914), an immigrant from Denmark, achieved fame exposing shameful slum conditions and advocating social reform as a journalist in New York City. He was a reporter for the *New York Tribune* (1877–88) and the *New York Evening Sun* (1888–99), much of that time specializing in police reporting on the Lower East Side of Manhattan. In 1888, to enhance his reporting, he began taking photographs of people and places on his "beat," using the new technique of flash photography. Many of the images Riis preserved—some of which are among the more than 90 illustrations in *The Battle With the Slum*—have become emblematic of the social reform efforts of the times.

In the book's preface, Riis alludes to a "collection of papers" he published (in 1900) as *A Ten Years' War*. Eight of those papers became chapters in *The Battle With the Slum*. Nine more chapters (plus an introductory section and an index) were added to cover the exceptionally active 1900–1902 period of political and social reform. For the 1998 edition, new footnotes (preceded by a dagger symbol; Riis's original footnotes are numbered) have been added to identify people, places, and events familiar in Riis's time.

When *The Battle With the Slum* first was published, in 1902, New York City was in a ferment of political and social change, much of it involving considerable conflict. On January 1, 1898, in accordance with an act of the state legislature, Greater New York had come into being, uniting five diverse "boroughs" as the new New York City. (Prior to 1874, New York City had consisted of Manhattan alone. In that year, part of what is now the west Bronx had been annexed from Westchester County.) The 1898 consolidation joined to that nucleus the populous city of Brooklyn, dozens of villages and towns in Queens County, and largely rural Staten Island. After a brief reform era under Republican mayor William L. Strong, elected in 1894, the corrupt Tammany organization that controlled the Democratic Party in New York City had elected its last mayor, Robert A. Van Wyck, in 1897. He took office in 1898, as the advent of Greater New York added Brooklyn's substantial municipal treasury to the New York City revenues to be plundered. (The formation of Greater New York, decided by the Republican-controlled state legislature, also added numerous Republicans to the City's voter rolls.)

In 1901, multimillionaire industrialist Andrew Carnegie had offered The New York Public Library (then consisting only of research collections; the foundation was laid in 1900 for what is now known as the Central Research Library, at Fifth Avenue from Fortieth to Forty-second Street) a gift of $5.2 million to build 65 branch libraries to lend books to the public, if New York City would provide the sites and pledge to maintain the buildings. By the end of 1905 seventeen public libraries were lending books. One of them had a reading room in a roof garden. Branch libraries such as Chatham Square, Hamilton Fish Park, Seward Park, and Tompkins Square are part of the living legacy of social reform on the east side of Manhattan below Fourteenth Street.

As Riis mentions in *The Battle With the Slum*, by 1902 crucial improvements in public transportation were enabling people to leave crowded slums to live in less-populated parts of the newly expanded city and commute to jobs in Manhattan's business districts. The book was published midway between the start (in March 1900) of excavations for New York City's first electric subway line, and the opening (in October 1904) of the first Interborough Rapid Transit (IRT) line, which extended from City Hall to 145th Street. Subway service, at first privately operated but later City-owned, had been delayed for decades by wealthy men who had major financial interests in the existing horse-drawn streetcars and elevated railways, and the New York Central Railroad.

As Riis reports, the greedy, callous Tammany Hall leaders of the Democratic Party were responsible in large part for the perpetuation of slum conditions in Manhattan. While buying immigrants' votes with liquor, jobs, and favors, they accepted bribes from landlords and businessmen to overlook violations of the law, and they filled City agencies with incompetent and dishonest men who were rewarded only for loyalty to Tammany. Most slum landlords were wealthy *before* they made "killings" (literally) from tenement rents. While New York City was controlled by corrupt Democratic politicians for decades, New York State was controlled by Republicans beholden to financiers, industrialists, and merchants. Slum battlers made some progress during Mayor William L. Strong's term (1895–1897), but lost ground rapidly during Tammany's last orgy of profiteering from the public treasury, 1898–1901. (The mayor's term of office changed from three years to four, when Greater New York was formed.)

In 1902 the longtime Tammany boss, Richard Croker, was about to retire to Ireland. Seth Low, a reform Democrat who was a former mayor of Brooklyn (1881–85) and president of Columbia University (1890–1901), was mayor of New York City. Benjamin O'Dell was governor of New York State (1901–1904) and Theodore Roosevelt, a Republican who had served as the very active anti-corruption president of New York City's police commission from 1895 to 1897 after declining to run for Mayor in 1894, was president of the United States. Riis admired Roosevelt's courage and energy in "cleaning up" a corrupt police force. Roosevelt had been governor of New York State, 1899–1900, during the "to hell with reform" Tammany administration in New York City that Riis vocally opposed. Republican Party state boss and U.S. Senator Thomas Platt, who could not control the independent Roosevelt, had arranged his nomination as Republican candidate for vice president in 1900, to remove him from New York State politics. When President William McKinley was assassinated in 1901, early in his second term, Roosevelt had become president.

After the Civil War, industrial monopolies had enormously changed the landscape, the locations and conditions of people's homes and workplaces, and the economic and social class structure of the United States. After 1880, especially, immigration from southern and eastern Europe had increased hugely. Social and political reform mainly was engaged in by wealthy men (and sometimes, in terms of "charitable" activities or "social work" considered to be separate from politics, by their wives). It was not considered the responsibility of the municipal government to provide what now is referred to as a "social safety net" for people who, for various reasons, were unable to earn an income sufficient to provide adequate food, clothing, and shelter. Although some beginnings had been made, with the establishment of settlement houses, for example, relatively few not-for-profit organizations functioned with a broad base of middle-class supporters. Settlement houses were designed to bring college-educated, middle-class people into the slums to live among the residents and work *with* them to improve conditions and develop thriving communities. Riis pointed out that slum dwellers should not be viewed as needy recipients of charity, but rather as people who have the ideas, energy, and motivation to better their lot, and have much to teach those who wish to help them.

At the turn of the century the majority of Manhattan's population still lived below Fourteenth Street—and the majority was poor. Two factors defined housing and working conditions in the slum areas: tenements and the "sweating" system. The word "tenement" denotes nothing more than a building in which separate dwellings are rented, but even before the Civil War it had the connotation of an apartment building with conditions inimical to happy or healthful living. The "sweating" system meant having production and assembly work done by workers in their (tenement) homes, and paying the workers by the piece at very low rates. Riis spotlighted the destructive effects on health and on family life of using the already dark, crowded, poorly ventilated, unsanitary tenement rooms as factories or workshops—and the danger to consumers, as tuberculosis and other infectious diseases could be transmitted by products made or processed at home.

The vast majority who lived in squalid tenements were immigrants or their children. Virtually all of the others were African Americans who remained trapped in the worst tenements because of racial prejudice when successive immigrant ethnic groups moved into better housing. Riis, an immigrant himself who never attended college, was free of some prevalent prejudices, such as considering immigrants not from northern Europe to be a lower order of human being. He believed that civic pride and patriotism—based on a sense of belonging, and respect for self and others—could cure the social ills bred in slums. He seemed to think that most self-defeating and socially destructive behavior was caused by nurture (environmental conditions) rather than nature (intellectual or moral inferiority). Riis recognized that slum dwellers—as voters, parents, city workers, citizen activists, and even elected officials—could change their own living conditions and society in general, but he did not link this potential to women's gaining the right to vote, which occurred in 1920, after Riis's death. He focused on male slum dwellers' problems, though he thought women had a morally uplifting influence. Riis continually referred to the needs of "the boy" for public education and recreational opportunities, barely mentioning girls' experience in the home, on the street, and in school.

At least four issues deeply important to Riis in the 1880s

and 1890s were controversial—again or still—in New York City during the 1980s and 1990s. These were: access to public schools as sites of cultural and social activities sponsored by community groups; providing public parks (including along shorelines) for all to enjoy natural beauty and recreational facilities; operating subsidized after-school programs in all public elementary schools daily; and preserving community gardens on the Lower East Side (Loísaida to Puerto Rican residents) and throughout Manhattan, on City-owned lots.

Jacob A. Riis exposed and helped *change* the tenement-based slum system in which people with few material resources were exploited. His best-known book continues to be *How the Other Half Lives* (1890). Riis was a sought-after lecturer who used slides to sharpen the impact of his words. Before he, by chance, became a newspaper reporter in 1873, Riis was homeless and hungry in Lower Manhattan. By the late 1880s he was a respected citizen who still moved freely in the tenement districts he knew so well, though he lived with his family in bucolic Richmond Hill, Queens County. Not a radical "muckraker," Riis avoided political involvement, hoping to aid the urban poor through the force of public opinion. His memory is honored in New York City by the Jacob Riis Community School (P.S./I.S. 126), a self-described "multicultural" public school on the Lower East Side; Jacob A. Riis Park, a beach and recreation area on the Rockaway Peninsula in Queens, opened in 1937 and now part of Gateway National Recreation Area; and the Jacob A. Riis Neighborhood Settlement House in Long Island City, Queens.

WHAT THE FIGHT IS ABOUT

THE slum is as old as civilization. Civilization implies a race to get ahead. In a race there are usually some who for one cause or another cannot keep up, or are thrust out from among their fellows. They fall behind, and when they have been left far in the rear they lose hope and ambition, and give up. Thenceforward, if left to their own resources, they are the victims, not the masters, of their environment; and it is a bad master. They drag one another always farther down. The bad environment becomes the heredity of the next generation. Then, given the crowd, you have the slum ready-made.

The battle with the slum began the day civilization recognized in it her enemy. It was a losing fight until conscience joined forces with fear and self-interest against it. When common sense and the golden rule obtain among men as a rule of practice, it will be over. The two have not always been classed together, but here they are plainly

I

seen to belong together. Justice to the individual is accepted in theory as the only safe groundwork of the commonwealth. When it is practised in dealing with the slum, there will shortly be no slum. We need not wait for the millennium, to get rid of it. We can do it now. All that is required is that it shall not be left to itself. That is justice to it and to us, since its grievous ailment is that it cannot help itself. When a man is drowning, the thing to do is to pull him out of the water; afterward there will be time for talking it over. We got at it the other way in dealing with our social problems. The wise men had their day, and they decided to let bad enough alone; that it was unsafe to interfere with "causes that operate sociologically," as one survivor of these unfittest put it to me. It was a piece of scientific humbug that cost the age which listened to it dear. "Causes that operate sociologically" are the opportunity of the political and every other kind of scamp who trades upon the depravity and helplessness of the slum, and the refuge of the pessimist who is useless in the fight against them. We have not done yet paying the bills he ran up for us. Some time since we turned to, to pull the drowning man out, and it was time. A little while longer, and we should hardly have escaped being dragged down with him.

The slum complaint had been chronic in all ages,

but the great changes which the nineteenth century saw, the new industry, political freedom, brought on an acute attack which put that very freedom in jeopardy. Too many of us had supposed that, built as our commonwealth was on universal suffrage, it would be proof against the complaints that harassed older states; but in fact it turned out that there was extra hazard in that. Having solemnly resolved that all men are created equal and have certain inalienable rights, among them life, liberty, and the pursuit of happiness, we shut our eyes and waited for the formula to work. It was as if a man with a cold should take the doctor's prescription to bed with him, expecting it to cure him. The formula was all right, but merely repeating it worked no cure. When, after a hundred years, we opened our eyes, it was upon sixty cents a day as the living wage of the working-woman in our cities; upon "knee pants" at forty cents a dozen for the making; upon the Potter's Field taking tithe of our city life, ten per cent each year for the trench, truly the Lost Tenth of the slum. Our country had grown great and rich; through our ports was poured food for the millions of Europe. But in the back streets multitudes huddled in ignorance and want. The foreign oppressor had been vanquished, the fetters stricken from the black man at home; but his white brother, in his bitter plight,

sent up a cry of distress that had in it a distinct
note of menace.   Political freedom we had won;
but the problem of helpless poverty, grown vast
with the added offscourings of the Old World,
mocked us, unsolved.   Liberty at sixty cents a
day set presently its stamp upon the government
of our cities, and it became the scandal and the
peril of our political system.

So the battle began.   Three times since the war
that absorbed the nation's energies and attention
had the slum confronted us in New York with its
challenge.   In the darkest days of the great struggle it was the treacherous mob;[1] later on, the
threat of the cholera, which found swine foraging
in the streets as the only scavengers, and a swarming host, but little above the hog in its appetites
and in the quality of the shelter afforded it, peo-
pling the back alleys.   Still later, the mob, caught
looting the city's treasury with its idol, the thief
Tweed,[†] at its head, drunk with power and plunder, had insolently defied the outraged community
to do its worst.   There were meetings and pro-
tests.   The rascals were turned out for a season;
the arch-chief died in jail.   I see him now, going
through the gloomy portals of the Tombs, whither,
as a newspaper reporter, I had gone with him, his
stubborn head held high as ever.   I asked myself

---

[1] The draft riots of 1863.

[†]William Marcy Tweed (1823–1878), a Tammany politician who
gained control of New York City's finances after the Civil War and stole
huge amounts of money through fraud. The Tweed Ring was exposed in

more than once, at the time when the vile prison was torn down, whether the comic clamor to have the ugly old gates preserved and set up in Central Park had anything to do with the memory of the " martyred " thief, or whether it was in joyful celebration of the fact that others had escaped. His name is even now one to conjure with in the Sixth Ward. He never " squealed," and he was " so good to the poor "— evidence that the slum is not laid by the heels by merely destroying Five Points and the Mulberry Bend. There are other fights to be fought in that war, other victories to be won, and it is slow work. It was nearly ten years after the Great Robbery before decency got a good upper grip. That was when the civic conscience awoke in 1879.

And after all that, the Lexow disclosures of inconceivable rottenness of a Tammany police; the woe unto you! of Christian priests calling vainly upon the chief of the city " to save its children from a living hell," and the contemptuous reply on the witness-stand of the head of the party of organized robbery, at the door of which it was all laid, that he was " in politics, working for his own pocket all the time, same as you and everybody else ! "

Slow work, yes! but be it ever so slow, the battle has got to be fought, and fought out. For it is one thing or the other: either we wipe out the slum, or it wipes out us. Let there be no mistake about

1871 and collapsed in 1874. After being convicted and escaping to Cuba and Spain, Tweed returned to New York City and was imprisoned in the Tombs (the Manhattan House of Detention for Men), where he died.

this. It cannot be shirked. Shirking means surrender, and surrender means the end of government by the people.

If any one believes this to be needless alarm, let him think a moment. Government by the people must ever rest upon the people's ability to govern themselves, upon their intelligence and public spirit. The slum stands for ignorance, want, unfitness, for mob-rule in the day of wrath. This at one end. At the other, hard-heartedness, indifference, self-seeking, greed. It is human nature. We are brothers whether we own it or not, and when the brotherhood is denied in Mulberry Street we shall look vainly for the virtue of good citizenship on Fifth Avenue. When the slum flourishes unchallenged in the cities, their wharves may, indeed, be busy, their treasure-houses filled, — wealth and want go so together, — but patriotism among their people is dead.

As long ago as the very beginning of our republic, its founders saw that the cities were danger-spots in their plan. In them was the peril of democratic government. At that time, scarce one in twenty-five of the people in the United States lived in a city. Now it is one in three. And to the selfishness of the trader has been added the threat of the slum. Ask yourself then how long before it would make an end of us, if let alone.

Put it this way : you cannot let men live like pigs when you need their votes as freemen; it is not safe.[1] You cannot rob a child of its childhood, of its home, its play, its freedom from toil and care, and expect to appeal to the grown-up voter's manhood. The children are our to-morrow, and as we mould them to-day so will they deal with us then. Therefore that is not safe. Unsafest of all is any thing or deed that strikes at the home, for from the people's home proceeds citizen virtue, and nowhere else does it live. The slum is the enemy of the home. Because of it the chief city of our land came long ago to be called " The Homeless City." When this people comes to be truly called a nation without homes there will no longer be any nation.

Hence, I say, in the battle with the slum we win or we perish. There is no middle way. We shall win, for we are not letting things be the way our fathers did. But it will be a running fight, and it is not going to be won in two years, or in ten, or in twenty. For all that, we must keep on fighting, content if in our time we avert the punishment that waits upon the third and the fourth generation of those who forget the brotherhood. As a man does in dealing

---

[1] " The experiment has been long tried on a large scale, with a dreadful success, affording the demonstration that if, from early infancy, you allow human beings to *live* like brutes, you can degrade them down to their level, leaving them scarcely more intellect, and no feelings and affections proper to human hearts."— *Report on the Health of British Towns*.

with his brother so it is the way of God that his children shall reap, that through toil and tears we may make out the lesson which sums up all the commandments and alone can make the earth fit for the kingdom that is to come.

CHAPTER I

BATTLING AGAINST HEAVY ODDS

THE slum I speak of is our own. We made it, but let us be glad we have no patent on the manufacture. It is not, as one wrote with soul quite too patriotic to let the Old World into competition on any terms, "the offspring of the American factory system." Not that, thank goodness! It comes much nearer to being a slice of original sin which makes right of might whenever the chance offers. When to-day we clamor for air and light and water as man's natural rights because necessary to his being, we are merely following in the track Hippocrates trod twenty-five centuries ago. How like the slums of Rome were to those of New York any one may learn from Juvenal's Satires and Gibbon's description of Rome under Augustus. "I must live in a place where there are no fires, no nightly alarms," cries the poet, apostle of commuters. "Already is Ucalegon shouting for water, already is he removing his chattels; the third story in the house you live in is already in a blaze. You know nothing about it. For if the alarm begin from the bottom of the stairs, he will be the last to be burned whom a single tile protects from the rain where the tame pigeons lay their eggs." (Clearly they had no air-shafts in the Roman tenements!) "Codrus had a bed too small for his Procula; six little jugs, the ornament of his sideboard, and a little can, besides, beneath it. . . . What a height it is from the lofty roofs from which a potsherd tumbles on your brains. How often cracked and chipped earthenware falls from the windows. . . . Pray and bear about with you the miserable wish that they may be contented with throwing down only what the broad basins have held. . . . If you can tear yourself away from the games in the circus, you can buy a capital house at Sora, or Fabrateria, or Frasino, for the price at which you are now hiring your dark hole for one year. There you will have your little garden . . . live there enamoured of the pitchfork. . . . It is something to be able in any spot to have made oneself proprietor even of a single lizard. . . . None but the wealthy can sleep in Rome." [1]

One reads with a grim smile of the hold-ups of old : "'Where do you come from?' he (policeman?) thunders out. 'You don't answer? Speak or be kicked! Say, where do you hang out?' It is all one whether you speak or hold your tongue; they beat you just the same, and then, in a passion,

[1] Satire III, Juvenal.

force you to give bail to answer for the assault. . . .
I must be off.   Let those stay . . . for whom it is
an easy matter to get contracts for building temples,
clearing   rivers,   constructing   harbors,   cleansing
sewers, etc."[1]   Not even in the boss and his pull
can we claim exclusive right.

Rome had its walls, as New York has, its rivers,
and they played a like part in penning up the
crowds.   Within space became scarce and dear, and
when there was no longer room to build in rows
where the poor lived, they put the houses on top
of one another.   That is the first chapter of the
story of the tenement everywhere.   Gibbon quotes
the architect Vitruvius, who lived in the Augustan
age, as complaining of "the common though inconvenient practice of raising houses to a considcrable
height in the air.   But the loftiness of the buildings, which often consisted of hasty work and in-
sufficient material, was the cause of frequent and
fatal accidents, and it was repeatedly enacted by
Augustus as well as by Nero that the height of
private dwellings should not exceed the measure
of seventy feet above the ground."

" Repeatedly " suggests that the jerry-builder was
a hard nut to crack then as now.   As to Nero's
edict, New York enacted it for its own protection in
our own generation.

[1] Satire III, Juvenal.

Step now across eighteen centuries and all the chapters of the dreary story to the middle of the century we have just left behind, and look upon this picture of the New World's metropolis as it was drawn in public reports at a time when a legislative committee came to New York to see how crime

One of the Five Points Fifty Years ago.

and drunkenness came to be the natural crop of a population " housed in crazy old buildings, crowded, filthy tenements in rear yards, dark, damp basements, leaking garrets, shops, outhouses, and stables converted into dwellings, though scarcely fit to shelter brutes," or in towering tenements, " often carried up to a great height without regard to the strength of the foundation walls." What matter? They were not intended to last. The rent was high enough to make up for the risk — to the property. The tenant was not considered. Nothing was expected of him, and he came up to the expectation, as men have a trick of doing. "Reckless slovenliness, discontent, privation, and ignorance were left to work out their inevitable results, until the entire premises reached the level of tenant-house dilapidation, containing, but sheltering not, the miserable hordes that crowded beneath smouldering, water-rotted roofs, or burrowed among the rats of clammy cellars."[1]

We had not yet taken a lesson from Nero. That came later. But otherwise we were abreast. No doubt the Roman landlord, like his New York brother of a later day, when called to account, "urged the filthy habits of his tenants as an excuse for the condition of the property." It has been the landlord's plea in every age. "They utterly forgot," observes the sanitarian who was set to clean up, "that it was the tolerance of those habits which was the real evil, and that for this they themselves were alone responsible."[2]

Those days came vividly back to me last winter, when in a Wisconsin country town I was rehears-

[1] Report of Select Committee of Assembly, New York, 1857.
[2] New York Health Department Report, 1866, Appendix A, p. 6.

ing the story of the long fight, and pointing out
its meaning to us all.   In the audience sat a sturdy,
white-haired, old farmer who followed the recital
with keen interest, losing no word.   When he
saw this picture of one of the Five Points, he spoke
out loud: "Yes! that is right.   I was there."   It
turned out that he and his sister had borne a hand
in the attack upon that stronghold of the slum by
the forces of decency, in 1849 and 1850, which
ended in the wiping out of the city's worst disgrace.   It was the first pitched battle in the fight.
Soon after he had come west and taken homestead
land; but the daily repetition during a lifetime of
the message to men, which the woods and the
fields and God's open sky have in keeping, had
not dulled his ears to it, and after fifty years his
interest in his brothers in the great city was as
keen as ever, his sympathies as quick.   He had
driven twenty miles across the frozen prairie to
hear my story.   It is his kind who win such battles,
and a few of them go a long way.

A handful of Methodist women made the Five
Points decent.   To understand what that meant,
look at the "dens of death" in Baxter Street, which
were part of it, "houses," says the health inspector,[1]
"into which the sunlight never enters . . . that are
dark, damp, and dismal throughout all the days of

[1] Report of Board of Health, New York, 1869, p. 346.

The "Old Church" Tenement.

the year, and for which it is no exaggeration to say
that the money paid to the owners as rent is literally the 'price of blood.'" It took us twenty-four
years after that to register the conviction in the

form of law that that was good cause for the destruction of a tenement in cold blood; but we got rid of some at that time in a fit of anger. The mortality officially registered in those "dens of death" was 17.5 per cent of their population. We think now that the death-rate of New York is yet too high at 19 or 20 in a thousand of the living.

A dozen steps away in Mulberry Street, called "Death's Thoroughfare" in the same report, were the "Old Church Tenements," part of the Five Points and nearly the worst part. "One of the largest contributors to the hospitals," this repulsive pile had seen the day when men and women sat under its roof and worshipped God. When the congregation grew rich, it handed over its house to the devil and moved uptown. That is not putting it too strong. Counting in the front tenements that shut out what little air and sunshine might otherwise have reached the wretched tenants, it had a population of 360 according to the record, and a mortality of 75 per thousand!

The sketches of the Fourth Ward and Wooster Street barracks are reproduced from an old report of the Association for Improving the Condition of the Poor. They rightly made out, those early missionaries, that the improvement must begin with the people's homes, or not at all, and allowed no indifference on the part of the public to turn them from their path. It is worth the while of Chicago and the other Western cities that are growing with such joyful metropolitan ambitions, to notice that their slums look to-day very much as New York's

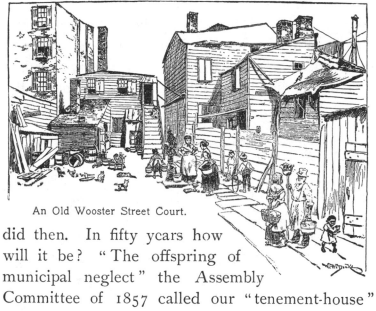

An Old Wooster Street Court.

did then. In fifty years how will it be? "The offspring of municipal neglect" the Assembly Committee of 1857 called our "tenement-house" system. "Forgetfulness of the poor" was the way a citizens' council put it. It comes to the same thing. Whether seen from the point of view of the citizen, the philanthropist, or the Christian, the slum is the poorest investment a city can make, and once made it is not easily unmade. In a Mississippi river town, when pleading for the turning over to the people's use of some vacant land on the river-shore that would make a fine breathing space, I was told that by and by they would consider it. Just now it was too valuable for factory purposes. When the city had grown opulent, in say twenty-five years, they would be willing to hand it over. Fatal delusion! Men do not grow that kind of sense as they grow rich. The land will be always "too valuable." When we in New York were scandalized at last into making a park of the Mulberry Bend, it cost us a million and a half, and it had made the

A Fourth Ward Colony in the
Bad Old Days.

slum a fixture, not to be dislodged. No! the way to fight the slum is to head it off. It is like fighting a fire. Chasing it up is hard and doubtful work; the chances are that you will not overtake it till the house is burned down.

There were those who thought when the Civil War was over, that a big fire would not be the worst thing that could happen to New York; and, if it could have burned sense into men's minds as it burned up the evidence of their lack of it, they would have been right. But forty per cent — the rent some of the barracks brought — is a powerful damper on sense and conscience, even with the cholera at the door. However, the fear of it gave us the Citizens' Council of Hygiene, and New York heard the truth for once.

"Not only," it ran, "does filth, overcrowding, lack of privacy and domesticity, lack of ventilation and lighting, and absence of supervision and of sanitary regulation still characterize the greater number of the tenements; but they are built to a greater height in stories; there are more rear houses built back to back with other buildings, correspondingly situated on parallel streets; the courts and alleys are more greedily encroached upon and narrowed into unventilated, unlighted, damp, and well-like holes between the many-storied front and rear tenements; and more fever-breeding wynds and *culs-de-sac* are created as the demand for the humble homes of the laboring poor increases."[1] The Council, which was composed of sixteen of New York's most distinguished physicians, declared that by ordinary sanitary management the city's death-rate should be reduced thirty per cent. Its judgment

[1] Council of Hygiene's Report, 1866.

has been more than borne out. In the thirty-five years that have passed since, it has in fact been reduced over fifty per cent.

Men and women were found living in cellars deep down under the ground. One or two of those holes are left still in Park Street near the Five Points Mission, but they have not been used as living-rooms for a generation. In cellars near the river the tide rose and fell, compelling the tenants "to keep the children in bed till ebb-tide." The plumber had come upon the field, but his coming brought no relief. His was not a case of conscience. " Untrapped soil pipes opened into every floor and poisoned the tenants."

Where the "dens of death" were in Baxter Street, big barracks crowded out the old shanties. More came every day. I remember the story of those shown in the picture. They had been built only a little while when complaint came to the Board of Health of smells in the houses. A sanitary inspector was sent to find the cause. He followed the smell down in the cellar and, digging there, discovered that the waste pipe was a blind. It had simply been run three feet into the ground and was not connected with the sewer.

The houses were built to sell. That they killed the tenants was no concern of builder's. His name, by the way, was Buddensiek. A dozen years after,

Dens of Death.

when it happened that a row of tenements he was building fell down ahead of time, before they were finished and sold, and killed the workmen, he was arrested and sent to Sing Sing for ten years, for manslaughter.

That time he had forgotten to put lime in the mortar. It was just sand. When the houses fell in the sight of men, the law was at last able to make him responsible. It failed in the matter of the soil pipe. It does sometimes to this very day. Knocking a man in the head with an axe, or sticking a knife into him, goes against the grain. Slowly poisoning a hundred so that the pockets of one be made to bulge may not even banish a man from respectable society. We are a queer lot in some things. However, that is hardly quite fair to society. It is a fact that that part of it which would deserve the respect of its fellow-citizens has got rid of its tenement-house property in recent years. It speculates in railway shares now.

Twenty cases of typhoid fever from a single house in one year was the record that had gone unconsidered. Bedrooms in tenements were dark closets, utterly without ventilation. There couldn't be any. The houses were built like huge square boxes, covering nearly the whole of the lot. Some light came in at the ends, but the middle was always black. Forty thousand windows, cut by order of the Health Board that first year, gave us a daylight view of the slum: "damp and rotten and dark, walls and banisters sticky with constant moisture." Think of living babies in such hell-holes; and make a note of it, you in the young cities who can still head off the slum where we have to wrestle with it for our sins. Put a brand upon the murderer who would smother babies in dark holes and bedrooms. He is nothing else. Forbid the putting of a house five stories high, or six, on a twenty-five foot lot, unless at least thirty-five per cent of the lot be reserved for sunlight and air. Forbid it absolutely, if you can. It is the devil's job, and you will have to pay his dues in the end, depend on it.

And while you are about it make a note of a fact we let go unheeded too long to our harm, and haven't grasped fully yet. The legislative committee of 1857 said it: "to prevent drunkenness provide every man with a clean and comfortable home." Call it paternalism, crankery, any other hard name you can think of, all the same it goes down underneath the foundation of things. I have known drunkards to wreck homes a plenty in my time; but I have known homes, too, that made drunkards by the shortest cut. I know a dozen now — yes, ten dozen — from which, if I had to live there, I should certainly escape to the saloon with its brightness and cheer as often and as long as I could to brood there perhaps over the fate which sowed desolation in one man's path that another might reap wealth and luxury. That last might not be my way, but it is a human way, and it breeds hatred which is not good mortar for us to build with. It does not bind. Let us remember that and just be sensible about things, or we shall not get anywhere.

By which I do not mean that we are not getting anywhere; for we are. Look at Gotham Court, described in the health reports of the sixties as a "packing-box tenement" of the hopeless back-to-back type, which meant that there was no ventilation and could be none. The stenches from the

"horribly foul cellars" with their "infernal system
of sewerage" must needs poison the tenants all the
way up to the fifth story. I knew the court well,

Gotham Court.

knew the gang that made its headquarters with the
rats in the cellar, terrorizing the helpless tenants;
knew the well-worn rut of the dead-wagon and the
ambulance to the gate, for the tenants died there
like flies in all seasons, and a tenth of its population

was always in the hospital. I knew the story of
how it had been built by a Quaker with good intentions, but without good sense, for the purpose of
rescuing people from the awful cellar-holes they
burrowed in around there, — this within fifty-one
years of the death of George Washington, who
lived just across the street on the crest of Cherry
Hill when he was President, — and how in a score
of years from the time it was built it had come to
earn the official description, "a nuisance which,
from its very magnitude, is assumed to be unremov-
able and irremediable."[1] That was at that time.
But I have lived to see it taken in hand three times,
once by the landlord under compulsion of the Board
of Health, once by Christian men bent upon proving
what could be done on their plan with the worst
tenement house. And a good deal was accom-
plished. The mortality was brought below the
general death-rate of the city, and the condition of
the living was made by comparison tolerable. Only
the best was bad in that spot, on account of the
good Quaker's poor sense, and the third time the
court was taken in hand it was by the authorities,
who destroyed it, as they should have done a generation before. Oh, yes, we are getting there; but that
sort of thing takes time.

Going through Whitechapel, London, about the

---

[1] Health Department Report, 1870, p. 111.

time we were making ready to deal with Gotham
Court as it deserved, I photographed Green Dragon
yard as typical of what I saw about me.   Compare
the court and the yard and see the difference be-

Green Dragon Yard, London.

tween our slum problem and that of Old World
cities.   Gotham Court contained 142 families when
I made a canvass of it in the old days, comprising
over 700 persons, not counting the vagrants who
infested the cellars.   The population of Green

Dragon Yard was greater than the sight of it would lead you to expect, for in Whitechapel one-room flats were the rule; but with its utmost crowding it came nowhere near the court. Sullen discontent was the badge of it. Gotham Court was in an active state of warfare at all hours, for its population was evenly divided between Irish and Italians, with only two German families, who caught it from both sides. But there was hope in that, for they were on the move; before the court was torn down, one-third of its tenants were Greeks. Their slum over yonder is dead, black, given over to smoky chimneys and bad draughts, with red-eyed and hopeless men and women forever blowing the bellows on ineffectual fires. Ours is alive if it *is* with fighting. There is yeast in it, and bright skies without, if not within. I don't believe there is a bellows to be had in New York. Our slum, with its greater crowd, has more urgent need of sharp attention, chiefly because of the overflow of theirs which it receives. But after all, even that represents what still had courage and manhood enough to make it want to get away and do better. We shall " get there" if we don't give up. It sometimes seems to me that *their* only hope is to get here.

Speaking of the fair beginning of Gotham Court reminds me of the Big Flat in Mott Street, a mighty tenement with room for a hundred families that was another instance of reform still-born; by which I mean that it came before we were ready for it, and willing to back it up; also before we knew just how.   That house was built by the philanthropists of those days on such a generous scale that it reached clear through the block to Elizabeth Street. It had not occurred to the builders that the neigh-

Flagged Hallway in the "Big Flat."

borhood was one in which such an arrangement might prove of special convenience to the lawbreakers with which it swarmed.   Thieves and thugs made it a runway, and decent people shunned it.   Other philanthropists, with the will but without the wisdom that was needed, took it up and tried to make a workingwoman's home of it; but that end was worse than the beginning.   The women would have none of the rules that went with the philanthropy, and the Big Flat lapsed back among the slum tenements and became the worst of a bad lot. I speak of.it here because just now the recollection of it is a kind of a milestone in the battle with the slum. Twenty years after, A. T. Stewart, the merchant prince, set another in the Park Avenue Hotel which he intended for his working-girls; and that was a worse failure than the first, for it never served the purpose he intended for it. And now, just as I am writing this, they are putting the finishing touches to a real woman's hotel up-town which will not be a failure, though it will hardly reach the same class which the remodellers of the Big Flat had in mind. However, we shall get there, too, now we know the way.

Slowly, with many setbacks, we battled our way into the light. A Board of Health had come with the cholera panic in 1866. The swine that ran at large in the streets, practically the only scavengers, were banished. The cholera and the yellow fever that had ravaged the city by turns never came back. The smallpox went its way, too,[1] and was heard

[1] They had "health wardens" in the old days, and the Council of Hygiene tells of the efficient way two of them fought the smallpox. One stood at the foot of the stairs and yelled to those minding a patient in the next story to "put pieces of camphor about the clothes of the sick and occasionally throw a piece on the hot stove." The other summoned the occupants of a smallpox smitten tenement to the hall door and cautioned them to say nothing about it to any one, or he would send them all to the pesthouse!

of again only once as an epidemic, till people had
forgotten what it was like, — enough to make them
listen to the anti-vaccination cranks, — and politics
had the health department by the throat again
and held the gate open. We acquired tenement
house laws, and the process of education that had
begun with the foraging ground of the swine was
extended step by step to the citizen's home. Short
steps and cautious were they. Every obstacle which
the landlord's cunning and the perversion of the
machinery of the law to serve his interests could
devise was thrown in the way. It was a new doctrine to that day that any power should intervene
between him and the tenants who represented his
income, and it was held to be a hardship if not
downright robbery. The builder took the same
view. Every tenement house plan was the subject
of hot debate between the Health Board and the
builder, or his architect. The smallest air-shaft had
to be wrung out of him, as it were, by main strength.
The church itself was too often on the side of the
enemy, where its material interests were involved.
Trinity,[†] the wealthiest church corporation in the
land, was in constant opposition as a tenement
house landlord, and finally, to save a few hundred
dollars, came near upsetting the whole structure of
tenement law that had been built up in the interest
of the toilers and of the city's safety with such infi-

[†]Trinity Church, at Broadway and Wall Street. The first church was
completed in 1698, for a Church of England congregation. By Riis's time
Trinity was part of the Episcopal Church in America. One hundred years
later, the Trinity Church Real Estate Department owns several valuable
office buildings in Lower Manhattan, rather than tenements.

nite pains. The courts were reluctant. Courts in such matters record rather than lead the state of the public mind, and now that the immediate danger of an epidemic was over, the public mind had a hard time grasping the fact that bettering the housing of the poor was simple protection for the community. When suit was brought against a bad landlord, judges demanded that the department must prove not only that a certain state of soil saturation, for instance, was dangerous to health, but that some one had been actually made sick by that specified nuisance. Fat-boilers, slaughter-house men, and keepers of other nuisances made common cause against the new decency, and with these obstacles in front, the Sanitarians found the enemy constantly recruited from the rear. With the immense immigration that poured in after the Civil War, the evil with which they were struggling grew enormously. Economic problems other than the old one of rent came to vex us. The sweater moved into the East Side tenements. Child-labor grew and swelled.

The tenement had grown its logical crop. In the sweating conspiracy it is a prime factor. Its extortionate rates make the need, and the need of the poor was ever the opportunity of their oppressor. What they have to take becomes the standard of all the rest. Sweating is only a modern name for it. The cause is as old as the slum itself.

However, the new light was not without its allies. Chief among them was the onward march of business that wiped out many a foul spot which had sorely tried the patience of us all. A carriage factory took the place of the Big Flat when it had become a disgusting scandal. Jersey Street, a short block

Jersey Street Rookeries.

between Mulberry and Crosby streets, to which no Whitechapel slum could hold a candle, became a factory street. No one lives there now. The last who did was murdered by the gang that grew as naturally out of its wickedness as a toadstool grows on a rotten log. He kept the saloon on the corner of Crosby Street. Saloon and tenements are gone together. Where they were are rows of factories,

The Survival of the Unfittest.

empty and silent at night. A man may go safely
there now at any hour. I should not have advised
strangers to try that when it was at its worst, though
Police Headquarters was but a block away.

I photographed that phase of the battle with the
slum just before they shut in the last tenement in
the block with a factory building in its rear. It
stood for a while after that down in a deep sort of
pocket with not enough light struggling down on
the brightest of days to make out anything clearly
in the rooms, — truly a survival of the unfittest;
but the tenants stayed. They had access through

a hallway on Crosby Street; they had never been used to a yard; as for the darkness, that they had always been used to. They were "manured to the soil," in the words of Mrs. Partington. But at length business claimed the last foot of the block, and peace came to it and to us.

All the while we were learning. It was emphatically a campaign of education. When the cholera threatened there was the old disposition to lie down under the visitation and pray. The council pointed to the fifteen hundred cases of smallpox ferreted out by its inspectors "in a few days," and sternly reminded the people of Lord Palmerston's advice to those who would stay an epidemic with a national fast, that they had better turn to and clean up. We pray nowadays with broom in hand, and the prayer tells. Do not understand me as discouraging the prayer; far from it. But I would lend an edge to it with the broom that cuts. That kind of foolishness we got rid of; the other kind that thinks the individual's interest superior to the public good — that is the thing we have got to fight till we die. But we made notches in that on which to hang arguments that stick. Human life then counted for less than the landlord's profits; to-day it is weighed in the scale against them. Property still has powerful pull. "Vested rights" rise up and confront you, and no matter how loudly you may protest that no man has the right to kill his neighbor, they are still there. No one will contradict you, but they won't yield — till you make them. In a hundred ways you are made to feel that vested rights are sacred, if human life is not. But the glory is that you *can* make them yield. You couldn't then.

We haven't reached the millennium yet. But let us be glad. A hundred years ago they hanged a woman on Tyburn Hill for stealing a loaf of bread. To-day we destroy the den that helped make her a thicf.

CHAPTER II

THE OUTWORKS OF THE SLUM TAKEN

I SAID that we got our grip when the civic conscience awoke in 1879. In that year the slum was arraigned in the churches. The sad and shameful story was told of how it grew and was fostered by avarice that saw in the homeless crowds from over the sea only a chance for business, and exploited them to the uttermost; how Christianity, citizenship, human fellowship, shook their skirts clear of the rabble that was only good enough to fill the greedy purse, and how the rabble, left to itself, improved such opportunities as it found after such fashion as it knew; how it ran elections merely to count its thugs in, and fattened at the public crib; and how the whole evil thing had its root in the tenements, where the home had ceased to be sacred, — those dark and deadly dens in which the family ideal was tortured to death, and character was smothered; in which children were " damned rather than born " into the world, thus realizing a slum kind of foreordination to torment, happily brief in many cases. The Tenement House Commission

long afterward called the worst of the barracks
"infant slaughter houses," and showed, by reference
to the mortality lists, that they killed one in every
five babies born in them.

The story shocked the town into action. Plans
for a better kind of tenement were called for, and
a premium was put on every ray of light and
breath of air that could be let into it. It was not
much, for the plans clung to the twenty-five-foot lot
which was the primal curse, and the type of tenement evolved, the double-decker of the "dumb-bell"
shape, while it seemed at the time a great advance
upon the black, old packing-box kind, came with the
great growth of our city to be a worse peril than
what had gone before. But what we got was
according to our sense. At least the will was there.
Money was raised to build model houses, and a bill
to give the health authorities summary powers in
dealing with tenements was sent to the legislature.
The landlords held it up until the last day of the
session, when it was forced through by an angered
public opinion, shorn of its most significant clause,
which proposed the licensing of tenements and so
their control and effective repression. However,
the landlords had received a real set-back. Many
of them got rid of their property, which in a large
number of cases they had never seen, and tried to
forget the source of their ill-gotten wealth. Light

The Rear Tenement grows up. An Alley condemned by the Council of Hygiene.

and air did find their way into the tenements in a half-hearted fashion, and we began to count the tenants as "souls." That is another of our milestones in the history of New York. They were never reckoned so before; no one ever thought of them as "souls." So, restored to human fellowship, in the twilight of the air-shaft that had penetrated to their dens, the first Tenement House Committee [1] was able to make them out "better than the houses" they lived in, and a long step forward was taken. The Mulberry Bend, the wicked core of the "bloody Sixth Ward," was marked for destruction, and all slumdom held its breath to see it go. With that gone, it seemed as if the old days must be gone too, never to return. There would not be another Mulberry Bend. As long as it stood, there

Professor Felix Adler.

was yet a chance. The slum had backing, as it were.

What was it like? says a man at my elbow, who never saw it. Like nothing I ever saw before, or hope ever to see again. A crooked three-acre lot built over with rotten structures that harbored the

[1] The Adler Tenement House Committee of 1884. It was the first citizens' commission. The legislative inquiry of 1856 was conducted by a Select Committee of the Assembly.

very dregs of humanity. Ordinary enough to look at from the street, but pierced by a maze of foul alleys, in the depths of which skulked the tramp and the outcast thief with loathsome wrecks that had once laid claim to the name of woman. Every foot of it reeked with incest and murder. Bandits' Roost, Bottle Alley, were names synonymous with robbery and red-handed outrage. By night, in its worst days, I have gone poking about their shuddering haunts with a policeman on the beat, and come away in a ferment of anger and disgust that would keep me awake far into the morning hours planning means of its destruction. That was what it was like. Thank God, we shall never see another such!

That was the exhibit that urged us on. But the civic conscience was not very robust yet, and required many and protracted naps. It slumbered fitfully eight long years, waking up now and then with a start, while the Bend lay stewing in its slime. I wondered often, in those years of delay, if it was just plain stupidity that kept the politicians from spending the money which the law had put within their grasp; for with every year that passed, a million dollars that could have been used for small park purposes was lost.[1] But they were wiser than I.

[1] The Small Parks law of 1887 allowed the expenditure of a million dollars a year for the making of neighborhood parks; but only as payment for work done or property taken. If not used in any one year, that year's appropriation was lost.

I understood when I saw the changes which letting in the sunshine worked. They were not of the kind that made for their good. We had all believed it, but they knew it all along. At the same time, they lost none of the chances that offered. They helped the landlords in the Bend, who considered themselves greatly aggrieved because

A Cellar Dive in the Bend.

their property was thereafter to front on a park instead of a pigsty, to transfer the whole assessment of half a million dollars for park benefit to the city. They undid in less than six weeks what it had taken considerably more than six years to do; but the park was cheap at the price. We could afford to pay all it cost to wake us up. When finally, upon the wave of wrath excited by the Parkhurst and Lexow disclosures, reform came with a shock that dislodged Tammany, it found us wide awake, and, it must be admitted, not a little astonished at our sudden access of righteousness.

The battle went against the slum in the three years that followed, until it found backing in the "odium of reform" that became the issue in the municipal organization of the greater city. Tammany made notes. The cry meant that we were tired of too much virtue. Of what was done, how it was done, and why, during those years, I shall have occasion to speak further in these pages. Here I wish to measure the stretch we have come since I wrote "How the Other Half Lives," thirteen years ago. Some of it we came plodding, and some at full speed; some of it in the face of every obstacle that could be thrown in our way, wresting victory from defeat at every step; some of it with the enemy on the run. Take it all together, it is a long way. Much of it will not have to be travelled over again. The engine of municipal progress, once started as it has been in New York, may slip many a cog with Tammany as the engineer; it may even be stopped for a season; but it can never be made to work backward. Even Tammany knows that, and gropes desperately for a new hold, a certificate of character. In the last election (1901) she laid loud claim to having built many new schools, though she had done little more than to carry out the plans of the previous reform administration, where they could not be upset. As a matter of fact we had fallen behind again, sadly. But even the claim was significant.

How long we strove for those schools, to no purpose! Our arguments, our anger, the anxious pleading of philanthropists who saw the young on the East Side going to ruin, the warning year after year of the superintendent of schools that the compulsory education law was but an empty mockery where it was most needed, the knocking of uncounted thousands of children for whom there was no room, — uncounted in sober fact; there was not even a way of finding out how many were adrift,[1] — brought only the response that the tax rate must be kept down. Kept down it was. "Waste" was successfully averted at the spigot; at the bunghole it went on unchecked. In a swarming population like that you must have either schools or jails, and the jails waxed fat with the overflow. The East Side, that had been orderly, became a hotbed of child crime. And when, in answer to the charge made by a legislative committee (1895) that the father forced his child into the shop, on a perjured age certificate, to labor

[1] The first school census was taken in 1895 by order of the legislature. It showed that there were 50,069 children of school age in New York City out of school and unemployed. The number had been variously estimated from 5000 to 150,000.

when he ought to have been at play, that father, bent and heavy-eyed with unceasing toil, flung back the charge with the bitter reproach that we gave him no other choice, that it was either the street or the shop for his boy, and that perjury for him was cheaper than the ruin of the child, we were mute. What, indeed, was there to say? The crime was ours, not his. That was seven years ago. Once since then have we been where we could count the months to the time when every child that knocked should find a seat in our schools; but Tammany came back. Once again, now, we are catching up. Yesterday Mayor Low's[†] reform government voted six millions of dollars for new schools. The school census law that was forgotten almost as soon as made (the census was to be taken once in two years, but was taken only twice) is to be enforced again so that we know where we stand. In that most crowded neighborhood in all the world, where the superintendent lately pleaded in vain for three new schools, half a dozen have been built, the finest in this or any other land, — great, light, and airy structures, with playgrounds on the roof; and all over the city the like are going up. The briefest of our laws, every word of which is like the blow of a hammer driving the nails home in the coffin of the bad old days, says that never one shall be built without its playground.

†Seth Low (1850–1916), a former mayor of the city of Brooklyn (1881–1885) and president of Columbia University (1890–1901), who was elected mayor of New York City as a reform (non-Tammany) Democrat in November 1901 and served in that capacity 1902–1903.

And not for the child's use only. The band
shall play there yet and neighbor meet neighbor
in such social contact as the slum has never known
to its undoing. Even as I write this the band is
tuning up and the children dancing to its strains
with shouts of joy. The president of the board of
education and members of the board lead in the
revolt against the old. Clergymen applaud the
opening of the school buildings on Sunday for concerts, lectures, and neighborhood meetings. Common sense is having its day. The streets are
cleaned.

The slum has even been washed. We tried that
on Hester Street years ago, in the age of cobble-
stone pavements, and the result fairly frightened
us. I remember the indignant reply of a well-
known citizen, a man of large business responsibility and experience in the handling of men, to
whom the office of street-cleaning commissioner
had been offered, when I asked him if he would
accept. "I have lived," he said, "a blameless life
for forty years, and have a character in the community. I cannot afford — no man with a reputation can afford — to hold that office; it will surely
wreck it." It made Colonel Waring's reputation.
He took the trucks from the streets. Tammany, in
a brief interregnum of vigor under Mayor Grant,
had laid the axe to the unsightly telegraph poles

and begun to pave the streets with asphalt, but it left the trucks and the ash barrels to Colonel Waring as hopeless. Trucks have votes; at least their drivers have. Now that they are gone, the drivers

It costs a Dollar a Month to sleep in these Sheds.

would be the last to bring them back; for they have children, too, and the rescued streets gave them their first playground. Perilous, begrudged by policeman and storekeeper, though it was, it was still a playground.

But one is coming in which the boy shall rule unchallenged. The Mulberry Bend Park kept its promise. Before the sod was laid in it two more

were under way in the thickest of the tenement
house crowding, and though the landscape gardener
has tried twice to steal them, he will not succeed.
Play piers and play schools are the order of the day.
We shall yet settle the "causes that operated sociologically" on the boy with a lawn-mower and a
sand heap.   You have got your boy, and the
heredity of the next one, when you can order his
setting.

Social halls for the older people's play are coming
where the saloon has had a monopoly of the cheer
too long.   The labor unions and the reformers work
together to put an end to sweating and child-labor.
The gospel of less law and more enforcement acquired standing while Theodore Roosevelt sat in
the governor's chair rehearsing to us Jefferson's
forgotten lesson that "the whole art and science
of government consists in being honest."   With a
back door to every ordinance that touched the lives
of the people, if indeed the whole thing was not the
subject of open ridicule or the vehicle of official
blackmail, it seemed as if we had provided a perfect municipal machinery for bringing the law into
contempt with the young, and so for wrecking
citizenship by the shortest cut.

Of free soup there is an end.   It was never food
for free men.   The last spoonful was ladled out by
yellow journalism with the certificate of the men

who fought Roosevelt[†] and reform in the police
board that it was good. It is not likely that it
will ever plague us again. Our experience has
taught us a new reading of the old word that
charity covers a multitude of sins. It does. Un-
covering some of them has kept us busy since
our conscience awoke, and there are more left.
The worst of them all, that awful parody on municipal charity, the police station lodging room, is
gone, after twenty years of persistent attack upon
the foul dens, — years during which they were arraigned, condemned, indicted by every authority
having jurisdiction, all to no purpose. The stale
beer dives went with them and with the Bend,
and the grip of the tramp on our throat has been
loosened. We shall not easily throw it off altogether, for the tramp has a vote, too, for which
Tammany, with admirable ingenuity, found a new
use, when the ante-election inspection of lodging
houses made them less available for colonization
purposes than they had been. Perhaps I should
say a new way of very old use. It was simplicity
itself. Instead of keeping tramps in hired lodgings
for weeks at a daily outlay, the new way was to
send them all to the island on short commitments
during the canvass, and vote them from there *en
bloc* at the city's expense.

Time and education must solve that, like so

†Theodore Roosevelt (1858–1919) was president of New York City's
four-man civilian police commission, 1895–1897. Jacob Riis, as a police
reporter, sometimes accompanied Roosevelt on nighttime prowls to
check on how well the police were fulfilling their duties.

many other problems which the slum has thrust
upon us.   They are the forces upon which, when
we have gone as far as our present supply of steam

Mulberry Street Police Station.   Waiting for the Lodging to open.

will carry us, we must always fall back; and this
we may do with confidence so long as we keep
stirring, if it is only marking time, when that is all
that can be done.   It is·in the retrospect that one
sees how far we have come, after all, and from that

gathers courage for the rest of the way. Thirty-two
years have passed since I slept in a police station
lodging house, a lonely lad, and was robbed, beaten,
and thrown out for protesting; and when the vagrant
cur that had joined its homelessness to mine, and
had sat all night at the door waiting for me to come
out, — it had been clubbed away the night before,
— snarled and showed its teeth at the doorman,
raging and impotent I saw it beaten to death on
the step. I little dreamed then that the friendless
beast, dead, should prove the undoing of the monstrous wrong done by the maintenance of these
evil holes to every helpless man and woman who
was without shelter in New York; but it did. It was
after an inspection of the lodging rooms, when I
stood with Theodore Roosevelt, then president of
the police board, in the one where I had slept that
night, and told him of it, that he swore they should
go. And go they did, as did so many another
abuse in those two years of honest purpose and
effort. I hated them. It may not have been a very
high motive to furnish power for municipal reform;
but we had tried every other way, and none of them
worked. Arbitration is good, but there are times
when it becomes necessary to knock a man down
and arbitrate sitting on him, and this was such a
time. It was what we started out to do with the
rear tenements, the worst of the slum barracks, and

it would have been better had we kept on that track. I have always maintained that we made a false move when we stopped to discuss damages with the land-lord, or to hear his side of it at all. His share in it was our grievance; it blocked the mortality records with its burden of human woe. The damage was all ours, the profit all his. If there are damages to collect, he should foot the bill, not we. Vested rights are to be protected, but, as I have said, no man has a right to be protected in killing his neighbor.

However, they are down, the worst of them. The community has asserted its right to destroy tenements that destroy life, and for that cause. We bought the slum off in the Mulberry Bend at its own figure. On the rear tenements we set the price, and set it low. It was a long step. Bottle Alley is gone, and Bandits' Roost. Bone Alley, Thieves' Alley, and Kerosene Row,— they are all gone. Hell's Kitchen and Poverty Gap have ac-quired standards of decency; Poverty Gap has risen even to the height of neckties. The time is fresh in my recollection when a different kind of necktie was its pride; when the boy-murderer — he was barely nineteen — who wore it on the gallows took leave of the captain of detectives with the cheerful invitation to "come over to the wake. They'll have a hell of a time." And the event fully re-

deemed the promise. The whole Gap turned out
to do the dead bully honor. I have not heard from
the Gap, and hardly from Hell's Kitchen, in five
years. The last news from the Kitchen was when
the thin wedge of a column of negroes, in their up-

Night in Gotham Court.

town migration, tried to squeeze in, and provoked
a race war; but that in fairness should not be laid
up against it. In certain local aspects it might be
accounted a sacred duty; as much so as to get
drunk and provoke a fight on the anniversary of the
battle of the Boyne. But on the whole the Kitchen
has grown orderly. The gang rarely beats a police-

man nowadays, and it has not killed one in a long
while.

So, one after another, the outworks of the slum
have been taken.   It has been beaten in many
battles; even to the double-decker tenement on
the twenty-five-foot lot have we put a stop.   But
its legacy is with us in the habitations of two
million souls.   This is the sore spot, and as against
it all the rest seems often enough unavailing.   Yet
it cannot be.   It is true that the home, about
which all that is to work for permanent progress
must cluster, is struggling against desperate odds
in the tenement, and that the struggle has been
reflected in the morals of the people, in the corruption of the young, to an alarming extent; but it
must be that the higher standards now set up on
every hand, in the cleaner streets, in the better
schools, in the parks and the clubs, in the settlements, and in the thousand and one agencies for
good that touch and help the lives of the poor
at as many points, will tell at no distant day, and
react upon the homes and upon their builders.   In
fact, we know it is so from our experience last fall,
when the summons to battle for the people's homes
came from the young on the East Side.   It was
their fight for the very standards I spoke of, their
reply to the appeal they made to them.

To any one who knew that East Side ten years

ago, the difference between that day and this in the
appearance of the children whom he sees there must
be striking.   Rags and dirt are now the exception
rather than the rule.   Perhaps the statement is a
trifle too strong as to the dirt; but dirt is not harm-
ful except when coupled with rags; it can be
washed off, and nowadays is washed off where such
a thing would have been considered affectation in
the days that were.   Soap and water have worked a
visible cure already that goes more than skin-deep.
They are moral agents of the first value in the slum.
And the day is coming soon now, when with real
rapid transit and the transmission of power to suburban workshops the reason for the outrageous crowding shall cease to exist.   It has been a long while,
a whole century of city packing, closer and more
close; but it looks as if the tide were to turn at
last.   Meanwhile, philanthropy is not sitting idle
and waiting.   It is building tenements on the humane plan that lets in sunshine and air and hope.
It is putting up hotels deserving of the name for the
army that but just now had no other home than the
cheap lodging houses which Inspector Byrnes fitly
called "nurseries of crime."   These also are standards from which there is no backing down, even if
coming up to them is slow work: and they are here
to stay, for they pay.   That is the test.   Not charity,
but justice, — that is the gospel which they preach.

Flushed with the success of many victories, we challenged the slum to a fight to the finish in 1897, and bade it come on. It came on. On our side fought the bravest and best. The man who marshalled the citizen forces for their candidate had been foremost in building homes, in erecting baths for the people, in directing the self-sacrificing labors

A Mulberry Bend Alley.

of the oldest and worthiest of the agencies for improving the condition of the poor. With him battled men who had given lives of patient study and effort to the cause of helping their fellow-men. Shoulder to shoulder with them stood the thoughtful workingman from the East Side tenement. The slum, too, marshalled its forces. Tammany produced its notes. It pointed to the increased tax rate, showed what it had cost to build schools and parks and to clean house, and called it criminal recklessness. The issue was made sharp and clear. The war cry of the slum was characteristic: " To hell with reform ! " We all remember the result. Politics interfered, and turned victory into defeat. We were beaten. I shall never forget that election night. I walked home through the Bowery in the midnight hour, and saw it gorging itself, like a starved wolf, upon the promise of the morrow. Drunken men and women sat in every doorway, howling ribald songs and curses. Hard faces I had not seen for years showed themselves about the dives. The mob made merry after its fashion. The old days were coming back. Reform was dead, and decency with it.

A year later, I passed that same way on the night of election.[1] The scene was strangely changed. The street was unusually quiet for such a time. Men stood in groups about the saloons, and talked in whispers, with serious faces. The name of Roosevelt was heard on every hand. The dives were running, but there was no shouting, and violence was discouraged. When, on the following day, I met the proprietor of one of the oldest con-cerns in the Bowery, — which, while doing a legiti-

[1] 1898, when Roosevelt was elected Governor after a fierce fight with Tammany.

"In the hallway I ran across two children, little tots, who were inquiring their way to 'the commissioner.'"

mate business, caters necessarily to its crowds, and therefore sides with them, — he told me with bitter reproach how he had been stricken in pocket. A gambler had just been in to see him, who had come on from the far West, in anticipation of a wide-open town, and had got all ready to open a house in the Tenderloin. " He brought $40,000 to put in the business, and he came to take it away to Baltimore. Just now the cashier of —— Bank told me that two other gentlemen — gamblers? yes, that's what you call them — had drawn $130,000 which they would have invested here, and had gone after him. Think of all that money gone to Baltimore! That's what you've done!"

I went over to police headquarters, thinking of the sad state of that man, and in the hallway I ran across two children, little tots, who were inquiring their way to "the commissioner." The older was a hunchback girl, who led her younger brother (he could not have been over five or six years old) by the hand. They explained their case to me. They came from Allen Street. Some "bad ladies" had moved into the tenement, and when complaint was made that sent the police there, the children's father, who was a poor Jewish tailor, was blamed. The tenants took it out of the boy by punching his nose till it bled. Whereupon the children went straight to Mulberry Street to see "the commissioner" and get justice. It was the first time in twenty years that I had known Allen Street to come to police headquarters for justice and in the discovery that the legacy of Roosevelt had reached even to the little children I read the doom of the slum, despite its loud vauntings.

No, it was not true that reform was dead, with decency. We had our innings four years later and proved it; of which more farther on. It was not the slum that had won; it was we who had lost. We were not up to the mark, — not yet. We may lose again, more than once, but even our losses shall be our gains, if we learn from them. And we are doing that. New York is a many times cleaner and better city to-day than it was twenty or even ten years ago. Then I was able to grasp easily the whole plan for wresting it from the neglect and indifference that had put us where we were. It was chiefly, almost wholly, remedial in its scope. Now it is preventive, constructive, and no ten men could gather all the threads and hold them. We have made, are making, headway, and no Tammany has the power to stop us. They know it, too, at the Hall, and were in such frantic haste to fill their pockets this last time that they abandoned their old ally, the tax rate, and the pretence of making bad government cheap government. Tammany dug its arms into the treasury fairly up to the elbows, raising taxes, assessments, and salaries all at once, and collecting blackmail from everything in sight. Its charges for the lesson it taught us came high; but we can afford to pay them. If to learning it we add common sense, we shall discover the bearings of it all without trouble. Yesterday I picked up a book, — a learned disquisition on government, — and read on the title-page, " Affectionately dedicated to all who despise politics." That was not common sense. To win the battle with the slum, we must not begin by despising politics. We have been doing that too long. The politics of the slum are apt to be like the slum itself, dirty. Then they must be cleaned. It is what the fight is about. Politics are the weapon. We must learn to use it so as to cut straight and sure. That is common sense, and the golden rule as applied to Tammany.

Some years ago, the United States government conducted an inquiry into the slums of great cities. To its staff of experts was attached a chemist, who gathered and isolated a lot of bacilli with fearsome Latin names, in the tenements where he went. Among those he labelled were the *Staphylococcus pyogenes albus*, the *Micrococcus fervidosus*, the *Saccharomyces rosaceus*, and the *Bacillus buccalis fortuitus*. I made a note of the names at the time, because of the dread with which they inspired me.

But I searched the collection in vain for the real bacillus of the slum. It escaped science, to be identified by human sympathy and a conscience-stricken community with that of ordinary human selfishness. The antitoxin has been found, and it is applied successfully. Since justice has replaced charity on the prescription the patient is improving. And the improvement is not confined to him; it is general. Conscience is not a local issue in our day. A few years ago, a United States senator sought reëlection on the platform that the decalogue and the golden rule were glittering generalities that had no place in politics, and lost. We have not quite reached the millennium yet, but since then a man was governor in the Empire State, elected on the pledge that he would rule by the ten commandments. These are facts that mean much or little, according to the way one looks at them. The significant thing is that they are facts, and that, in spite of slipping and sliding, the world moves forward, not backward. The poor we shall have always with us, but the slum we need not have. These two do not rightfully belong together. Their present partnership is at once poverty's worst hardship and our worst blunder.

CHAPTER III

THE DEVIL'S MONEY

THAT was what the women called it, and the name stuck and killed the looters. The young men of the East Side began it, and the women finished it. It was a campaign of decency against Tammany, that one of 1901 of which I am going to make the record brief as may be, for we all remember it; and also, thank God, that decency won the fight.

If ever inhuman robbery deserved the name, that which caused the downfall of Tammany surely did. Drunk with the power and plunder of four long unchallenged years, during which the honest name of democracy was pilloried in the sight of all men as the active partner of blackmail and the brothel, the monstrous malignity reached a point at last where it was no longer to be borne. Then came the crash. The pillory lied. Tammany is no more a political organization than it is the benevolent concern it is innocently supposed to be by some people who never learn. It neither knows nor cares for principles. " Koch ?"[†]said its President of the Health Department when mention was made in

†Robert Koch (1843–1910), a German physician, identified the tuberculosis and cholera bacilli; he won a Nobel Prize in 1905.

his hearing of the authority of the great German doctor, "who is that man Koch you are talking about?" And he was typical of the rest. His function was to collect the political revenue of the department, and the city was overrun with smallpox for the first time in thirty years. The police force, of whom Roosevelt had made heroes, became the tools of robbers. Robbery is the business of Tammany. For that, and for that only, is it organized. Politics are merely the convenient pretence. I do not mean that every Tammany man is a thief. Probably the great majority of its adherents honestly believe that it stands for something worth fighting for,—for personal freedom, for the people's cause,—and their delusion is the opportunity of scoundrels. They have never understood its organization or read its history.

For a hundred years that has been an almost unbroken record of fraud and peculation. Its very founder, William Mooney,[†] was charged with being a deserter from the patriot army to the British forces. He was later on removed from office as superintendent of the almshouse for swindling the city. Aaron Burr plotted treason within its councils. The briefest survey of the administration of the metropolis from his day down to that of Tweed shows a score of its conspicuous leaders removed, indicted, or tried, for default, bribe-taking, or theft;

†William Mooney (1756–1831) founded the New York Society of Tammany in 1786 as a fraternal organization. Decades later, as superintendent of the City's almshouse, he spent little on the residents' needs and much on rum.

and the fewest were punished. The civic history of New York to the present day is one long struggle to free itself from its blighting grip. Its people's parties, its committees of seventy, were ever emergency measures to that end, but they succeeded only for a season. There have been decent Tammany mayors, but not for long. There have been attempts to reform the organization from within, but they have been failures. You cannot reform an " organized appetite " except by reforming it away. And then there would be nothing left of the organization.

For whatever the rank and file have believed, the organization has never been anything else but the means of satisfying the appetite that never will be cloyed. Whatever principles it has professed, they have served the purpose only of filling the pockets of the handful of men who rule its inner councils and use it to their own enrichment and our loss and disgrace. We have heard its most successful leader testify brazenly before the Mazet legislative committee[†] that he was in politics working for his own pocket all the time. That was his principle. And his followers applauded till the room rang.

That is the Tammany which has placed murderers and gamblers in its high seats. That is the Tammany which you have to fight at every step when battling with the slum; the Tammany which, un-

†This committee of the Republican-controlled New York State legislature conducted hearings on corruption in New York City government during 1900.

masked and beaten by the Parkhurst and Lexow disclosures,[†] came back with the Greater New York to exploit the opportunity reform had made for itself, and gave us a lesson we will not soon forget. For at last it dropped all pretence and showed its real face to us.

Civil service reform was thrown to the winds; the city departments were openly parcelled out among the district leaders: a $2000 office to one, — two $1000 to another to even up. That is the secret of the "organization" which politicians admire. It does make a strong body. How it served the city in one department, the smallpox epidemic bore witness. That department, the pride of the city and its mainstay in days of danger, was wrecked. The first duty of the new president, when the four years were over and Tammany out again, was to remove more than a hundred and fifty useless employees. Their only function had been to draw the salaries which the city paid. The streets that had been clean became dirty — the "voter" was back "behind the broom" — and they swarmed once more with children for whom there was no room in school. Officials who drew big salaries starved the inmates of the almshouse on weak tea and dry bread, and Bellevue, the poor people's hospital, became a public scandal. In one night there were five drunken fights, one of them between two of the attendants

†The Rev. Dr. Charles H. Parkhurst (1842–1933), rector of Madison Square Presbyterian Church, began preaching against political corruption, police collusion with criminals, and their damaging social

who dropped the corpse they were carrying to the morgue and fought over it. The tenements were plunged back into the foulness of their worst day; the inspectors were answerable, not to the Health Board, but to the district leader, and the landlord who stood well with him thumbed his nose at them and at their orders to clean up. The neighborhood parks, acquired at such heavy sacrifice, lay waste. Tammany took no step toward improving them. One it did take up at Fort George; and though the property only cost the city $600,000, the bills for taking it were $127,467. That is the true Tammany style. In the Seward Park, where the need of relief was greatest, Tammany election district captains built booths, rent free, for the sale of dry goods and fish. That was "their share." Wealthy corporations were made to pay heavily for "peace"; timid storekeepers were blackmailed. One, a Jew, told his story: he was ordered to pay five dollars a week for privilege of keeping open Sundays. He paid, and they asked ten. When he refused, he was told that it would be the worse for him. He closed up. The very next week he was sued for a hundred dollars by a man of whom he had never borrowed anything. He did not defend the suit, and it went against him. In three days the sheriff was in his store. He knew the hopelessness of it then, and went out and mortgaged his store and paid the bill. The next week

effects on Valentine's Day, 1892. His influence led Clarence Lexow (1852–1910), an upstate Republican state senator, to conduct 1894 hearings on corruption in New York City's government and police force.

another man sued him for a hundred dollars he did not owe. He went and threw himself on his mercy, and the man let him off for the costs.

He was one of the many thousands of toilers who look with fear to the approaching summer because it is then the hot tenement kills their babies. Their one chance of life then depends upon the supply of ice that is hawked from door to door in small pieces, since tenements have rarely other refrigerator than the draughty airshaft. The greed of politicians plotted to deprive them of even this chance. They had control of docks and means of transportation and they cornered the supply, raising the price from thirty to sixty cents a hundred pounds and suppressing the five-cent piece. Some of them that sat in high official station grew rich, but the poor man's babies died and he saw at last the quality of the friendship Tammany professed for him. The push-cart pedlers, blackmailed and driven from pillar to post, saw it. They had escaped from unbearable tyranny in their old home to find a worse where they thought to be free; for to their oppressors yonder at least their women were sacred.

It is difficult to approach calmly what is left of the diabolical recital. The police, set once more to collecting blackmail from saloon keepers, gambling hells, policy shops, and houses of ill fame,

under a chief who on a policeman's pay became
in a few short years fairly bloated with wealth, sank
to the level of their occupation or into helpless or
hopeless compliance with the apparently inevitable.
The East Side, where the home struggled against
such heavy odds, became a sinkhole of undreamt-of
corruption.   The tenements were overrun with lewd
women who paid the police for protection and received it.   Back of them the politician who controlled
all and took the profits.   This newspaper arraignment published in January, 1901, tells the bald truth:

" Imagine, if you can, a section of the city territory
completely dominated by one man, without whose
permission neither legitimate nor illegitimate business can be conducted ; where illegitimate business
is encouraged and legitimate business discouraged ;
where the respectable residents have to fasten their
doors and windows summer nights and sit in their
rooms with asphyxiating air and one hundred degrees temperature, rather than try to catch the faint
whiff of breeze in their natural breathing places —
the stoops of their homes ; where naked women
dance by night in the streets, and unsexed men
prowl like vultures through the darkness on " business" not only permitted, but encouraged, by the
police ; where the education of infants begins with
the knowledge of prostitution and the training of
little girls is training in the arts of Phryne ; where
American girls brought up with the refinements
of American homes are imported from small towns
up-state, Massachusetts, Connecticut, and New
Jersey, and kept as virtually prisoners as if they

were locked up behind jail bars until they have lost all semblance of womanhood; where small boys are taught to solicit for the women of disorderly houses; where there is an organized society of young men whose sole business in life is to corrupt young girls and turn them over to bawdy houses; where men walking with their wives along the street are openly insulted; where children that have adult diseases are the chief patrons of the hospitals and dispensaries; where it is the rule, rather than the exception, that murder, rape, robbery, and theft go unpunished — in short, where the premium of the most awful forms of vice is the profit of the politicians.

"There is no 'wine, woman, and song' over there. The 'wine' is stale beer, the 'woman' is a degraded money-making machine, and the 'song' is the wail of the outraged innocent. The political backers have got it down to what has been called a 'cash-register, commutation-ticket basis,' called so from the fact that in some of these places they issued tickets, on the plan of a commutation meal-ticket, and had cash registers at the entries."

Lest some one think the newspaper exaggerating after all, let me add Bishop Potter's[†] comment before his Diocesan Convention. He will not be suspected of sensationalism:

"The corrupt system, whose infamous details have been steadily uncovered to our increasing horror and humiliation, was brazenly ignored by those who were fattening on its spoils; and the world was presented with the astounding spectacle

[†]Bishop Henry Codman Potter, Episcopal bishop of New York, who said the benediction at the Statue of Liberty's 1886 dedication, began building the Cathedral Church of St. John the Divine at W. 112th Street and Amsterdam Avenue. Bishop Potter presided over the Episcopal Church in New York City from the Pro-Cathedral on Stanton Street on the Lower East Side, which Riis mentions several times.

of a great municipality whose civic mechanism was largely employed in trading in the bodies and souls of the innocent and defenceless. What has been published in this connection is but the merest hint of what exists — and exists, most appalling of all, as the evidence has come to me under the seal of confidence in overwhelming volume and force to demonstrate — under a system of terrorism which compels its victims to recognize that to denounce it means the utter ruin, so far as all their worldly interests are concerned, of those who dare to do so. This infamous organization for making merchandise of girls and boys, and defenceless men and women, has adroitly sought to obscure a situation concerning which all honest people are entirely clear, by saying that vice cannot be wholly suppressed. Nobody has made upon the authorities of New York any such grotesque demand. All that our citizens have asked is that the government of the city shall not be employed to protect a trade in vice, which is carried on for the benefit of a political organization. The case is entirely clear. No Mephistophelian cunning can obscure it, and I thank God that there is abundant evidence that the end of such a condition of things is not far off."

It was, indeed, coming. But Tammany, gorged with power and the lust of it, neither saw nor heeded. At a meeting of young men on the East Side, one of them, responding to an address by Felix Adler,[†] drew such a heart-rending picture of the conditions prevailing there that the echoes of the meeting found its way into the farthest places:

†Felix Adler, Ph.D. (1851–1933), born in Germany to Jewish parents and educated at Columbia University and in Germany, was a professor and a lecturer on politics, ethics, and philosophy who founded the New York Society for Ethical Culture in 1876.

" Now you go," he said, "to your quiet home in
a decent street where no harm comes to you or
your wife or children in the night, for it is their
home. And we — we go with our high resolves,
the noble ambitions you have stirred, to our tenements where evil lurks in the darkness at every
step, where innocence is murdered in babyhood,
where mothers bemoan the birth of a daughter as
the last misfortune, where virtue is sold into a worse
slavery than ever our fathers knew, and our sisters
betrayed by paid panders; where the name of home
is as a bitter mockery, for alas! we have none.
These are the standards to which we go from here."
And then followed the whole amazing story of damning conspiracy between power and vice in those
tenements before which a whole city stood aghast.

A meeting was called the following day by Dr.
Adler, of men and women who had the welfare of
their city at heart, and when they had heard the
story, they resolved that they would not rest till
those things were no longer true. One of their
number was the Rev. Robert Paddock, the priest
in charge of Bishop Potter's Pro-Cathedral, right in
the heart of it all in Stanton Street. He set about
gathering evidence that would warrant the arraignment of the evil-doers in his district; but when he
brought it to the police he was treated with scorn
and called liar.

The measure was nearly full. Bishop Potter came back from the East, where he had been travelling, and met his people. Out of that meeting came the most awful arraignment of a city government which the world has ever heard. " Nowhere else on earth," the Bishop wrote to the Mayor of New York, "certainly not in any civilized or Christian community, does there exist such a situation as defiles and dishonors New York to-day."

" In the name of these little ones," his letter ran, "these weak and defenceless ones, Christian and Hebrew alike, of many races and tongues, but homes in which God is feared and His law revered, and virtue and decency honored and exemplified, I call upon you, sir, to save these people, who are in a very real way committed to your charge, from a living hell, defiling, deadly, damning, to which the criminal supineness of the constituted authorities set for the defence of decency and good order, threatens to doom them."

The Mayor's virtual response was to put the corrupt Chief of Police in practically complete and irresponsible charge of the force. Richard Croker,[†] the boss of Tammany Hall, had openly counselled violence at the election then pending (1900), and the Chief in a general order to the force repeated the threat. But they had reckoned without Governor Roosevelt. He compelled the Mayor to

†Richard Croker (1841–1922), brought to New York from Ireland as a child, controlled Democratic politics with the Tammany "machine" by 1886. The major corruption scandal of 1894, focused on police protection of prostitution, did not dislodge him. He was power broker until 1901, when a non-Tammany Democrat, Seth Low, was elected Mayor.

have the order rescinded, and removed the District Attorney who had been elected on the compact platform "to hell with reform." The whole city was aroused. The Chamber of Commerce formed a Committee of Fifteen which soon furnished evidence without stint of the corruption that was abroad. The connection between the police and the gambling dens was demonstrated, and also that the police were the mere tools of "politics." In 237 tenements that were investigated 290 flats were found harboring prostitutes in defiance of law. The police were compelled to act. The "Cadets," who lived by seducing young girls and selling them to their employer at $25 a head, were arrested and sent to jail for long terms. They showed fight, and it developed that they had a regular organization with political affiliations.

The campaign of 1901 approached. Judge Jerome† went upon the stump and rattled the brass checks from the cash-register that paid for the virtue of innocent girls, the daughters of his hearers. The mothers of the East Side, the very Tammany women themselves, rose and denounced the devil's money, and made their husbands and brothers go to the polls and vote their anger.[1] The world knows

---

[1] Up to that time I wrote of Tammany as "she"; but I dropped it then as an outrage upon the sex. "It" it is and will remain hereafter. I am ashamed of ever having put the stigma on the name of woman.

†William Travers Jerome (1859–1934), a Democrat, served as District Attorney for New York County, 1901–1909, after his judgeship. Jerome Avenue, a major Bronx thoroughfare, is named for him.

the rest. The "Red Light" of the East Side damned Tammany to defeat. Seth Low was elected mayor.[†] Decency once more moved into the City Hall and into the homes of the poor. Croker abdicated and went away, and a new day broke for our harassed city.

That, in brief, is the story of the campaign that discharged the devil as paymaster, and put his money out of circulation — for good, let us all hope.

[†]Seth Low (1850–1916), a reformer, had served as mayor of the City of Brooklyn (1881–1885) and president of Columbia University (1890–1901). He had been defeated by the Tammany candidate in the 1897 mayoral election, for the term that began with Greater New York on January 1, 1898. His victory in the 1901 election foretold the end of Tammany control of New York City politics and government.

CHAPTER IV

THE BLIGHT OF THE DOUBLE-DECKER

In a Stanton Street tenement, the other day, I stumbled upon a Polish capmaker's home. There were other capmakers in the house, Russian and Polish, but they simply "lived" there. This one had a home. The fact proclaimed itself the moment the door was opened, in spite of the darkness. The rooms were in the rear, gloomy with the twilight of the tenement although the day was sunny without, but neat, even cosey. It was early, but the day's chores were evidently done. The tea-kettle sang on the stove, at which a bright-looking girl of twelve, with a pale but cheery face, and sleeves brushed back to the elbows, was busy poking up the fire. A little boy stood by the window, flattening his nose against the pane, and gazed wistfully up among the chimney pots where a piece of blue sky about as big as the kitchen could be made out. I remarked to the mother that they were nice rooms.

"Ah yes," she said, with a weary little smile that struggled bravely with hope long deferred, "but it

"With his whole hungry little soul in his eyes."

is hard to make a home here. We would so like to live in the front, but we can't pay the rent."

I knew the front with its unlovely view of the tenement street too well, and I said a good word for the air-shaft — yard or court it could not be called, it was too small for that — which rather surprised myself. I had found few virtues enough in it before. The girl at the stove had left off poking the fire. She broke in the moment I finished, with eager enthusiasm: "Why, they have the sun in there. When the door is opened the light comes right in your face."

"Does it never come here?" I asked, and wished I had not done so, as soon as the words were spoken. The child at the window was listening, with his whole hungry little soul in his eyes.

Yes, it did, she said. Once every summer, for a little while, it came over the houses. She knew the month and the exact hour of the day when its rays shone into their home, and just the reach of its slant on the wall. They had lived there six years. In June the sun was due. A haunting fear that the baby would ask how long it was till June — it was February then — took possession of me, and I hastened to change the subject. Warsaw was their old home. They kept a little store there, and were young and happy. Oh, it was a fine city, with parks and squares, and bridges over the beautiful river,—and grass and flowers and birds and soldiers, put in the girl breathlessly. She remembered. But the children kept coming, and they went across the sea to give them a better chance. Father made fifteen dollars a week, much money; but there were long seasons when there was no work. She, the mother, was never very well here,—she hadn't any strength; and the baby! She glanced at his grave white face, and took him in her arms. The picture of the two, and of the pale-faced girl longing back to the fields and the sunlight, in their prison of gloom and gray walls, haunts me yet. I have not had the courage to go back since. I recalled the report of an English army surgeon, which I read years ago, on the many more soldiers that died — were killed would be more correct— in barracks into which the sun never shone than in those that were open to the light. They have yet two months to the sun in Stanton Street.

The capmaker's case is the case of the nineteenth century of civilization against the metropolis of America. The home, the family, are the rallying points of civilization. The greatness of a city is to be measured, not by its balance sheets of exports and imports, not by its fleet of merchantmen, or by its miles of paved streets, nor even by its colleges, its art museums, its schools of learning, but by its homes. New York has all these, but its people live

in tenements where " all the conditions which sur-
round childhood, youth, and womanhood make for
unrighteousness."[1] This still, after forty years of
battling, during which we have gone on piling layer
upon layer of human beings and calling *that* home !
The 15,309 tenements the Council of Hygiene found
in 1864 have become 47,000, and their population of
495,592 has swelled into nearly a million and three-
quarters.[2] There were four flights of stairs at most
in the old days. Now they build tenements six and
seven stories high, and the street has become a mere
runway. It cannot take up the crowds for which
it was never meant. Go look at those East Side
streets on a summer evening or on any fair Sunday
when, at all events, some of the workers are at
home, and see what they are like. In 1880 the
average number of persons to each dwelling in New
York, counting them all in, the rich and the poor,
was 16.37 ; in 1890 it was 18.52 ; in 1900, according to
the United States census, the average in the old city
was 20.4. It all means that there are so many more
and so much bigger tenements, and four families
to the floor where there were two before. Statistics

---

[1] Report of Tenement House Commission, 1900.

[2] Tenement house census of 1900 : Manhattan and the Bronx boroughs (the old city), 46,993 tenements, with a population of 1,701,643.
The United States census of the two boroughs gave them a population
of 2,050,600. In the Greater New York there are 82,000 tenements,
and two-thirds of our nearly four millions of people live in them.

are not my hobby. I like to get their human story out of them. Anybody who wants them can get the figures in the census books. But as an instance of the unchecked drift — unchecked as yet — look at this record of the Tenth Ward, the "most crowded spot in the world." In 1880, when it had not yet attained to that bad eminence, it contained 47,554 persons, or 432.3 to the acre. In 1890 the census showed a population of 57,596, which was 522 to the acre. The police census of 1895 found 70,168 persons living in 1514 houses, which was 643.08 to the acre. The Health Department's census for the first half of 1898 gave a total of 82,175 persons living in 1201 tenements, with 313 inhabited buildings yet to be heard from. This is the process of doubling up, — literally, since the cause and the vehicle of it all is the double-decker tenement, — which in the year 1900 had crowded a single block in that ward at the rate of 1724 persons per acre, and one in the Eleventh Ward at the rate of 1894.[1] It goes on not in the Tenth Ward or on the East Side only, but throughout the city. When, in 1897, it was proposed to lay out a small park in the Twenty-second Ward, up on the far West Side, it was shown that five blocks in that section, between Forty-ninth and

[1] Police census of 1900, block bounded by Canal, Hester, Eldridge, and Forsyth streets: size 375 × 200, population 2969, rate per acre 1724. Block bounded by Stanton, Houston, Attorney, and Ridge streets: size 200 × 300, population 2609, rate per acre 1894.

Sixty-second streets and Ninth and Eleventh avenues, had a population of more than 3000 each. The block between Sixty-first and Sixty-second streets and Tenth and Eleventh avenues harbored 4254 when the police made a count in 1900, which meant 1158 persons to the acre.

These are the facts. The question is, are they beyond our control? Let us look at them squarely and see. In the first place, it is no answer to the charge that New York's way of housing its workers is the worst in the world to say that they are better off than they were where they came from. It is not true, in most cases, as far as the home is concerned; a shanty is better than a flat in a slum tenement, any day. Even if it were true, it would still be beside the issue. In Poland my capmaker counted for nothing. Nothing was expected of him. Here he ranks, after a few brief years, politically equal with the man who hires his labor. A citizen's duty is expected of him, and home and citizenship are convertible terms. The observation of the Frenchman who had watched the experiment of herding two thousand human beings in eight tenement barracks over yonder, that the result was the "exasperation of the tenant against society," is true the world over. We have done as badly in New York. Social hatefulness is not a good soil for citizenship to grow in, where political equality rules.

Nor is it going to help us any to charge it all to the tenant " who *will* herd." He herds because he has no other chance; because it puts money into some one's pockets to let him. We never yet have passed a law for his relief that was not attacked in the same or the next legislature in the interest of the tenement-house builder. Commission after commission has pointed out that the tenants are " better than the houses they live in "; that they " respond quickly to improved conditions." Those are not honest answers. The man who talks that way is a fool, or worse.

The truth is that if we cannot stop the crowds from coming, we *can* make homes for those who come, and at a profit on the investment. That has been proved, is being proved now every day. It is not a case of transforming human nature in the tenant, but of reforming it in the landlord builder. It is a plain question of the per cent he is willing to take.

So then, we have got it on the moral ground where it belongs. Let the capmaker's case be ever so strong, we shall yet win. We shall win his fight and our own together; they are one. This is the way it stands at the outset of the twentieth century: New York's housing is still the worst in the world. We have the biggest crowds. We have been killing the home that is our very life at the most reckless rate. But, badly as we are off and shall be off for years to come, — allowing even that we are getting worse off in the matter of crowding, — we know now that we can do better. We have done it. We are every year wresting more light and air from the builder. He no longer dares come out and fight in the open, for he knows that public sentiment is against him. The people understand — to what an extent is shown in a report of a Tenement House Committee in the city of Yonkers, which the postman put on my table this minute. The committee was organized "to prevent the danger to Yonkers of incurring the same evils that have fallen so heavily upon New York and have cost that city millions of money and thousands of lives." It sprang from the Civic League, was appointed by a Republican mayor and indorsed by a Democratic council! That is as it should be. So, we shall win.

In fact, we are winning now, backed by this very understanding. The double-decker is doomed, and the twenty-five-foot lot has had its day. We are building tenements in which it is possible to rear homes. We are at last in a fair way to make the slum unprofitable, and that is the only way to make it go. So that we may speed it the more let us go with the capmaker a while and get his point of view. After all, that is the one that counts; the community is not nearly as much interested in the profits of the landlord as in the welfare of the workers.

That we may get it fairly, suppose we take a stroll through a tenement-house neighborhood and see for ourselves. We were in Stanton Street. Let us start there, then, going east. Towering barracks on either side, five, six stories high. Teeming crowds. Push-cart men " moved on " by the policeman, who seems to exist only for the purpose. Forsyth Street: there is a church on the corner, Polish and Catholic, a combination that strikes one as queer here on the East Side, where Polish has come to be synonymous with Jewish. I have cause to remember that corner. A man killed his wife in this house, and was hanged for it. Just across the street, on the stoop of that brown-stone tenement, the tragedy was reënacted the next year; only the murderer saved the county trouble and expense by taking himself off also. That other stoop in the same row witnessed a suicide.

Why do I tell you these things ? Because they are true. The policeman here will bear me out. They belong to the ordinary setting of life in a crowd such as this. It is never so little worth living, and therefore held so cheap along with the fierce, unceasing battle that goes on to save it. You will go no further unless I leave it out ? Very well; I shall leave out the murder after we have passed the block yonder. The tragedy of that is of a kind that comes too close to the everyday life of tenement-house people to be omitted. The house caught fire in the night, and five were burned to death,—father, mother, and three children. The others got out; why not they? They stayed, it seems, to make sure none was left; they were not willing to leave one behind, to save themselves. And then it was too late; the stairs were burning. There was no proper fire escape. That was where the murder came in; but it was not all chargeable to the landlord, nor even the greater part. More than thirty years ago, in 1867, the state made it law that the stairs in every tenement four stories high should be fireproof, and forbade the storing of any inflammable material in such houses. I do not know when the law was repealed, or if it ever was. I only know that in 1892 the Fire Department, out of pity for the tenants and regard for the safety of its own men, forced through an amendment to the building law, requiring the stairs of the common type of five-story tenements to be built of fireproof material, and that they are still of wood, just as they always were. Ninety-seven per cent of the tenements examined by the late Tenement House Commission (1900) in Manhattan had stairs of wood. In Brooklyn they were *all* of wood. Once, a couple of years ago, I looked up the Superintendent of Buildings and asked him what it meant. I showed him the law, which said that the stairs should be "built of slow-burning construction or fireproof material"; and he put his finger upon the clause that follows, "as the Superintendent of Buildings shall decide." The law gave him discretion, and that is how he used it. "Hard wood burns slowly," said he.

The fire of which I speak was a "cruller fire," if I remember rightly, which is to say that it broke out in the basement bakeshop, where they were boiling crullers (doughnuts) in fat, at 4 A.M., with a hundred tenants asleep in the house above them. The fat went into the fire, and the rest followed. I suppose that I had to do with a hundred such fires, as a police reporter, before, under the protest of the Gilder Tenement House Commission[†] and the Good Government Clubs, the boiling of fat in tenement bakeshops was forbidden. The Chief of the Fire Department, in his testimony before the commission, said that "tenements are erected mainly with a view of returning a large income for the amount of capital invested. It is only after a fire in which great loss of life occurs that any interest whatever is taken in the safety of the occupants." The Superintendent of Buildings, after such a fire in March, 1896, said that there were thousands of tenement firetraps in the city.

[†]Richard Watson Gilder (1844–1909) was managing editor of *Scribner's Monthly* and editor-in-chief when it was continued as *The Century* magazine. He was chairman of the New York Tenement House Commission, 1894.

My reporter's notebook bears witness to the correct-
ness of his statement, and it has many blank leaves
that are waiting to be put to that use yet.   The
reckoning for eleven years showed that, of 35,844
fires in New York, 53.18 per cent were in tenement
houses, though they were only a little more than
31 per cent of all the buildings, and that 177 occupants were killed, 523 maimed, and 625 rescued by
the firemen.   Their rescue cost the lives of three of
these brave men, and 453 were injured in the effort.
And when all that is said, not the half is told.   A
fire in the night in one of those human beehives,
with its terror and woe, is one of the things that
live in the recollection ever after as a terrible nightmare.   The fire-chief thought that every tenement
house should be fireproof, but he warned the commission that such a proposition would "meet with
strong opposition from the different interests,
should legislation be requested."   He was right.
It is purely a question of the builder's profits.   Up
to date we have rescued the first floor from him.
That must be fireproof.   We shall get the whole
structure yet if we pull long enough and hard
enough, as we will.

Here is a block of tenements inhabited by poor
Jews.   Most of the Jews who live over here are
poor; and the poorer they are, the higher rent do
they pay, and the more do they crowd to make it

up between them.   " The destruction of the poor is
their poverty."   It is only the old story in a new
setting.   The slum landlord's profits were always
the highest.   He spends nothing for repairs, and lays
the blame on the tenant.   The " district leader "
saves him, when Tammany is at the helm, unless
he is on the wrong side of the political fence, in
which case the Sanitary Code comes handy, to
chase him into camp.   A big " order " on his house
is a very effective way of making a tenement-house
landlord discern political truth on the eve of an
important election.   Just before the election which
put Theodore Roosevelt in the Governor's chair at
Albany[†]the sanitary force displayed such activity as
had never been known till then in the examination
of tenements belonging very largely, as it happened,
to sympathizers with the gallant Rough Rider's
cause; and those who knew did not marvel much
at the large vote polled by the Tammany candidate
in the old city.

The halls of these tenements are dark.   Under
the law there should be a light burning, but it is
one of the rarest things to find one.   The thing
seems well-nigh impossible of accomplishment.
When the Good Government Clubs set about backing up the Board of Health in its efforts to work
out this reform, which comes close to being one of
the most necessary of all, — such untold mischief

[†]The New York State election of 1898.

is abroad in the darkness of these thoroughfares, —
the sanitary police reported 12,000 tenement halls
unlighted by night, even, and brought them, by
repeated orders, down to less than 1000 in six
months. I doubt that the light burned in 1000 of
them all a month after the election that brought
Tammany back. It is so easy to put it out when
the policeman's back is turned. Gas costs money.
Let what doesn't take care of itself.

We had a curious instance, at the time, of the
difficulties that sometimes beset reform. Certain
halls that were known to be dark were reported
sufficiently lighted by the policeman of the district,
and it was discovered that it was his standard that
was vitiated. He himself lived in a tenement, and
was used to its gloom. So an order was issued
defining darkness to the sanitary police: if the sink
in the hall could be made out, and the slops over-
flowing on the floor, and if a baby could be seen
on the stairs, the hall was light; if, on the other
hand, the baby's shrieks were the first warning that
it was being trampled upon, the hall was dark.
Some days later the old question arose about an
Eldridge Street tenement. The policeman had
reported the hall light enough. The President of
the Board of Health, to settle it once for all, went
over with me, to see for himself. The hall was
very dark. He sent for the policeman.

" Did you see the sink in that hall ? " he asked.

The policeman said he did.

" But it is pitch dark.   How did you see it ? "

" I lit a match," said the policeman.

Four families live on these floors, with heaven knows how many children.   It was here the police commissioners were requested, in sober earnest, some years ago, by a committee of very practical woman philanthropists, to have the children tagged, as they do in Japan, I am told, so as to save the policeman wear and tear in taking them back and forth between the Eldridge Street police station and headquarters, when they got lost.   If tagged, they could be assorted at once and taken to their homes.   Incidentally, the city would save the expense of many meals.   It was shrewdly suspected that the little ones were lost on purpose in a good many cases, as a way of getting them fed at the public expense.

That the children preferred the excitement of the police station, and the distinction of a trip in charge of a brass-buttoned guardian, to the Ludlow Street flat is easy enough to understand.   A more unlovely existence than that in one of these tenements it would be hard to imagine.   Everywhere is the stench of the kerosene stove that is forever burning, serving for cooking, heating, and ironing alike, until the last atom of oxygen is burned out of the

close air.   Oil is cheaper than coal.   The air shaft
is too busy carrying up smells from below to bring
any air down, even if it is not hung full of washing
in every story, as it ordinarily is.   Enterprising

One Family's Outlook on the Air Shaft.   The Mother said, "Our
Daughter does not care to come Home to Sleep."

tenants turn it to use as a refrigerator as well.
There is at least a draught of air, such as it is.
When fire breaks out, this draught makes of the
air shaft a flue through which the fire roars fiercely
to the roof, so transforming what was meant for the
good of the tenants into their greatest peril.   The

stuffy rooms bring to mind this denunciation of the tenement builder of fifty years ago by an angry writer, " He measures the height of his ceilings by the shortest of the people, and by thin partitions divides the interior into as narrow spaces as the leanest carpenter can work in." Most decidedly, there is not room to swing the proverbial cat in any one of them. In one I helped the children, last holiday, to set up a Christmas tree, so that a glimpse of something that was not utterly sordid and mean might for once enter their lives. Three weeks after, I found the tree standing yet in the corner. It was very cold, and there was no fire in the room. " We were going to burn it," said the little woman, whose husband was then in the insane asylum, "and then I couldn't. It looked so kind o' cheery-like there in the corner." My tree had borne the fruit I wished.

It remained for the New York slum landlord to assess the exact value of a ray of sunlight, — upon the tenant, of course. Here are two back-to-back rear tenements, with dark bedrooms on the south. The flat on the north gives upon a neighbor's yard, and a hole two feet square has been knocked in the wall, letting in air and sunlight; little enough of the latter, but what there is is carefully computed in the lease. Six dollars for this flat, six and a half for the one with the hole in the wall. Six dollars a year per ray. In half a dozen houses in this block have I found the same rate maintained. The modern tenement on the corner goes higher: for four front rooms, "where the sun comes right in your face," seventeen dollars; for the rear flat of three rooms, larger and better every other way, but always dark, like the capmaker's, eleven dollars. From the landlord's point of view, this last is probably a concession. But he is a landlord with a heart. His house is as good a one as can be built on a twenty-five-foot lot. The man who owns the corner building in Orchard Street, with the two adjoining tenements, has no heart. In the depth of last winter I found a family of poor Jews living in a coop under his stairs, an abandoned piece of hallway, in which their baby was born, and for which he made them pay eight dollars a month. It was the most outrageous case of landlord robbery I had ever come across, and it gave me sincere pleasure to assist the sanitary policeman in curtailing his profits by even this much. The hall is not now occupied.

The Jews under the stairs had two children. The shoemaker in the cellar next door had three. They were fighting and snarling like so many dogs over the coarse food on the table before them, when we looked in. The baby, it seems, was the cause of the row. He wanted it all. He was a very dirty and a very fierce baby, and the other two children were no match for him. The shoemaker grunted fretfully at his last, " Ach, he is all de time hungry!" At the sight of the policeman, the young imp set up such a howl that we beat a hasty retreat. The cellar "flat" was undoubtedly in violation of law, but it was allowed to pass. In the main hall, on the ground floor, we counted seventeen children. The facts of life here suspend ordinary landlord prejudices to a certain extent. Occasionally it is the tenant who suspends them. The policeman laughed as he told me of the case of a mother who coveted a flat into which she well knew her family would not be admitted; the landlord was particular. She knocked, with a troubled face, alone. Yes, the flat was to let; had she any children? The woman heaved a sigh. " Six, but they are all in Greenwood." The landlord's heart was touched by such woe. He let her have the flat. By night he was amazed to find a flock of half a dozen robust youngsters domiciled under his roof. They had indeed been in Greenwood; but they had come back from the cemetery to stay. And stay they did, the rent being paid.

High rents, slack work, and low wages go hand in hand in the tenements as promoters of overcrowding. The rent is always one-fourth of the family income, often more. The fierce competition

for a bare living cuts down wages; and when loss
of work is added, the only thing left is to take in
lodgers to meet the landlord's claim.   The Jew
usually takes them singly, the Italian by families.
The midnight visit of the sanitary policeman dis-
closes a state of affairs against which he feels himself helpless.   He has his standard: 400 cubic feet
of air space for each adult sleeper, 200 for a child.
That in itself is a concession to the practical neces-
sities of the case.   The original demand was for
600 feet.   But of 28,000 and odd tenants canvassed
in New York, in the slumming investigation prose-
cuted by the general government in 1894, 17,047
were found to have less than 400 feet, and of these
5526 slept in unventilated rooms with no windows.
No more such rooms have been added since; but
there has come that which is worse.

It was the boast of New York, till a few years
ago, that at least that worst of tenement depravities,
the one-room house, too familiar in the English
slums, was practically unknown here.   It is not so
any longer.   The evil began in the old houses in
Orchard and Allen streets, a bad neighborhood, infested by fallen women and the thievish rascals who
prey upon their misery, — a region where the whole
plan of humanity, if plan there be in this disgusting
mess, jars out of tune continually.   The furnished-
room house has become an institution here, speeded

on by a conscienceless Jew who bought up the old buildings as fast as they came into the market, and filled them with a class of tenants before whom charity recoils, helpless and hopeless. When the houses were filled, the crowds overflowed into the yard. In one, I found, in midwinter, tenants living in sheds built of odd boards and roof tin, and paying a dollar a week for herding with the rats. One of them, a red-faced German, was a philosopher after his kind. He did not trouble himself to get up, when I looked in, but stretched himself in his bed, — it was high noon, — responding to my sniff of disgust that it was "sehr schoen! ein bischen kalt, aber was!" His neighbor, a white-haired old woman, begged, trembling, not to be put out. She would not know where to go. It was out of one of these houses that Fritz Meyer, the murderer, went to rob the poor box in the Redemptorist Church, the night when he killed policeman Smith. The policeman surprised him at his work. In the room he had occupied I came upon a brazen-looking woman with a black eye, who answered the question of the officer, " Where did you get that shiner?" with a laugh. " I ran up against the fist of me man," she said. Her " man," a big, sullen lout, sat by, dumb. The woman answered for him that he was a mechanic.

" What does he work at?" snorted the policeman,

restraining himself with an effort from kicking the fellow.

She laughed scornfully, "At the junk business." It meant that he was a thief.

Young men, with blotched faces and cadaverous looks, were loafing in every room. They hung their heads in silence. The women turned their faces away at the sight of the uniform. They cling to these wretches, who exploit their starved affections for their own ease, with a grip of desperation. It is their last hold. Women have to love something. It is their deepest degradation that they must love these. Even the wretches themselves feel the shame of it, and repay them by beating and robbing them, as their daily occupation. A poor little baby in one of the rooms gave a shuddering human touch to it all.

The old houses began it, as they began all the tenement mischief that has come upon New York. But the opportunity that was made by the tenant's need was not one to be neglected. In some of the newer tenements, with their smaller rooms, the lodger is by this time provided for in the plan, with a special entrance from the hall. "Lodger" comes, by an easy transition, to stand for "family." One winter's night I went with the sanitary police on their midnight inspection through a row of Elizabeth Street tenements which I had known since they were built, seventeen or eighteen years ago. That is the neighborhood in which the recent Italian immigrants crowd. In the house which we selected for examination, in all respects the type of the rest, we found forty-three families where there should have been sixteen. Upon each floor were four flats, and in each flat three rooms that measured respectively 14×11, 7×11, and $7 \times 8\frac{1}{2}$ feet. In only one flat did we find a single family. In three there were two to each. In the other twelve each room had its own family living and sleeping there. They cooked, I suppose, at the one stove in the kitchen, which was the largest room. In one big bed we counted six persons, the parents and four children. Two of them lay crosswise at the foot of the bed, or there would not have been room. A curtain was hung before the bed in each of the two smaller rooms, leaving a passageway from the hall to the room with the windows. The rent for the front flats was twelve dollars; for that in the rear ten dollars. The social distinctions going with the advantage of location were rigidly observed, I suppose. The three steps across a tenement hall, from the front to " the back," are often a longer road than from Ludlow Street to Fifth Avenue.

They were sweaters' tenements.[†] But I shall keep that end of the story until I come to speak of the tenants. The houses I have in mind now. They

---

[†]"Sweaters" and "sweating" were terms referring to the practice of manufacturers (who might also be tenement landlords) having merchandise produced or assembled in the tenement homes of workers who were paid by the piece, at rates so low that every man, woman, and child had to work long hours merely to gain enough income to subsist.

were Astor leasehold property,[†] and I had seen them
built upon the improved plan of 1879, with air shafts
and all that. There had not been water in the tenements for a month then, we were told by the one
tenant who spoke English that could be understood.
The cold snap had locked the pipes. Fitly enough,
the lessee was an undertaker, an Italian himself, who
combined with his business of housing his people
above and below the ground also that of the padrone,
to let no profit slip. He had not taken the trouble
to make many or recent repairs. The buildings had
made a fair start; they promised well. But the
promise had not been kept. In their premature decay they were distinctly as bad as the worst. I had
the curiosity to seek out the agent, the middleman,
and ask him why they were so. He shrugged his
shoulders. With such tenants nothing could be
done, he said. I have always held that Italians are
most manageable, and that, with all the surface in-
dications to the contrary, they are really inclined to
cleanliness, if cause can be shown, and I told him so.
He changed the subject diplomatically. No doubt it
was with him simply a question of the rent. They
might crowd and carry on as they pleased, once that
was paid; and they did. It used to be the joke of
Elizabeth Street that when the midnight police came,
the tenants would keep them waiting outside, pre-

†Property that was part of the vast real estate holdings of the
descendants of John Jacob Astor (1763–1848), who made his fortune in
the fur trade and was by far the richest man in the United States at his
death. His son, William Backhouse Astor (1792–1875), known as "the
landlord of New York," refused to improve the many notoriously fetid
tenements he owned, until the period 1861–1873.

tending to search for the key, until the surplus population of men had time to climb down the fire-escape. When the police were gone they came back. We surprised them all in bed.

Like most of the other tenements we have come across on our trip, these were double-deckers. That is the type of tenement that is responsible for the crowding that till now has gone on unchecked. For twenty years it has been replacing the older barracks everywhere, as fast as they rotted or were torn down.

This double-decker was thus described by the Tenement House Commission of 1894: "It is the one hopeless form of tenement construction. It cannot be well ventilated, it cannot be well lighted; it is not safe in case of fire. It is built on a lot 25 feet wide by 100 or less in depth, with apartments for four families in each story. This necessitates the occupation of from 86 to 90 per cent of the lot's depth. The stairway, made in the centre of the house, and the necessary walls and partitions reduce the width of the middle rooms (which serve as bedrooms for at least two people each) to 9 feet each at the most, and a narrow light and air shaft, now legally required in the centre of each side wall, still further lessens the floor space of these middle rooms. Direct light is only possible for the rooms at the front and rear. The middle rooms must borrow what light they can from dark hall-

ways, the shallow shafts, and the rear rooms.
Their air must pass through other rooms or the
tiny shafts, and cannot but be contaminated before
it reaches them.   A five-story house of this character contains apartments for eighteen or twenty
families, a popu-
lation frequently
amounting to 100
people, and some-
times increased by
boarders or lodg-
ers   to   150   or
more."

The commis-
sion, after looking
in vain through
the slums of the
Old World cities
for something to
compare the
double - deckers
with, declared that,

The only Bath-tub in the Block: it hangs in
the Air Shaft.

in their setting, the separateness and sacredness of
home life were interfered with, and evils bred,
physical and moral, that "conduce to the corruption of the young."   "Make for unrighteousness"
said the commission of 1900, six years later.

Yet it is for these that the "interests" of which

the fire-chief spoke have rushed into battle at almost every session of the legislature, whenever a step was taken to arraign them before the bar of public opinion. No winter has passed, since the awakening conscience of the people of New York City manifested itself in a desire to better the lot of the other half, that has not seen an assault made, in one shape or another, on the structure of tenement-house law built up with such anxious solicitude. Once a bill to exempt from police supervision, by withdrawing them from the tenement-house class, the very worst of the houses, whose death-rate threatened the community, was sneaked through the legislature all unknown, and had reached the executive before the alarm was sounded. The Governor, put upon his guard, returned the bill, with the indorsement that he was unable to understand what could have prompted a measure that seemed to have reason and every argument against it and none for it.

But the motive is not so obscure, after all. It is the same old one of profit without conscience. It took from the Health Department the supervision of the light, ventilation, and plumbing of the tenements, which by right belonged there, and put it in charge of a compliant Building Department, "for the convenience of architects and their clients, and the saving of time and expense to them." For the convenience of the architect's client, the builder, the lot was encroached upon, until of one big block which the Gilder Commission measured only 7 per cent was left open to the air; 93 per cent of it was covered with brick and mortar. Rear tenements, to the number of nearly 100, have been condemned as "slaughter-houses," with good reason, but this block was built practically solid. The average of space covered in 34 tenement blocks was shown to be 78.13 per cent. The law allowed only 65. The "discretion" that penned tenants in a burning tenement with stairs of wood for the builder's "convenience" cut down the chance of life of their babies unmoved. Sunlight and air mean just that, where three thousand human beings are packed into a single block. That was why the matter was given into the charge of the health officials, when politics was yet kept out of their work.

Of such kind are the interests that oppose betterment of the worker's hard lot in New York, that dictated the appointment by Tammany of a commission composed of builders to revise its code of tenement laws, and that sneered at the "laughable results of the Gilder Tenement House Commission." Those results made for the health and happiness and safety of a million and a half of souls, and were accounted, on every humane ground, the longest step forward that had been taken by this com-

The Old Style of Tenements, with Yards.

munity. For the old absentee landlord, who did not know what mischief was afoot, we have got the speculative builder, who does know, but does not care, so long as he gets his pound of flesh. Half of the just laws that have been passed for

As a Solid Block of Double-deckers, Lawful until now, would appear.

the relief of the people he has paralyzed with his
treacherous discretion clause, carefully nursed in
the school of practical politics to which he gives
faithful adherence.   The thing has been the curse
of our city from the day when the earliest struggle
toward better things began.   Among the first man-
ifestations of that was the prohibition of soap
factories below Grand Street by the Act of 1797,
which created a Board of Health with police
powers.   The act was passed in February, to take
effect in July; but long before that time the same
legislature had amended it by giving the authorities
discretion in the matter.   And the biggest soap
factory of them all is down there to this day, and
is even now stirring up a rumpus among the latest
immigrants, the Syrians, who have settled about it.
No doubt it is all a question of political education;
but is not a hundred years enough to settle this
much, that compromise is out of place where the
lives of the people are at stake, and that it is time
our years of " discretion " were numbered?

At last there comes for the answer an emphatic
yes.   This year the law has killed the discretionary
clause and spoken out plainly.   No more stairs of
wood; no more encroachment on the tenants' sunlight; and here, set in its frame of swarming tenements, is a wide, open space, yet to be a real park,
with flowers and grass and birds to gladden the

hearts of those to whom such things have been as tales that are told, all these dreary years, and with a playground in which the children of yonder big school may roam at will, undismayed by landlord or policeman. Not all the forces of reaction can put back the barracks that were torn down as one of the "laughable results" of that very Tenement House Commission's work, or restore to the undertaker his profits from Bone Alley of horrid memory. It was the tenant's turn to laugh, that time. Half a dozen blocks away, among even denser swarms, is another such plot, where there will be football and a skating pond before another season. They are breaking ground to-day. Seven years of official red tape have we had since the plans were first made, and it isn't all unwound yet; but it will be speedily now, and we shall hear the story of those parks and rejoice that the day of reckoning is coming for the builder without a soul. Till then let him deck the fronts of his tenements with bravery of plate glass and brass to hide the darkness within. He has done his worst.

We can go no farther. Yonder lies the river. A full mile we have come, through unbroken ranks of tenements with their mighty, pent-up multitudes. Here they seem, with a common impulse, to overflow into the street. From corner to corner it is crowded with girls and children, dragging babies nearly as big as themselves, with desperate endeavor to lose nothing of the show. There is a funeral in the block. Unnumbered sewing-machines cease for once their tireless rivalry with the flour mill in the next block, that is forever grinding in a vain effort to catch up. Heads are poked from windows. On the stoops hooded and shawled figures have front seats. The crowd is hardly restrained by the policeman and the undertaker in holiday mourning, who clear a path by main strength to the plumed hearse. The eager haste, the frantic rush to see, — what does it not tell of these starved lives, of the quality of their aims and ambitions? The mill clatters loudly; there is one mouth less to fill. In the midst of it all, with clamor of urgent gong, the patrol wagon rounds the corner, carrying two policemen precariously perched upon a struggling "drunk," a woman. The crowd scatters, following the new sensation. The tragedies of death and life in the slum have met together.

Many a mile I might lead you along these rivers, east and west, through the island of Manhattan, and find little else than we have seen. The great crowd is yet below Fourteenth Street, but the northward march knows no slackening of pace. As the tide sets up-town, it reproduces faithfully the scenes of the older wards, though with less of their human interest than here, where the old houses, in all their ugliness, have yet some imprint of the individuality of their tenants.   Only on feast days does Little Italy, in Harlem, recall the Bend when it put on holiday attire.   Anything more desolate and disheartening than the unending rows of tenements, all alike and all equally repellent, of the up-town streets, it is hard to imagine.   Hell's Kitchen in its ancient wickedness was picturesque, at least, with its rocks and its goats and shanties.   Since the negroes took possession it is only dull, except when, once in a while, the remnant of the Irish settlers make a stand against the intruders.   Vain hope! Perpetual eviction is their destiny.   Negro, Italian, and Jew, biting the dust with many a bruised head under the Hibernian's stalwart fist, resistlessly drive him before them, nevertheless, out of house and home.   The landlord pockets the gate money.   The old robbery still goes on.   Where the negro pitches his tent, he pays more rent than his white neighbor next door, and is a better tenant.   And he is good game forever.   He never buys the tenement, as the Jew or the Italian is likely to do when he has scraped up money enough to reënact, after his own fashion, the trick taught him by his oppressor.   The black column has reached the hundredth street on the East Side, and the sixties on the West,[1] and

---

[1] There is an advanced outpost of blacks as far up as One Hundred and Forty-fifth Street, but the main body lingers yet among the sixties.

there for the present it halts.   Jammed between
Africa, Italy, and Bohemia, the Irishman has abandoned the East Side up-town.   Only west of Central Park does he yet face his foe, undaunted in
defeat as in victory.   The local street nomenclature,
in which the directory has no hand, — Nigger Row,
Mixed Ale Flats, etc., — indicates the hostile camps
with unerring accuracy.

Up-town or down-town, as the tenements grow
taller, the thing that is rarest to find is the home of
the olden days, even as it was in the shanty on the
rocks.   "No home, no family, no manhood, no
patriotism!" said the old Frenchman.   Seventy-
seven per cent of their young prisoners, say the
managers of the state reformatory, have no moral
sense, or next to none.   "Weakness, not wickedness, ails them," adds the prison chaplain; no manhood, that is to say.   It is the stamp of the home
that is lacking, and we need to be about restoring
it, if we would be safe.   Years ago, roaming through
the British Museum, I came upon an exhibit that
riveted my attention as nothing else had.   It was a
huge stone arm, torn from the shoulder of some
rock image, with doubled fist and every rigid muscle
instinct with angry menace.   Where it came from
or what was its story I do not know.   I did not
ask.   It was its message to us I was trying to read.
I had been spending weary days and nights in the

slums of London, where hatred grew, a noxious crop, upon the wreck of the home. Lying there, mute and menacing, the great fist seemed to me like a shadow thrown from the gray dawn of the race into our busy day with a purpose, a grim, un-heeded warning. What was it? In the slum the question haunts me yet. They perished, the em-pires those rock-hewers built, and the governments reared upon their ruins are long since dead and forgotten. They were born to die, for they were not built upon human happiness, but upon human terror and greed. We built ours upon the bed rock, and its cornerstone is the home. With this bitter mockery of it that makes the slum, can it be that the warning is indeed for us?

CHAPTER V

"DRUV INTO DECENCY"

I STOOD at Seven Dials and heard the policeman's account of what it used to be. Seven Dials is no more like the slum of old than is the Five Points to-day. The conscience of London wrought upon the one as the conscience of New York upon the other. A mission house, a children's refuge, two big schools, and, hard by, a public bath and a wash-house, stand as the record of the battle with the slum, which, with these forces in the field, has but one ending. The policeman's story rambled among the days when things were different. Then it was dangerous for an officer to go alone there at night.

Around the corner there came from one of the side streets a procession with banners, parading in honor and aid of some church charity. We watched it pass. In it marched young men and boys with swords and battle-axes, and upon its outskirts skipped a host of young roughs — so one would have called them but for the evidence of their honest employment — who rattled collection boxes, reaping a harvest of pennies from far and near. I looked at the battle-axes and the collection boxes, and thought of forty years ago. Where was the Seven Dials of that day, and the men who gave it its bad name? I asked the policeman.

" They were druv into decency, sor," he said, and answered from his own experience the question ever asked by faint-hearted philanthropists. " My father, he done duty here afore me in '45. The worst dive was where that church stands. It was always full of thieves," — whose sons, I added mentally, have become collectors for the church. The one fact was a whole chapter on the slum.

London's way with the tenant we adopted at last in New York with the slum landlord. He was " druv into decency." We had to. Moral suasion had been stretched to the limit. The point had been reached where one knock-down blow out-weighed a bushel of arguments. It was all very well to build model tenements as object lessons to show that the thing could be done; it had become necessary to enforce the lesson by demonstrating that the community had power to destroy houses which were a menace to its life. The rear tene-ments were chosen for this purpose.

They were the worst, as they were the first, of New York's tenements. The double-deckers of which I have spoken had, with all their evils, at least this to their credit, that their death-rate was not nearly as high as that of the old houses. That was not because of any virtue inherent in the double-deckers, but because the earlier tenements were old, and built in a day that knew nothing of sanitary restrictions, and cared less. Hence the showing that the big tenements had much the lowest mortality. The death-rate does not sound the depths of tenement-house evils, but it makes a record that is needed when it comes to attacking property rights. The mortality of the rear tenements had long been a scandal. They are built in the back yard, generally back to back with the rear buildings on abutting lots. If there is an open space between them, it is never more than a slit a foot or so wide, and gets to be the receptacle of garbage and filth of every kind; so that any opening made in these walls for purposes of ventilation becomes a source of greater danger than if there were none. The last count that was made, in 1900, showed that among the 44,850 tenements in Manhattan and the Bronx there were still 2143 rear houses left.[1] Where they are the death-rate rises, for reasons that are apparent. The sun cannot reach them. They are damp and dark, and the tenants, who are always the poorest and most crowded, live "as in a cage open only toward the front." A canvass made of the

[1] That was, however, a reduction of 236 since 1898, when the census showed 2379 rear houses.

mortality records by Dr. Roger S. Tracy, the regis-
trar of records, showed that while in the First Ward
(the oldest), for instance, the death-rate in houses
standing singly on the lot was 29.03 per 1000 of the
living, where there were rear houses it rose to 61.97.
The infant death-rate is a still better test; that rose
from 109.58 in the single tenements of the same
ward to 204.54 where there were rear houses.[1]   One
in every five babies had to die; that is to say, the
house killed it.   No wonder the Gilder commission
styled the rear tenements "slaughter-houses," and
called upon the legislature to root them out, and
with them every old, ramshackle, disease-breeding
tenement in the city.

A law which is in substance a copy of the English act for destroying slum property was passed
in the spring of 1895.   It provided for the seizure
of buildings that were dangerous to the public
health or unfit for human habitation, and their destruction upon proper proof, with compensation to
the owner on a sliding scale down to the point of
entire unfitness, when he might claim only the
value of the material in his house.   Up to that
time, the only way to get rid of such a house had
been to declare it a nuisance under the sanitary
code; but as the city could not very well pay for
the removal of a nuisance, to order it down seemed

[1] Report of Gilder Tenement House Commission, 1894.

too much like robbery; so the owner was allowed to keep it. It takes time and a good many lives to grow a sentiment such as this law expressed. The Anglo-Saxon respect for vested rights is strong in us also. I remember going through a ragged school in London, once, and finding the eyes of the children in the infant class red and sore. Suspecting some contagion, I made inquiries, and was told that a collar factory next door was the cause of the trouble. The fumes from it poisoned the children's eyes.

Richard Watson Gilder, Chairman of the Tenement House Commission of 1894.

"And you allow it to stay, and let this thing go on?" I asked, in wonder.

The superintendent shrugged his shoulders. "It is their factory," he said.

I was on the point of saying something that might not have been polite, seeing that I was a guest, when I remembered that, in the newspaper which I carried in my pocket, I had just been reading a plea of some honorable M. P. for a much-needed reform in the system of counsel fees, then being agitated in the House of Commons. The reply of the solicitor general had made me laugh. He was inclined to agree with the honorable member, but still preferred to follow precedent by referring the matter to the Inns of Court. Quite incidentally, he mentioned that the matter had been hanging fire in the House two hundred years. It seemed very English to me then; but when we afterward came to tackle our rear tenements, and in the first batch there was a row which I knew to have been picked out by the sanitary inspector twenty-five years before as fit only to be destroyed, I recognized that we were kin, after all.

That was Gotham Court. It was first on the list, and the Mott Street Barracks came next, when, as executive officer of the Good Government Clubs, I helped the Board of Health put the law to the test the following year. Roosevelt was Police President and Health Commissioner; nobody was afraid of the landlord. The Health Department kept a list of 66 old houses, with a population of 5460 tenants, in which there had been 1313 deaths in a little over five years (1889–94). From among them we picked our lot, and the department drove the tenants out. The owners went to law, one and all; but, to their surprise and dismay, the courts held with the health officers. The moral effect was instant and overwhelming. Rather than keep up the fight, with no rent coming in, the landlords surrendered at discretion. In consideration of this, compensation was allowed them at the rate of about a thousand dollars a house, although they were really entitled only to the value of the old bricks. The buildings all came under the head of "wholly unfit." Gotham Court, with its sixteen buildings, in which, many years before, a health inspector counted 146 cases of sickness, including "all kinds of infectious disease," was bought for $19,750, and Mullen's Court, adjoining, for $7251. To show the character of all, let two serve; in each case it is the official record, upon which seizure was made, that is quoted:

No. 98 Catherine Street: "The floor in the apartments and the wooden steps leading to the second-floor apartment are broken, loose, saturated with filth. The roof and eaves gutters leak, rendering the apartments wet. The two apartments on the first floor consist of one room each, in which the tenants are compelled to cook, eat, and sleep. The back walls are defective, the house wet and damp, and unfit for human habitation. It robs the surrounding houses of light."

"The sunlight never enters" was the constant refrain.

No. 17 Sullivan Street: "Occupied by the lowest

whites and negroes, living together. The houses are decayed from cellar to garret, and filthy beyond description, — the filthiest, in fact, we have ever seen. The beams, the floors, the plaster on the walls, where there is any plaster, are rotten, and alive with vermin. They are a menace to the public health, and cannot be repaired. Their annual death-rate in five years was 41.38."

The sunlight enters where these stood, at all events, and into 58 other yards that once were plague spots. Of 94 rear tenements seized that year, 60 were torn down, 33 of them voluntarily by the owners; 29 were remodelled and allowed to stand, chiefly as workshops; 5 other houses were standing empty, and yielding no rent, when I last heard of them. I suppose they have been demol-ished since. The worst of them all, the Mott Street Barracks, were taken into court by the owner; but all the judges and juries in the land had no power to put them back when it was decided upon a technicality that they should not have been destroyed offhand. It was a case of "They can't put you in jail for that." — "Yes, but I am in jail." They were gone, torn down under the referee's decision that they ought to go, before the Appellate Division called a halt. We were not in a mood to trifle with the Barracks, or risk any of the law's delays. In 1888 I counted 360 tenants in these tenements,

The Mott Street Barracks.

front and rear, all Italians, and the infant death-
rate of the Barracks that year was 325 per 1000.
There were forty babies, and one in three of them
had to die. The general infant death-rate for the
whole tenement-house population that year was
88.38. In the four years following, during which
the population and the death-rate of the houses
were both reduced with an effort, fifty-one funerals
went out of the Barracks. With entire fitness,
a cemetery corporation held the mortgage upon
the property. The referee allowed it the price of
opening one grave, in the settlement, gave one dollar to the lessee, and one hundred and ten dollars
to the landlord, who refused to collect and took his
case into the courts. We waited to see the landlord attack the law itself on the score of constitutionality, but he did not. The Court of Appeals
decided that it had not been shown that the Barracks might not have been used for some other
purpose than a tenement and that therefore we had
been hasty. The city paid damages, but it was all
right. It was emphatically a case of haste making
for speed. So far the law stands unchallenged,
both here and in Massachusetts, where they destroyed twice as many unfit houses as we did in
New York and stood their ground on its letter,
paying the owners the bare cost of the old timbers.

As in every other instance, we seized only the

rear houses at the Barracks; but within a year or two the front houses were also sold and destroyed too, and so disappeared quite the worst rookery that was left on Manhattan Island. Those of us who had explored it with the "midnight police" in its worst days had no cause to wonder at its mortality. In Berlin they found the death-rate per thousand to be 163.5 where a family occupied one room, 22.5 where it lived in two rooms, 7.5 in the case of three-room dwellers, and 5.4 where they had four rooms.[1] Does any one ask yet why we fight the slum in Berlin and New York? The Barracks in those days suggested the first kind.

I have said before that I do not believe in paying the slum landlord for taking his hand off our throats, when we have got the grip on him in turn. Mr. Roger Foster, who as a member of the Tenement House Committee drew the law, and as counsel for the Health Department fought the landlords successfully in the courts, holds to the opposite view. I am bound to say that instances turned up in which it did seem a hardship to deprive the owners of even such property. I remember especially a tenement in Roosevelt Street, which was the patrimony and whole estate of two children. With the rear house taken away, the income from the front would not be enough to cover the interest on the mortgage. It

[1] "Municipal Government in Continental Europe," by Albert Shaw.

was one of those things that occasionally make standing upon abstract principle so very uncomfortable. I confess I never had the courage to ask what was done in their case. I know that the tenement went, and I hope — well, never mind what I hope. It has nothing to do with the case. The house is down, and the main issue decided upon its merits.

In the 94 tenements (counting the front houses in; they cannot be separated from the rear tenements in the death registry) there were in five years 956 deaths, a rate of 62.9 at a time when the general city death-rate was 24.63. It was the last and heaviest blow aimed at the abnormal mortality of a city that ought, by reason of many advantages, to be one of the healthiest in the world. With clean streets, pure milk, medical school inspection, antitoxin treatment of deadly diseases, and better sanitary methods generally; with the sunlight let into its slums, and its worst plague spots cleaned out, the death-rate of New York came down from 26.32 per 1000 inhabitants in 1887 to 19.53 in 1897. Inasmuch as a round half million was added to its population within the ten years, it requires little figuring to show that the number whose lives were literally saved by reform would people a city of no mean proportions. The extraordinary spell of hot weather in the summer of 1896, when the temperature hung for ten consecutive days in the nineties, with days and nights of extreme discomfort, brought out the full meaning of this. While many were killed by sunstroke, the population as a whole was shown to have acquired, in better hygienic surroundings, a much greater power of resistance. It yielded slowly to the heat. Where two days had been sufficient, in former years, to send the death-rate up, it now took five; and the infant mortality remained low throughout the dreadful trial. Perhaps the substitution of beer for whiskey as a summer drink had something to do with it; but Colonel Waring's broom and unpolitical sanitation had more. Since it spared him so many voters, the politician ought to have been grateful for this; but he was not. Death-rates are not as good political arguments as tax rates, we found out. In the midst of it all, a policeman whom I knew went to his Tammany captain to ask if Good Government Clubs were political clubs within the meaning of the law which forbade policemen joining such. The answer he received set me to thinking: "Yes, the meanest, worst kind of political clubs, they are." Yet they had done nothing worse than to save the babies, the captain's with the rest.

The landlord read the signs better, and ran to cover till the storm should blow over. Houses that had hardly known repairs since they were built were put in order with all speed. All over the

city, he made haste to set his house to rights, lest it
be seized or brought to the bar in other ways. The
Good Government Clubs had their hands full that
year (1896–97). They made war upon the dark hall
in the double-decker, and upon the cruller bakery.
They compelled the opening of small parks, or the
condemnation of sites for them anyway, exposed
the abuses of the civil courts, the "poor man's
courts," urged on the building of new schools,
cleaned up in the Tombs prison and hastened the
demolition of the wicked old pile, and took a hand
in evolving a sensible and humane system of dealing
with the young vagrants who were going to waste
on free soup. The proposition to establish a farm
colony for their reclamation was met with the challenge at Albany that "we have had enough reform
in New York City," and, as the event proved, for the
time being we had really gone as far as we could.
But even that was a good long way. Some things
had been nailed that could never again be undone;
and hand in hand with the effort to destroy had
gone another to build up, that promised to set us
far enough ahead to appeal at last successfully to
the self-interest of the builder, if not to his humanity; or, failing that, to compel him to decency. If
that promise has not been all kept, the end is not
yet. I believe it will be kept.

The movement for reform, in the matter of hous-

ing the people, had proceeded upon a clearly out-
lined plan that apportioned to each of several forces
its own share of the work.   At a meeting held under
the auspices of the Association for Improving the

Condition of the Poor,
early in the days of
the movement, the field
had been gone over
thoroughly.   To the
Good Government
Clubs fell the task, as
already set forth, of
compelling the enforce-
ment of the existing
tenement-house laws.
D. O. Mills, the phi-
lanthropic banker, de-
clared his purpose to
build hotels which
should prove that a

R. Fulton Cutting, Chairman of the
Citizens' Union.

bed and lodging as good as any could be furnished
to the great army of homeless men at a price that
would compete with the cheap lodging houses, and
yet yield a profit to the owner.   On behalf of a
number of well-known capitalists, who had been
identified with the cause of tenement-house reform
for years, Robert Fulton Cutting,[†] the president of
the Association for Improving the Condition of the

†Robert Fulton Cutting (1852–1934), a financier and civic leader, was
elected the first chairman of the Citizens Union and served 1897–1908.

Poor, offered to build homes for the working people that should be worthy of the name, on a large scale. A company was formed, and chose for its president Dr. Elgin R. L. Gould,[†] author of the government report on the "Housing of the Working People," the standard work on the subject. A million dollars was raised by public subscription, and operations were begun at once.

Two ideas were kept in mind as fundamental: one, that charity that will not pay will not stay; the other, that nothing can be done with the twenty-five-foot lot. It is the primal curse of our housing system, and any effort toward better things must reckon with it first. Nineteen lots on Sixty-eighth and Sixty-ninth streets, west of Tenth Avenue, were purchased of Mrs. Alfred Corning Clark, who took one tenth of the capital stock of the City and Suburban Homes Company; and upon these was erected the first block of tenements. This is the neighborhood toward which the population has been setting with ever increasing congestion. Already in 1895 the Twenty-second Ward contained nearly 200,000 souls. I gave figures in the previous chapter that showed a crowding of more than 1100 persons per acre in some of the blocks here where the conditions of the notorious Tenth Ward are certain to be reproduced, if indeed they are not exceeded. In the Fifteenth Assembly Dis-

†Dr. Elgin R. L. Gould (1860–1915), a professor of political economy, was active in civic and philanthropic activities in New York City from 1896, when he was chosen as president of the City and Suburban Homes Company.

trict, some distance below, but on the same line, the first sociological canvass of the Federation of Churches had found the churches, schools, and other educational agencies marshalling a frontage of 756 feet on the street, while the saloon fronts stretched themselves over nearly a mile; so that, said the compiler of these pregnant facts, " saloon social ideals are minting themselves on the minds of the people at the ratio of seven saloon thoughts to one educational thought."   It would not have been easy to find a spot better fitted for the experiment of restoring the home to its place.

The Alfred Corning Clark buildings, as they were called in recognition of the effort of this public-spirited woman, have at this writing been occupied five years.   They harbor nearly four hundred families, as contented a lot as I ever saw anywhere. The one tenant who left in disgust was a young doctor who had settled on the estate, thinking he could pick up a practice among so many.   But he couldn't.   They were not often sick, those tenants. Last year only three died, and they were all killed while away from home.   So he had good cause of complaint.   The rest had none, and having none, they stay, which is no mean blow struck for the home in the battle with the slum.   The home feeling can never grow where people do not stay long enough to feel at home, any more than the

Alfred Corning Clark Buildings.

plant can which the child is pulling up every two
or three days to "see if it has roots."

Half the tenement house population — and I am
not sure that I ought not to say the whole of it —
is everlastingly on the move.   Dr. Gould quotes as
an instance of it the experience of an assembly district leader in distributing political circulars among
the people in a good tenement neighborhood.   In
three months after the enrolment lists had been
made out, one-third of the tenants had moved.   No
doubt the experience was typical.   How can the
one who hardly knows what a home means be
expected to have any pride or interest in his home
in the larger sense: the city?   And to what in
such men is one to appeal in the interests of civic
betterment?   That is why every effort that goes to
help tie the citizen to one spot long enough to give
him the proprietary sense in it which is the first
step toward civic interest and pride, is of such
account.   It is one way in which the public schools
as neighborhood houses in the best sense could be
of great help, and a chief factor in the success of
the social settlement.   And that is why model tenements, which pay and foster the home, give back
more than a money interest to the community.

They must pay, for else, as I said, they will not
stay.   These pay four per cent, and are expected to
pay five, the company's limit.   So it is not strange

that the concern has prospered. It has since raised more than one million of dollars, and has built another block, with room for 338 families, on First Avenue and on Sixty-fourth and Sixty-fifth streets, within hail of Battle Row, of anciently warlike memory. Still another block is going up at Avenue A and Seventy-eighth Street, and in West Sixty-second Street, where the colored population crowds, the company is erecting two buildings for negro tenants, where they will live as well as their white fellows do in *their* model tenements, — a long-delayed act of justice, for as far back as any one can remember the colored man has been paying more and getting less for his money in New York than whites of the same grade, who are poorer tenants every way. The Company's " city homes " come as near being that as any can. There is light and air in abundance, steam heat in winter in the latest ones, fire-proof stairs, and deadened partitions to help on the privacy that is at once the most needed and hardest to get in a tenement. The houses do not look like barracks. Any one who has ever seen a row of factory tenements that were just houses, not homes, will understand how much that means. I can think of some such rows now, with their ugly brick fronts, straight up and down without a break and without a vine or a window-box of greens or flowers, and the mere thought of them gives me the blues for the rest of the day. There is nothing of that about these tenements, unless it be the long play-yard between the buildings in Sixty-eighth and Sixty-ninth streets. It is too narrow to have anything in it but asphalt. But the rest makes up for it in part.

All together, the company has redeemed its promise of real model tenements; and it has had no trouble with its tenants. The few and simple rules are readily understood as being for the general good, and so obeyed. It is the old story, told years and years ago by Mr. Alfred T. White when he had built his Riverside tenements in Brooklyn. The tenants "do not have to come up" to the landlord's standard. They are more than abreast of him in his utmost endeavor, if he will only use common sense in the management of his property. They do that in the City and Suburban Homes Company's buildings. They give their tenants shower-baths and a friend for a rent-collector, their children playrooms and Christmas parties, and the whole neighborhood feels the stimulus of the new and humane plan. In all Battle Row there has not been a scrap, let alone an old-time shindy, since the "accommodation flats" came upon the scene. That is what they call them. It is an everyday observation that the Row has "come up" since some of the old houses have been remodelled. The new that are being built aim visibly toward the higher standard.

The company's rents average a dollar a week per room, and are a trifle higher than those of the old tenements round about; but they have so much more in the way of comfort that the money is eagerly paid; nor is the difference so great that the "picking of tenants" amounts to more than the putting of a premium on steadiness, sobriety, and cleanliness, which in itself is a service to render. One experience of the management which caused some astonishment, but upon reflection was accepted as an encouraging sign, was the refusal of the tenants to use the common wash-tubs in the laundry. They are little used to this day. The women will use the drying racks, but they object to rubbing elbows with their neighbors while they wash their clothes. It is, after all, a sign that the tenement that smothers individuality left them this useful handle, and if the experience squashed the hopes of some who dreamed of municipal wash-houses on the Glasgow plan, there is nothing to grieve over. Every peg of personal pride rescued from the tenement is worth a thousand theories for hanging the hope of improvement on.

With $2,300,000 invested by this time, the company has built city homes for 1450 families, and has only made a beginning. All the money that

is needed for going on with its work is in sight.
Nor are the rich the only investors. Of the 400
stockholders 250 have small lots, ten shares and less
each, a healthy sign that the company is holding
the confidence of the community. It has fairly
earned it. No one could have done a greater and
better thing for the metropolis than to demonstrate
that it is possible to build homes for the toilers as
a business and net a business interest upon the
investment.

The statement is emphasized by the company's
experience with the suburban end of its work. It
bought sites for two or three hundred little cottages
out on Long Island, but within the greater city, and
only half an hour by trolley or elevated from the
City Hall. A hundred houses were built, neat and
cosey homes of brick and timber, each in its own
garden; and a plan was devised under which the
purchaser had twenty years to pay for the property.
A life insurance policy protected the seller and
secured the house to the widow should the bread-
winner die. The plan has worked well in Bel-
gium under the eyes of the government, but it
failed to attract buyers here. Of those whom it
did attract at the outset, not a few have given up
and gone away. When I went out to have a
look at the place the year after Homewood had
been settled, seventy-two houses had found owners

under the company's plans.   After four years fifty-six only are so held, ten have been bought outright, and three sold under contract.   Practically the company has had to give up its well-thought-out plan and rent as many of the houses as it could. Nine were vacant this last spring.

So what we all thought the "way out" of the slum seems barred for the time being.   For there is no other explanation of the failure than that the people will not go "among the stumps."   Lack of facilities for getting there played a part, possibly, but a minor one, and now there is no such grievance.   The simple fact is that the home-feeling that makes a man rear a home upon the soil as the chief ambition of his life was not there.   The tenement and the flat have weakened that peg among the class of workers for whom Homewood was planned.   I hate to say that they have broken the peg, for I do not believe it.   But it has been hurt without doubt.   They longed for the crowds.   The grass and the trees and the birds and the salt breath of the sea did not speak to them in a language they understood.   The brass bands and the hand-organs, the street cries and the rush and roar of the city, had made them forget their childhood's tongue. For the children understood, even in the gutter.

"It means, I suppose," said Dr. Gould to me, when we had talked it all over, "that we are and always shall be a tenement house city, and that we have got to reckon with and plan for that only."

I think not. I believe he is mistaken. And yet I can give no other ground for my belief than my unyielding faith that things will come right yet, if it does take time. They are not right as they are. Man is not made to be born and to live all his life in a box, packed away with his fellows like so many herring in a barrel. He is here in this world for something that is not attained in that way; but is, if not attained, at least perceived when the daisies and the robins come in. If to help men perceive it is all we can do in our generation, that is a good deal. But I believe that before our children have come to the divide, perhaps before we are gone, we shall see the tide of the last century's drift to the cities turn, under the impulse of the new forces that are being harnessed for man's work, and Homewood come to its rights. I say I believe it. I wish I could say I knew; but then you would ask for my proofs, and I haven't any. For all that, I still believe it.

Meanwhile Dr. Gould's advice is good sense. If he is right, it is of the last importance; if I am right, it is still the way to proving me so by holding on to what is left of the home in the tenement and making the most of it. That we have taken the advice is good ground for hope, in the face of the fact that New York has still the worst housing in

the world. We can now destroy what is not fit to
stand. We have done it, and the republic yet sur-
vives. The slum landlord would have had us
believe that it must perish with his rookeries. We
are building model tenements and making them
pay. Alfred T. White's Riverside tenements are as
good to-day as when they were built a dozen years
ago — better if anything, for they were honestly built
— and in all that time they have paid five and six
per cent, and even more. Dr. Gould found that only
six per cent of all the great model housing operations which he examined for the government here
and abroad had failed to pay. All the rest were
successful. And by virtue of the showing we have
taken the twenty-five-foot lot itself by the throat.

Three years ago, speaking of it as the one thing
that was in the way of progress in New York, I
wrote: "It will continue to be in the way. A
man who has one lot will build on it; it is his
right. The state, which taxes his lot, has no right
to confiscate it by forbidding him to make it yield
him an income, on the plea that he might build
something which would be a nuisance. But it can
so order the building that it shall not be a nuisance ;
that is not only its right, but its duty."

That duty has been done since ; let me tell how.
Popular sentiment, taking more and more firmly
hold of the fact that there is a direct connection

The Riverside Tenements in Brooklyn.

between helpless poverty and bad housing, shaped itself in 1898 into a volunteer Tenement House Committee which, as an effective branch of the Charity Organization Society, drew up and presented to the municipal authorities a reform code of building ordinances affecting the dwellings of the poor. But Tammany was back, and they would not listen at the City Hall. Seeing which, the committee made up its mind to appeal to the people themselves in such fashion that it should be heard. That was the way the Tenement House Exhibition of the winter of 1900 came into existence.

Rich and poor came to see that speaking record of a city's sorry plight, and at last we all understood. Not to understand after one look at the poverty and disease maps that hung on the wall was to declare oneself a dullard. The tenements were all down in them, with the size of them and the air space within, if there was any. Black dots upon the poverty maps showed that for each one five families in that house had applied for charity within a given time. There were those that had as many as fifteen of the ominous marks, showing that seventy-five families had asked aid from the one house. To find a tenement free from the taint one had to search long and with care. Upon the disease maps the scourge of tuberculosis lay like a black pall over the double-decker districts. A year later the State Commission, that continued the work then begun, said: "There is hardly a tenement house in which there has not been at least one case of pulmonary tuberculosis within the last five years, and in some houses there have been as many as twenty-two different cases of this terrible disease. There are over 8000 deaths a year in New York City from this disease alone, at least 20,000 cases of well-developed and recognized tuberculosis, and in addition a large number of obscure and incipient cases. The connection between tuberculosis and the character of the tenement houses in which the poor people live is of the very closest." [1]

A model was shown of a typical East Side block, containing 2781 persons on two acres of land, nearly every bit of which was covered with buildings. There were 466 babies in the block (under five years), but not a bath-tub except one that hung in an air shaft. Of the 1588 rooms 441 were dark, with no ventilation to the outer air except through other rooms; 635 rooms gave upon twilight "air shafts." In five years 32 cases of tuberculosis had been reported from that block, and in that time 660 different families in the block had

[1] Report of the Tenement House Commission of 1900. The secretary of that body said: "Well might those maps earn for New York the title of the City of the Living Death."

A Typical East Side Block.

applied for charity. The year before the Bureau of Contagious Diseases had registered 13 cases of diphtheria there. However, the rent-roll was all right. It amounted to $113,964 a year.

Those facts told. New York — the whole country — woke up. More than 170 architects sent in plans in the competition for a humane tenement that should be commercially profitable. Roosevelt was governor, and promptly appointed a Tenement House Commission, the third citizen body appointed for such purposes by authority of the state. Mr. Robert de Forest, a distinguished lawyer and a public-spirited man,[†] who had been at the head of the Charity

Robert W. de Forest, Chairman of the Tenement House Commission of 1900.

Organization Society and of the relief efforts I spoke of, in time became its chairman, and commissioner of the new Tenement House Department that was created by the new charter of the city to carry into effect the law the commission drew up.

†Robert W. de Forest (1848–1931), among other civic activities, was president of the National Housing Association and presided over the 1903 National Conference on Charities and Correction.

At this writing, with the department not yet fully organized, it is too early to say with any degree of certainty exactly how far the last two years have set us ahead; but this much is certain:

"Discretion" is dead — at last.   In Manhattan, no superintendent of buildings shall have leave after this to pen tenants in a building with stairs of wood because he thinks with luck it might burn slowly; nor in Brooklyn shall a deputy commissioner rate a room with a window opening on a hall, or a skylight covered over at the top, "the outer air." [1]   Of these things there is an end.   The air shaft that was a narrow slit between towering walls has become a "court," a yard big enough for children to run in.   Thirty per cent of the tenement-house lot must be open to the sun.   The double-decker has had its day, and it is over.   A man may still build a tenement on a twenty-five-foot lot if he so chooses, but he can hardly pack four families on each floor of it and keep within the law.   He can do much better, and make an ample profit, by crossing the lot line and building on forty or fifty feet; in consequence of which, building being a business, he does so.   In a lot of half a hundred tenement plans I looked over at the department yesterday, there were only two for single houses, and they had but three families on the floor.

[1] Report of Tenement House Commission of 1900.

So it seems as if the blight of the twenty-five-foot lot were really wiped out with the double-decker. And no one is hurt. The speculative builder weeps — for the poor, he says. He will build no more, he avers, and rents will go up, so they will have to sleep on the streets. But I notice the plans I spoke of call for an investment of three millions of dollars, and that they are working over-time at the department to pass on them, so great is the rush. Belike, then, they are crocodile tears. Anyway, let him weep. He has laughed long enough.

As for the rents, he will put them as high as he can, no doubt. They were too high always, for what they bought. In the case of the builder the state can add force to persuasion, and so urge him along the path of righteousness. When it comes to the rent collector the case is different. It may yet be necessary for the municipality to enter the field as a competing landlord on the five-per-cent basis; but I would rather we, as a community, learned first a little more of the art of governing ourselves without scandal. With Tammany liable to turn up at any moment — no, no! Political tenements might yet add a chapter to the story of our disgrace to make men weep. I have not forgotten the use Tammany made of the people's baths erected in the Hamilton Fish Park on the East Side

1. Old Knickerbocker dwelling.
2. The same made over into a tenement.
3. The rear tenement caves.
4. Packing-box tenement built for revenue only.
5. The limit; the air shaft—first concession to tenant.
6. The double-decker, where the civic conscience began to stir in 1879.
7. Evolution of double-decker up to date.
8. Prize plan of Tenement House Exhibition, 1900 (fifty-foot lot).

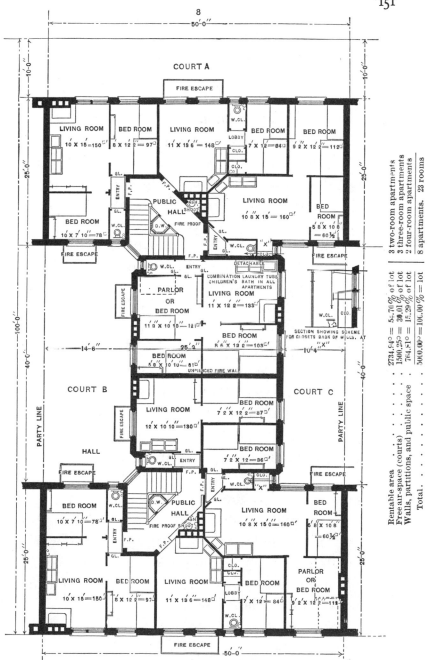

Plan of a Typical Floor in Class First of the Competition in the C. O. S.
Plans of Model Tenements.

— the Ham-fish, locally. They were shut from the day they were opened, I came near saying; I mean from the day they should have been opened; and two stalwart watchmen drew salaries for sitting in the door to keep the people out. That was a perfectly characteristic use of the people's money, and is not lightly to be invited back. Rather wait awhile yet, and see what our bridges and real rapid transit, and the "philanthropy and five per cent" plan, will do for us. When that latter has been grasped so by the tenant that a little extra brass and plate-glass does not tempt him over into the enemy's camp, the usurious rents may yet follow the double-decker, as they have clung to it in the past.

But if the city may not be the landlord of tenements, I have often thought it might with advantage manage them to the extent of building them to contain so many tenements on basis of air space, and no more. The thing was proposed when the tenement house question first came up for discussion, but was dropped then. The last Tenement House Commission considered it carefully, but decided to wait and see first how the new department worked. The whole expense of that, with its nearly two hundred inspectors, might easily be borne by the collection of a license fee so small that even the tenement house landlord could not complain.

Lodging houses are licensed, and workshops in the tenements likewise, to secure efficient control of them. If that is not secured in the case of the workshops, as it is not, it is no fault of the plan, but of the working out of it. I do not expect the licensing of tenements to dispose of all the evils in them. No law or system will ever do that. But it ought to make it easier to get the grip on them that has been wanting heretofore, to our hurt.

CHAPTER VI

THE MILLS HOUSES

SITTING by my window the other day, I saw a boy
steering across the street for my little lad, who was
laying out a base-ball diamond on the lawn. It
seems that he knew him from school.

"Hey," he said, as he rounded to at the gate,
"we've got yer dad's book to home; yer father was
a bum onct."

Proof was immediately forthcoming that whatever
the father might have been, his son was able to up-
hold the family pride, and I had my revenge. Some
day soon now my boy will read his father's story[1]
himself, and I hope will not be ashamed. They
read it in their way in the other boy's house, and
got out of it that I was a "bum" because once I
was on the level of the Bowery lodging house.
But if he does not stay there, a man need not be
that; and for that matter, there are plenty who
do whom it would be a gross injury to call by such
a name. There are lonely men, who, with no kin of
their own, prefer even such society as the cheap

[1] "The Making of an American."

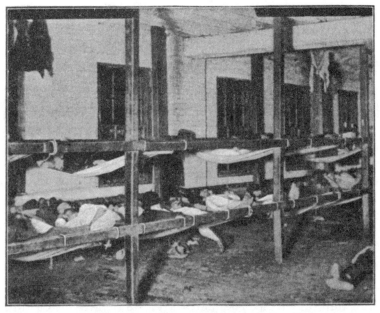

A Seven-cent Lodging House in the Bowery.

lodging house has to offer to the desolation of the
tenement; and there are plenty of young lads from
the country, who, waiting in the big city for the
something that is sure to turn up and open their
road to fortune, get stranded there. Beginning,
perhaps, at the thirty-cent house, they go down,
down, till they strike the fifteen or the ten cent
house, with the dirty sheets and the ready club in
the watchman's hand. And then some day, when
the last penny is gone, and the question where the
next meal is going to come from looms larger than
the Philippine policy of the nation, a heavy-browed

man taps one on the shoulder with an offer of an easy job — easy and straight enough in the mood the fellow is in just then; for does not the world owe him a living? It is one of the devil's most tempting baits to a starving man that makes him feel quite a moral hero in taking that of which his more successful neighbor has deprived him. The heavy-browed fellow is a thief, who is out recruiting his band which the police have broken up in this or some other city. By and by his victim will have time, behind prison bars, to make out the lie that caught him. The world owes no man a living except as the price of honest work. But, wrathful and hungry, he walks easily into the trap.

That was what Inspector Byrnes meant by calling the cheap lodging houses nurseries of crime. I have personally, as a police reporter, helped trace many foul crimes to these houses where they were hatched. They were all robberies to begin with, but three of them ended in murder. Most of my readers will remember at least one of them, the Lyman S. Weeks murder in Brooklyn, a thoroughly characteristic case of the kind I have described. A case they never heard of, because it was nipped in the bud, was typical of another kind. Two young Western fellows had come on, on purpose to hold up New York, and were practising in their lodging, but not, it seems, with much success, for the police pulled them in at their second or third job. When searched, a tintype, evidently of Bowery make, was found in the pocket of one, showing them at rehearsal. They grinned when asked about it. "We done a fellow up easy that way," they said, "and we'd a mind to see how it looked." They were lucky in being caught so soon. A little while, and the gallows would have claimed them, on the road they were travelling.

They had a Mind to see how it looked.

I mention this to show the kind of problem we have in our Bowery lodging houses, with their army of fifteen or sixteen thousand lodgers, hanging on to the ragged edge most of them, and I have only skimmed the surface of it at that. The political boss searches the depths of it about election time when he needs votes; the sanitary policeman in times of epidemic, when small-pox or typhus fever threatens. All other efforts to reach it had proved unavailing when D. O. Mills, the banker,

built his two "Mills Houses," No. 1 in Bleecker
Street for the West Side and No. 2 in Rivington
Street for the homeless of the East Side.   They did
reach it, by a cut 'cross lots as it were, by putting
the whole thing on a neighborly basis.   It had been
just business before, and, like the keeping of slum
tenements, a mighty well-paying one.   The men
who ran it might well have given more, but they
didn't.   It was the same thing over again: let the
lodgers shift as they could; their landlord lived in
style on the avenue.   What were they to him except
the means of keeping it up?

The Mills Houses do not neglect the business
end.   Indeed, they insist upon it.   "No patron,"
said Mr. Mills at the opening, "will receive more
than he pays for, unless it be my hearty good-will
and good wishes.   It is true that I have devoted
thought, labor, and capital to a very earnest effort
to help him, but only by enabling him to help himself.   In doing the work on so large a scale, and in
securing the utmost economies in purchases and in
administration, I hope to give him a larger equiva-
lent for his money than has hitherto been possible.
He can, without scruple, permit me to offer him
this advantage; but he will think better of himself,
and will be a more self-reliant, manly man and a
better citizen, if he knows that he is honestly paying for what he gets."   That had the right ring to

it, and from the beginning so have the houses had. Big, handsome hotels, as fine as any, with wide marble stairs for the dark hole through which one dived into the man-traps of old. Mr. Mills gave to the lodger a man's chance, if he *is* poor. His room is small, but the bed for which he pays twenty cents is clean and good. Indeed, it is said that the spring in

it was made by the man who made the springs for the five-dollar beds in the Waldorf-Astoria, and that it is just the same. However that may be, it is comfortable enough, as comfortable as any need have it in Bleecker Street or on Fifth Avenue. The guest at the Mills House has all the privi-

Doorway of the Mills House, No. 1

leges the other has, except to while away the sunlit hours in his bed. Then he is expected to be out hustling. At nine o'clock his door is barred against him, and is not again opened until five in the afternoon. But there are smoking and writing rooms, and a library for his use; games if he chooses, baths when he feels like taking one, and a laundry where he may wash his own clothes if he has to save the pennies, as he likely has to. It is a good place to do it, too, for he can sleep comfortably and have two square meals a day for fifty cents all told. There is a restaurant in the basement where his dinner costs him fifteen cents.

I will not say that the dinner is as savory as the one they would serve at Delmonico's, but he comes to it probably with a good deal better appetite, and that is the thing after all. I ate with him once, and here is the bill of fare of that day. I kept it.

Soup   One Meat Dish   Two Vegetables
        Dessert   Tea, Coffee or Milk
                        15 cents

SOUPS
Consommé with Noodles   Purée of Tomatoes

HOT MEATS
Roast Turkey, Cranberry Sauce
        Roast Beef, Dish Gravy
                Fricasseed Spring Lamb with Mushrooms

COLD MEAT
Boiled Fresh Beef Tongue

FISH
Fried Smelts, Tartare Sauce
Boiled Cod, Egg Sauce

VEGETABLES
Boiled Sweet Potatoes   Mashed Potatoes
Cauliflower, Hollandaise Sauce   Fried Egg Plant
Celery Salad

DESSERT

Plum Pudding, Hard or Lemon Sauce

Pumpkin Pie   Baked Apples

Tea   Coffee   Milk

I will own the turkey seemed to me to taste of codfish and the codfish of turkey, as if it were all cooked in one huge dish; but there was enough of it, and it was otherwise good. And the fault may have been with my palate, probably was. It is getting to be quite the thing for clubs with a social inquiry turn to meet and take their dinners at Mills House No. 1 in Bleecker Street, so it must be all right. Perhaps I struck the cook's off day.[1]

No. 1 is the largest, with rooms for 1554 guests, and usually there are 1554 there. No. 2 in Rivington Street has 600 rooms. Together they are capable of housing about twelve per cent of all who nightly seek the cheap lodging houses, not counting the Raines law hotels, which are chiefly used for purposes of assignation. The Bowery houses have felt the competition, and have been compelled to make concessions that profit the lodger. The greatest gain to him is the chance of getting away from there. At the Mills Houses he is reasonably

---

[1] Since reading this proof I have been over and verified my diagnosis. The trouble must have been with me. The soup and the mutton and the pie had each its proper savor, and the cook is all right. So is the lunch. There is no fifty-cent lunch in the city that I know of which is better.

safe from the hold-up man and the recruiting thief. Though the latter often gives the police the Bleecker Street house as his permanent address on the principle that makes the impecunious seeker of a job conduct his correspondence from the Fifth Avenue Hotel or the Savoy, he is rarely found there, and if found, is not kept long. If he does get in, he is quiet and harmless because he has to be. Crooks in action seek crooked houses kept by crooked men, and they find them along the Bowery more readily than anywhere. There are the shows and the resorts that draw the young lads, who, away from home, are all too easily drawn, to their undoing. The getting them out of their latitude is the greatest gain, and this service the Mills House performs, to a salutary extent. The more readily since its fame has gone abroad, and the Mills House has become a type. There is scarcely a mail now that does not bring me word from some city in the West or East that a Mills House has been started there in the effort to grapple with the problem of the floating population. The fear that their reputation may help increase that problem by drawing greater crowds from the country is rather strained, it seems to me. The objection would lie against free shelters, but hardly against a business concern that simply strives to give the poor lodger his money's worth. As to him, the

Evening in One of the Courts in the Mills House, No. 1.

everlasting pessimist predicted, when the Mills Houses were opened, that they would have to "make bathing compulsory." The lodger has given him the lie; the average has been over 400 bathers per day, — one in five, — and the record has passed 1000. No doubt soap may be cheap and salvation dear, but on the other hand cleanliness does and must ever begin godliness when fighting the slum, and no one who ever took a look into one of the old-style lodging houses will doubt that we are better off by so much. The Mills houses have paid four, even five, per cent on their owner's investment of a million and a half. It follows that the business will attract capital, which means that there will be an end of the old nuisance. Beyond this, they have borne and will bear increasingly a hand in settling with the saloon with which they compete on its strong ground — that of social fellowship. It has no rival in the Bowery house or in the boarding-house back bedroom. Every philanthropic effort to fight it on that ground has drawn renewed courage and hope from Mr. Mills's work and success.

Many years ago a rich merchant planned to do for his working women the thing Mr. Mills has done for lonely men. Out on Long Island he built a town for his clerks that was to be their very own. But it came out differently. The Long Island town became a cathedral city and the home of wealth and fashion; his woman's boarding house a great public hotel far beyond the reach of those he sought to benefit. The passing years saw his great house, its wealth, its very name, vanish as if they had never been, and even his bones denied by ghoulish thieves rest in the grave. There is no more pathetic page in the history of our city than that which records the eclipse of the house of Alexander T. Stewart,[†] merchant prince. I like to think of the banker's successful philanthropy as a kind of justice to the memory of the dead merchant, more eloquent than marble and brass in the empty crypt. Mills House No. 1 stands upon the site of Mr. Stewart's old home, where he dreamed his barren dream of benevolence to his kind.

His work lies undone yet. While I am writing this, they are putting the roof on a great structure in East Twenty-ninth Street that is to be the "Woman's Hotel" of the city and bear the name of Martha Washington. It is intended for business and professional women who can pay from seven or eight dollars a week up to almost anything for their board and lodging, and it is expected to fill so great a need as to be commercially profitable at once. That will be well, and we shall all be glad. But who will build the Mills House for lonely girls and women who cannot pay seven or eight dollars a week, and would not go to the Woman's Hotel if they

†Alexander T. Stewart (1803–1876), born in Ireland to Scottish Protestant parents, imported Irish laces from 1823 and expanded his dry goods business in New York City until he owned the world's largest retail

could? The social cleft between Madison Avenue
and Bleecker Street is too wide to be bridged by the
best intentions of a hotel company. I doubt if they
would know where to go in that strange uptown
country. When as an immigrant I paid two dollars
a day for board that was not worth fifty cents, in a
Greenwich Street house, I might have lodged in comfort in a Broadway hotel for less money, had I only
known where. There are hosts of half-starved women
and girls living in cheerless back rooms, — or, rather,
they do not live, they exist on weak coffee or tea,
laying up an evil day for the generation of which
they are to be the mothers, — to whom such a house
would be home, freedom, and life. Ask any working
girls' vacation society whence the need of their
labor early and late, if not to put a little life and
vigor into those ill-nourished bodies. Ask the
priest, or any one who knows the temptations of
youth, how much that bald and dreary life of theirs
counts for in the fight he has on hand. Who
will build the working women's hotel somewhere
between Stewart's old store and Twenty-third
Street, east of Broadway, that shall give them their
sadly needed chance? And while about it, let him
add a wing, or build a separate house, such as they
have in Glasgow, for widows with little children, that
shall answer another of our perplexing problems, —
a house, this latter, with nursery, kindergarten,

store. The Long Island town Riis refers to is Garden City (Stewart also
built adjacent Stewart Manor); the not-for-profit boardinghouse for
women workers that Stewart planned became the Park Avenue Hotel.

and laundry, where the mother might know her child safe while she provided for it with her work. Who will be the D. O. Mills of these helpless ones?

Lodging Room in the Leonard Street Police Station.

Or is there but one Mills? I have heard it said that he has been waiting, asking the same question. Let him wait no longer, then, if he would put the finishing touch to a practical philanthropy that will rank in days to come with the great benefactions to mankind.

I have dwelt upon the need of bracing up the home, or finding something to replace it as nearly like it as could be, where that had to be done, because the home is the key to good citizenship.

Unhappily for the great cities, there exists in them
all a class that has lost the key or thrown it away.
For this class, New York, until three years ago, had
never made any provision. The police station
lodging rooms, of which I have spoken, were not to
be dignified by the term. These vile dens, in
which the homeless of our great city were herded,
without pretence of bed, of bath, of food, on rude

Women's Lodging Room in Eldridge Street Police Station.

planks, were the most pernicious parody on municipal charity, I verily believe, that any civilized
community had ever devised. To escape physical
and moral contagion in these crowds seemed

humanly impossible. Of the innocently homeless lad they made a tramp by the shortest cut. To the old tramp they were indeed ideal provision, for they enabled him to spend for drink every cent he could beg or steal. With the stale beer dive, the free lunch counter, and the police lodging room at hand, his cup of happiness was full. There came an evil day, when the stale beer dive shut its doors and the free lunch disappeared for a season. The beer pump, which drained the kegs dry and robbed the stale beer collector of his ware, drove the dives out of business; the Raines law[†] forbade the free lunch. Just at this time Theodore Roosevelt shut the police lodging rooms, and the tramp was literally left out in the cold, cursing reform and its fruits. It was the climax of a campaign a generation old, during which no one had ever been found to say a word in defence of these lodging rooms; yet nothing had availed to close them.

The city took lodgers on an old barge in the East River, that winter (1896), and kept a register of them. We learned something from that. Of nearly 10,000 lodgers, one-half were under thirty years old and in good health — fat, in fact. The doctors reported them "well nourished." Among 100 whom I watched taking their compulsory bath, one night, only two were skinny; the others were stout, well-fed men, abundantly able to do a man's

†A New York State liquor tax law, written by State Senator John Raines (1840–1909), which stated that liquor could not be sold on premises where meals were not sold.

work. They all insisted that they were willing, too; but the moment inquiries began with a view of setting such to work as really wanted it, and sending the rest to the island as vagrants, their

A "Scrub" and her Bed — the Plank.

number fell off most remarkably. From between 400 and 500 who had crowded the barge and the pier sheds, the attendance fell on March 16, the day the investigation began, to 330, on the second day to 294, and on the third day to 171; by March

21 it had been cut down to 121. The problem of the honestly homeless, who were without means to pay for a bed even in a ten-cent lodging house, and who had a claim upon the city by virtue of residence in it, had dwindled to surprisingly small proportions. Of 9386 lodgers, 3622 were shown to have been here less than sixty days, and 968 more not a year. The old mistake, that there is always a given amount of absolutely homeless destitution in a city, and that it is to be measured by the number of those who apply for free lodging, had been reduced to a demonstration. The truth is that the opportunity furnished by the triple alliance of stale beer, free lunch, and free lodging at the police station was the open door to permanent and hopeless vagrancy. Men, a good bishop said, will do what you pay them to do: if to work, they will work; if you make it pay them to beg, they will beg; if to maim helpless children makes begging pay better, they will do that too. See what it is to encourage laziness in man whose salvation is work.

A city lodging house was established, with decent beds, baths, and breakfast, and a system of investigation of the lodger's claim that is yet to be developed to useful proportions. The link that is missing is a farm school, for the training of young vagrants to habits of industry and steady work, as the alternative of the workhouse. Efforts to forge this link

have failed so far, but in the good time that is coming, when we shall have learned the lesson that the
unkindest thing that can be done to a young tramp
is to let him go on tramping, and when magistrates
shall blush to discharge him on the plea that "it is
no crime to be poor in this country," they will

What a Search of the Lodgers brought forth.

succeed, and the tramp also we shall then have
"druv into decency." When I look back now to
the time, ten or fifteen years ago, when, night after
night, with every police station filled, I found the
old tenements in the "Bend" jammed with a reek-
ing mass of human wrecks that huddled in hall
and yard, and slept, crouching in shivering files, all
the way up the stairs to the attic, it does seem as if

we had come a good way, and as if all the turmoil and the bruises and the fighting had been worth while.   New York is no longer, at least when Tammany is out, a tramp's town.   And that is so much gained, to us and to the tramp.

CHAPTER VII

PIETRO AND THE JEW

WE have seen that the problem of the tenement is to make homes for the people, out of it if we can, in it if we must. Now about the tenant. How much of a problem is he? And how are we to go about solving it?

The government "slum inquiry," of which I have spoken before, gave us some facts about him. In New York it found 62.58 per cent of the population of the slum to be foreign-born, whereas for the whole city the percentage of foreigners was only 43.23. While the proportion of illiteracy in all was only as 7.69 to 100, in the slum it was 46.65 per cent. That with nearly twice as many saloons to a given number there should be three times as many arrests in the slum as in the city at large need not be attributed to nationality, except indirectly in its possible responsibility for the saloons. I say "possible" advisably. Anybody, I should think, whose misfortune it is to live in the slum might be expected to find in the saloon a refuge. I shall not quarrel with the other view of it. I am merely stating a personal impression.

The fact that concerns us here is the great proportion of the foreign-born. Though the inquiry covered only a small section of a tenement district, the result may be accepted as typical.

We shall not, then, have to do with an American element in discussing this tenant, for even of the "natives" in the census, by far the largest share is made up of the children of the immigrant. Indeed, in New York only 4.77 per cent of the slum population canvassed were shown to be of native parentage. The parents of 95.23 per cent had come over the sea, to better themselves, it may be assumed. Let us see what they brought us, and what we have given them in return.

The Italians were in the majority where this census-taker went. They were from the south of Italy, avowedly the worst of the Italian immigration, which in the eleven years from 1891 to 1902 gave us nearly a million of Victor Emmanuel's subjects. The exact number of Italian immigrants, as registered by the Emigration Bureau, from July 1, 1891, to June 1, 1902, a month short of eleven years, was 944, 345. And they come in greater numbers every year. In 1898, 58,613 came over, of whom 36,086 gave New York as their destination. In 1901 the Italian immigrants numbered 138,608, and as I write shiploads with thousands upon thousands are afloat, bound for our shores. Yet there is a gleam of promise in the showing of last year, for of the 138,608, those who came to stay in New York numbered only 67,231. Enough surely, but they were after all only one-half of the whole against two-thirds in 1898. If this means that they came to join friends elsewhere in the country — that other centres of immigration

Bedroom in the New City Lodging House.

have been set up — well and good. There is room for them there. Going out to break ground, they give us more than they get. The peril lies in their being cooped up in the city.

Of last year's intake 116,070 came from southern Italy, where they wash less, and also plot less against the peace of mankind, than they do in the north. Quite a lot were from Sicily, the island of the absentee landlord, where peasants die of hunger. I make no apology for quoting here the statement of an Italian officer, on duty in the island, to a staff correspondent of the *Tribuna* of Rome, a paper not to be suspected of disloyalty to United Italy. I take it from the *Evening Post*:

" In the month of July I stopped on a march by a threshing-floor where they were measuring grain. When the shares had been divided, the one who had cultivated the land received a single *tumolo* (less than a half bushel). The peasant, leaning on his spade, looked at his share as if stunned. His wife and their five children were standing by. From the painful toil of a year this was what was left to him with which to feed his family. The tears rolled silently down his cheeks."

These things occasionally help one to understand. Over against this picture there arises in my memory one from the barge office, where I had gone to see an Italian steamer come in. A family sat apart, ordered to wait by the inspecting officer; in the group was an old man, worn and wrinkled, who viewed the turmoil with the calmness of one having no share in it. The younger members formed a sort of bulwark around him.

" Your father is too old to come in," said the official.

Two young women and a boy of sixteen rose to

"Are we not young enough to work for him?"

their feet at once. "Are not we young enough to work for him?" they said. The boy showed his strong arms.

It is charged against this Italian immigrant that he is dirty, and the charge is true. He lives in the darkest of slums, and pays rent that ought to hire a decent flat. To wash, water is needed; and we have a law which orders tenement landlords to put it on every floor, so that their tenants may have the chance. And it is not yet half a score years since one of the biggest tenement-house landlords in the city, the wealthiest church corporation in the land, attacked the constitutionality of this statute rather than pay two or three hundred dollars for putting water into two old buildings, as the Board of Health had ordered, and so came near upsetting the whole structure of tenement-house law upon which our safety depends. Talk about the Church and the people; that one thing did more to drive them apart than all the ranting of atheists that ever were. Yesterday a magazine came in the mail in which I read: "On a certain street corner in Chicago stands a handsome church where hundreds of worshippers gather every Sabbath morning for prayer and praise. Just a little way off, almost within the shadow of its spire, lived, or rather herded, in a dark, damp basement, a family of eight — father, mother, and six children. For all the influence that the songs or the sermons or the prayers had upon them they might have lived there and died like rats in a hole. They did not believe in God, nor heaven, nor hell, other than that in which they lived. Church-goers were to them a lot of canting hypocrites who wrapped their comfortable robes about them and cared nothing for the sufferings of others. Hunger and misery were daily realities."

No, it was not a yellow newspaper. It was a religious publication, and it told how a warm human love did find them out, and showed them what the Church had failed to do — what God's love is like. And I am not attacking the Church either. God forbid! I would help, not hinder it; for I, too, am a churchman. Only — well, let it pass. It will not happen again. That same year I read in my paper the reply of the priest at the Pro-Cathedral in Stanton Street to a crank who scoffed at the kind of "religion" they had there: kindergartens, nurseries, boys' and girls' clubs, and mothers' meetings. "Yes," he wrote, "that is our religion. We believe that a love of God that doesn't forthwith run to manifest itself in some loving deed to His children is not worth having." That is how I came to be a churchman in Bishop Potter's camp. I "joined" then and there.

Our Italian is ignorant, it is said, and that charge

is also true. I doubt if one of the family in the
barge office could read or write his own name. Yet
would you fear especial danger to our institutions,
to our citizenship, from those four? He lives
cheaply, crowds, and underbids even the Jew in the
sweat shop. I can myself testify to the truth of
these statements. A couple of years ago I was the
umpire in a quarrel between the Jewish tailors and
the factory inspector whom they arraigned before
the governor on charges of inefficiency. The
burden of their grievance was that the Italians
were underbidding them in their own market,
which of course the factory inspector could not
prevent. Yet, even so, the evidence is not that the
Italian always gets the best of it. I came across
a family once working on " knee-pants." " Twelve
pants, ten cents," said the tailor, when there was
work. " Ve work for dem sheenies," he explained.
" Ven dey has work, ve gets some; ven dey hasn't,
ve don't." He was an unusually gifted tailor as to
English, but apparently not as to business capacity.
In the Astor tenements, in Elizabeth Street, where
we found forty-three families living in rooms intended for sixteen, I saw women finishing "pants "
at thirty cents a day. Some of the garments were
of good grade, and some of poor; some of them
were soldiers' trousers, made for the government;
but whether they received five, seven, eight, or ten

cents a pair, it came to thirty cents a day, except in
a single instance, in which two women, sewing from
five in the morning till eleven at night, were able,
being practised hands, to finish forty-five "pants"
at three and a half cents a pair, and so made
together over a dollar and a half. They were
content, even happy. I suppose it seemed wealth
to them, coming from a land where a Parisian
investigator of repute found three lire (not quite
sixty cents) *per month* a girl's wages.

I remember one of those flats, poor and dingy,
yet with signs of the instinctive groping toward orderly arrangement which I have observed so many
times, and take to be evidence that in better surroundings much might be made of these people.
Clothes were hung to dry on a line strung the
whole length of the room. Upon couches by the
wall some men were snoring. They were the boarders. The "man" was out shovelling snow with the
midnight shift. By a lamp with brown paper shade,
over at the window, sat two women sewing. One
had a baby on her lap. Two sweet little cherubs,
nearly naked, slept on a pile of unfinished "pants,"
and smiled in their sleep. A girl of six or seven
dozed in a child's rocker between the two workers,
with her head hanging down on one side; the
mother propped it up with her elbow as she sewed.
They were all there, and happy in being together

even in such a place. On a corner shelf burned a
night lamp before a print of the Mother of God,
flanked by two green bottles, which, seen at a certain angle, made quite a festive show.

Complaint is made that the Italian promotes child
labor. His children work at home on "pants" and
flowers at an hour when they ought to have been long
in bed. Their sore eyes betray the little flower-mak-
ers when they come tardily to school. Doubtless
there are such cases, and quite too many of them;
yet, in the very block which I have spoken of, the
investigation conducted for the Gilder Tenement
House Commission by the Department of Sociology
of Columbia University, under Professor Franklin H.
Giddings,[†] discovered, of 196 children of school age,
only 23 at work or at home, and in the next block
only 27 out of 215. That was the showing of the
foreign population all the way through. Of 225
Russian Jewish children only 15 were missing from
school, and of 354 little Bohemians only 21. The
overcrowding of the schools and their long waiting
lists occasionally furnished the explanation why they
were not there. Professor Giddings reported, after
considering all the evidence: "The foreign-born
population of the city is not, to any great extent,
forcing children of legal school age into money-
earning occupations. On the contrary, this population shows a strong desire to have its children

†The 1894 New York Tenement House Commission, chaired by
Richard Watson Gilder. Franklin H. Giddings (1855–1931), a journalist
as well as a sociologist, was the author of nearly a dozen books on
sociology.

acquire the common rudiments of education. If the city does not provide liberally and wisely for the satisfaction of this desire, the blame for the civic and moral dangers that will threaten our community, because of ignorance, vice, and poverty, must rest on the whole public, not on our foreign-born residents." And Superintendent Maxwell of the Department of Education adds, six years later, that with a shortage of 28,000 seats, and worse coming, "it is difficult to avoid the conclusion that the insufficiency of school accommodation in New York City is a most serious menace to our universal welfare."[1]   For we have reached the stage again, thanks be to four years of Tammany, when, after all the sacrifices of the past, we are once more face to face with an army of enforced truants, and all they stand for.

He is clannish, this Italian; he gambles and uses a knife, though rarely on anybody not of his own people; he "takes what he can get," wherever anything is free, as who would not, coming to the feast like a starved wolf? There was nothing free where he came from. Even the salt was taxed past a poor man's getting any of it. Lastly, he buys fraudulent naturalization papers, and uses them. I shall plead guilty for him to every one of these counts. They are all proven. Gambling is his besetting sin. He is sober, industrious, frugal, enduring beyond belief;

[1] Superintendent Maxwell in *Municipal Affairs*, December, 1900.

but he will gamble on Sunday and quarrel over his cards, and when he sticks his partner in the heat of the quarrel, the partner is not apt to tell. He prefers to bide his time. Yet there has lately been evidence once or twice, in the surrender of an assassin by his countrymen, that the old vendetta is being shelved and a new idea of law and justice is breaking through. As to the last charge: our Italian is not dull. With his intense admiration for the land where a dollar a day waits upon the man with a shovel, he can see no reason why he should not accept the whole "American plan" with ready enthusiasm. It is a good plan. To him it sums itself up in the statement: a dollar a day for the shovel; two dollars for the shovel with a citizen behind it. And he takes the papers and the two dollars.

He came here for a chance to live. Of politics, social ethics, he knows nothing. Government in his old home existed only for his oppression. Why should he not attach himself with his whole loyal soul to the plan of government in his new home that offers to boost him into the place of his wildest ambition, a "job on the streets," — that is, in the Street Cleaning Department, — and asks no other return than that he shall vote as directed? Vote! Not only he, but his cousins and brothers and uncles will vote as they are told, to get Pietro the job he covets.

If it pleases the other man, what is it to him for whom he votes? He is after the job.

Here, ready-made to the hand of the politician, is such material as he never saw before. For Pietro's loyalty is great. As a police detective, one of his own people, once put it to me, " He got a kind of an idea, or an old rule: an eye for an eye; do to another as you'd be done by; if he don't squeal on you, you stick by him, no matter what the consequences." This " kind of an idea " is all he has to draw upon for an answer to the question if the thing is right. But the question does not arise. Why should it? Was he not told by the agitators whom the police jailed at home that in a republic all men are made happy by means of the vote? And is there not proof of it? It has made him happy, has it not? And the man who bought his vote seems to like it. Well, then?

Very early Pietro discovered that it was every man for himself, in the chase of the happiness which this powerful vote had in keeping. He was robbed by the padrone — that is, the boss — when he came over, fleeced on his steamship fare, made to pay for getting a job, and charged three prices for board and lodging and extras while working in the railroad gang. The boss had a monopoly, and Pietro was told that it was maintained by his "divvying" with some railroad official.

Rumor said, a very high-up official, and that the railroad was in politics in the city; that is to say, dealt in votes. When the job gave out, the boss packed him into the tenement he had bought with his profits on the contract; and if Pietro had a family, told him to take in lodgers and

The Play School. Dressing Dolls for a Lesson.

crowd his flat, as the Elizabeth Street tenements were crowded, so as to make out the rent, and to never mind the law. The padrone was a politician, and had a pull. He was bigger than the law, and it was the votes he traded in that did it all. Now it was Pietro's turn. With his vote he could buy what to him seemed wealth;

two dollars a day. In the muddle of ideas, that was the one which stood out clearly. When citizen papers were offered him for $12.50, he bought them quickly, and got his job on the street.

It was the custom of the country. If there was any doubt about it, the proof was furnished when Pietro was arrested through the envy and plotting of the opposition boss. Distinguished counsel, employed by the machine, pleaded his case in court. Pietro felt himself to be quite a personage, and he was told that he was safe from harm, though a good deal of dust might be kicked up; because, when it came down to that, both the bosses were doing the same kind of business. I quote from the report of the State Superintendent of Elections of January, 1899: " In nearly every case of illegal registration, the defendant was represented by eminent counsel who were identified with the Democratic organization, among them being three assistants to the corporation counsel. My deputies arrested Rosario Calecione and Giuseppe Marrone, both of whom appeared to vote at the fifth election district of the Sixth Assembly District; Marrone being the Democratic captain of the district, and, it was charged, himself engaged in the business of securing fraudulent naturalization papers. In both of these cases Farriello had procured the naturalization papers for the men for a consideration. They were subsequently indicted. Marrone and Calecione were bailed by the Democratic leader of the Sixth Assembly District."

The business, says the state superintendent, is carried on "to an enormous extent." It appears, then, that Pietro has already "got on to" the American plan as the slum presented it to him, and has in good earnest become a problem. I guessed as much from the statement of a Tammany politician to me, a year ago, that every Italian voter in his district got his "old two" on election day. He ought to know, for he held the purse. Suppose, now, we speak our minds as frankly, for once, and put the blame where it belongs. Will it be on Pietro? And upon this showing, who ought to be excluded, when it comes to that?

The slum census taker did not cross the Bowery. Had he done so, he would have come upon the refugee Jew, the other economic marplot of whom complaint is made with reason. If his Nemesis has overtaken him in the Italian, certainly he challenged that fate. He did cut wages by his coming. He was starving, and he came in shoals. In eighteen years more than half a million Jewish immigrants have landed in New York.[1] They had

[1] According to the register of the United Hebrew Charities, between October 1, 1884, and June 1, 1902, the number was 539,067, and it is again on the increase. The year 1902 will probably show an increase in this class of immigration over 1901 of quite 15,000.

to have work and food, and they got both as they could. In the strife they developed qualities that were anything but pleasing. They herded like cattle. They had been so herded by Christian rulers, a despised and persecuted race, through the centuries. Their very coming was to escape from their last inhuman captivity in a. Christian state. They lied, they were greedy, they were charged with bad faith. They brought nothing, neither money nor artisan skill, — nothing but their consuming energy, to our land, and their one gift was their greatest offence. One might have pointed out that they had been trained to lie, for their safety; had been forbidden to work at trades, to own land; had been taught for a thousand years, with the scourge and the stake, that only gold could buy them freedom from torture. But what was the use? The charges were true. The Jew was — he still is — a problem of our slum.

And yet, if ever there was material for citizenship, this Jew is such material. Alone of all our immigrants he comes to us without a past. He has no country to renounce, no ties to forget. Within him there burns a passionate longing for a home to call his, a country which will own him, that waits only for the spark of such another love to spring into flame which nothing can quench. Waiting for it, all his energies are turned into his business. He is not always choice in method; he often offends. He crowds to the front in everything, no matter whom he crowds out. The land is filled with his clamor. "If the East Side would shut its mouth and the West Side get off the saloon corner, we could get somewhere," said a weary philanthropist to me the other day, and made me laugh, for I knew what he meant. But the Jew heeds it not. He knows what he wants and he gets it. He succeeds. He is the yeast of any slum, if given time. If it will not let him go, it must rise with him. The charity managers in London said it, when we looked through their slums some years ago, "The Jews have renovated Whitechapel." I, for one, am a firm believer in this Jew, and in his boy. Ignorant they are, but with a thirst for knowledge that surmounts any barrier. The boy takes all the prizes in the school. His comrades sneer that he will not fight. Neither will he when there is nothing to be gained by it. Yet, in defence of his rights, there is in all the world no such fighter as he. Literally, he will die fighting, by inches, too, from starvation. Witness his strikes. I believe that, should the time come when the country needs fighting men, the son of the despised immigrant Jew will resurrect on American soil, the first that bade him welcome, the old Maccabee type, and set an example for all the rest of us to follow.

This long while he has been in the public eye as the vehicle and promoter of sweating, and much severe condemnation has been visited upon him with good cause. He had to do something, and he took to the clothes-maker's trade as that which was most quickly learned. The increasing crowds, the tenement, and his grinding poverty made the soil wherein the evil grew rank. But the real sweater does not live in Ludlow Street; he keeps the stylish shop on Broadway, and he does not always trouble himself to find out how his workers fare, much as that may have to do with the comfort and security of his customers.

"We do not have to have a license," said the tenants in one wretched flat where a consumptive was sewing on coats almost with his last gasp; "we work for a first-class place on Broadway."

And so they did. Sweating is simply a question of profit to the manufacturer. By letting out his work on contract, he can save the expense of running his factory and delay longer making his choice of styles. If the contractor, in turn, can get along with less shop room by having as much of the work as can profitably be so farmed out done in the tenements by cheap home labor, he is so much better off. And tenement labor is always cheap because of the crowds that clamor for it and must have bread. The poor Jew is the victim of the mischief

quite as much as he has helped it on.   Back of the
manufacturer and the contractor there is still another sweater, — the public.   Only by its sufferance
of the bargain counter and of sweat-shop-made goods
has the nuisance existed as long as it has.   I am
glad I have lived to see the day of its passing, for,
unless I greatly mistake, it is at hand now that the
old silent partner is going out of the firm.

I mean the public.   We tried it in the old days,
but the courts said the bill to stop tenement cigar-
making was unconstitutional.   Labor was property,
and property is inviolable — rightly so until it itself becomes a threat to the commonwealth.   Child
labor is such a threat.   It has been stopped in the
factories, but no one can stop it in the tenement so
long as families are licensed to work there.   The
wrecking of the home that is inevitable where the
home is turned into a shop with thirty cents as a
woman's wage is that; the overcrowding that goes
hand in hand with home-work is that; the scourge
of consumption which doctors and Boards of Health
wrestle with in vain while dying men and women
" sew on coats with their last gasp " and sew the
death warrant of the buyer into the lining, is a
threat the gravity of which we have hardly yet made
out.   Courts and constitutions reflect the depth of
public sentiment on a moral or political issue.   We
have been doing a deal of dredging since then, and

we are at it yet. While I am writing a Tuberculosis Committee is at work sifting the facts of tenement-house life as they bear on that peril. A Child Labor Committee is preparing to attack the slum in its centre, as we stopped the advance guard when we made the double-decker unprofitable. The factory inspector is gathering statistics of earnings and hours of labor in sweat shop and tenement to throw light on the robbery that goes on there. When they have told us what they have to tell, it may be that we shall be able to say to the manufacturer: "You shall not send out goods to be made in sweat shop or tenement. You shall make them in your own shop or not at all." He will not be hurt, for all will have to do alike. I am rather inclined to think that he will be glad to take that way out of a grisly plight.

For he has seen the signs of a flank movement that goes straight for his pocket-book, an organized public sentiment that is getting ready to say to him, "We will buy no clothes or wear them, or any other thing whatsoever, that is made at the price of the life and hope of other men or women." Wherever I went last winter, through the length and breadth of the land, women were stirring to organize branches of the Consumers' League. True, they were the well-to-do, not yet the majority. But they were the very ones who once neither knew nor cared. Now they do both. That is more than half the fight. Whatever may be the present results of the agitation, in the long run I would rather take my chances with a vigorous Consumers' League and not a law in the state to safeguard labor or the community's interests, than with the

Label of Consumers' League.

most elaborate code man has yet devised, and the bargain counter in full blast, unchallenged, from Monday to Saturday. Laws may be evaded, and too often are; tags betraying that goods are "tenement made" may be removed, and they make no appeal anyhow to a community deaf to the arraignment of the bargain counter. But an instructed public sentiment, such as that of which the Consumers' League [1] is the most recent expression, makes laws and enforces them too. By its aid

[1] The following is the declaration of principles of the National Consumers' League : —

SEC. 1. That the interests of the community demand that all workers shall receive fair living wages, and that goods shall be produced under sanitary conditions.

SEC. 2. That the responsibility for some of the worst evils from which producers suffer rests with the consumers who seek the cheapest markets regardless how cheapness is brought about.

SEC. 3. That it is, therefore, the duty of consumers to find out under what conditions the articles they purchase are produced and distributed, and insist that these conditions shall be wholesome, and consistent with a respectable existence on the part of the workers.

we have forced the children out of the factories, the sweat shops out of the tenements, and shut the door against the stranger there. Only to families are licenses granted. By its aid we shall yet drive work out of the home altogether; for goods are made to

Josephine Shaw Lowell,† Chairman of the Vagrancy Committee, and one of the Strongest Forces in Charity Organization, the Consumers' League, and every other Healthy Reform Effort.

sell, and none will be made which no one will buy.

Organized labor makes its own appeal to the same end. From this year (1892) on, the United Garment Workers of America resolved in national convention to give their stamp to no manufacturer who does not have all his work done on his own premises. If they faithfully live up to that compact with the public, they will win. Two winters ago I took their label, which was supposed to guarantee living wages and clean and healthy conditions, from the hip pocket of a pair of trousers which I found a man, sick with scarlet fever, using as a pillow in

†Josephine Shaw Lowell (1843–1905), was a commissioner of the New York State Board of Charities, 1877–1889. *Public Relief and Private Charity* was one of her two published books.

one of the foulest sweater's tenements I had ever
been in, and carried it to the headquarters of the
union to show them what a mockery they were
making of the mightiest engine that had come to
their hand.   I am glad to believe those days are
over for good; and when we all believe it their fight
will be won.   When the union label deserves public
confidence as a guarantee against such things, it
will receive it.   When I know that insisting on a
union plumber for my pipes means that the job will
be done right, then I will always send for a union
plumber and have no other.   That is the whole
story, and on that day the label will be mightier
than any law, because the latter will be merely the
effort to express by statute the principle it embodies.

Stragglers there will always be, I suppose.   It
was only the other day I read in the report of the
Consumers' League in my own city that " a benevolent institution," when found giving out clothing to
be made in tenement houses that were not licensed,
and taken to task for it, asked the agents of the
League to " show some way in which the law could
be evaded "; but it is just as well for that " benevolent institution " that name and address were wanting, or it might find its funds running short
unaccountably.   We *are* waking up.   This very
licensing of tenement workers is proof of it, though
it gives one a cold chill to see thirty thousand licenses

out, with hardly a score of factory inspectors to keep tab on them. Roosevelt, as governor, set the pace, going himself among the tenements to see how the law was enforced, and how it could be mended. Now we have a registry system copied from Massachusetts, where they do these things right and most others besides. An index is so arranged by streets that when the printed sheet comes every morning from the Bureau of Contagious Diseases, with name and house number of every case of small-pox, scarlet fever, diphtheria, etc. reported during the twenty-four hours, a clerk can check one off from the other in half an hour, and before noon have every infected flat quarantined. Word is sent to the manufacturer to stop sending any more supplies there, and the garments in the house are tagged till after disinfection. And by the same means all the cards are laid on the table. If a merchant in California or in Florida brags that he buys only factory-made goods, the customer can find out through the Consumers' League if it is true. If the register shows that the manufacturer has filed lists of the tenements where his goods are made up, it is not true. All of which helps.

But Massachusetts is Massachusetts, and New York is New York. A tenement-house population of more than two millions of souls makes its own problems, and there is no other like it. After all,

the chief function of the license must, in the end, be
to show that it cannot be done so — safely.   Even
with the active coöperation of the Board of Health,
and with the nearly two hundred tenement-house inspectors that are being turned loose this summer,
full of new zeal and desire to make a record, we
shall yet be whipping the devil around the stump
until the public sentiment fostered by the Consumers' League and its allies heads him off on the
other side.   The truth of the matter is that the job
is too big for the law alone.   It needs the gospel to
back it up.   Together they can do it.

CHAPTER VIII

ON WHOM SHALL WE SHUT THE DOOR?

THE Jew and the Italian have filled the landscape so far, because, as a matter of fact, that is what they do. Yesterday it was the Irishman and the Bohemian.[†] To-morrow it may be the Greek, who already undersells the Italian from his pushcart in the Fourth Ward, and the Syrian, who can give Greek, Italian, and Jew points at a trade. The rebellious Slovak holds his own corner in our industrial system, though never for long. He yearns ever for the mountain sides of his own Hungary. He remembers, where the Jew tries only to forget. From Dalmatia[††] comes a new emigration, and there are signs that the whole Balkan peninsula has caught the fever and is waiting only for cheap transportation to be established on the Danube to the Black Sea, when there is no telling what will be heading our way. I sometimes wonder what thoughts come to the eagle that perches over the great stone gateway on Ellis Island, as he watches the procession that files through it into the United States day after day, and never ends. He looks out

[†]Bohemia then was part of the Austro-Hungarian empire; after World War I it was part of the new nation of Czechoslovakia. The Bohemian people ethnically were Slovak.

[††]Dalmatia, on the Balkan Peninsula, became part of the nation of Yugoslavia formed after World War I.

One Door that has been opened: St. John's Park in Hudson Street, —
once a Graveyard.

of his grave, unblinking eye at the motley crowd,
but gives no sign. Does he ask: "Where are the
Pilgrim Fathers, the brave Huguenots, the patient
Puritans, the sturdy priests, and the others that
came for conscience' sake to build upon this conti-
nent a home for freedom? And these, why do
they come with their strange tongues — for gold?"
True, eagle! but look to the roster of those who
fought and died for the freedom those pioneers
planted, who watered the tree with their life blood,
and see how many you find inscribed there who
came through that gate. Go to the public school
and hear their children speak the tongue that is

sweet to your ear; hear their young voices as they salute the flag that is *theirs:*

" We give our heads and our hearts to our country. One country, one language, one flag! "

Fear not, eagle! While that gate is open let no one bar the one you guard. While the flag flies over the public school, keep it aloft over Ellis Island and have no misgivings. The school has the answer to your riddle.

About once a week I am asked: Would I shut out any, and whom and how and why? Sometimes, looking at it from the point of view of the tenement and the sweat shop, — that is to say, the city, — I think I would. And were that all, I certainly should. But then, there comes up the recollection of a picture of the city of Prague that hangs in a Bohemian friend's parlor, here in New York. I stood looking at it one day, and noticed in the foreground cannon that pointed in over the city. I spoke of it, unthinking, and said to my host that they should be trained, if against an enemy, the other way. The man's eye flashed fire. " Ha! " he cried, " here, yes! " When I think of that, I do not want to shut the door.

Again, there occurs to me an experience the police had a few years ago in Mulberry Street. They were looking for a murderer, and came upon a nest of Italian thugs who lived by blackmailing their countrymen. They were curious about them, and sent their names to Naples with a request for information.   There came back such a record as none of the detectives had ever seen or heard of before.   All of them were notorious criminals, who had been charged with every conceivable crime, from burglary to kidnapping and "maiming," and some not to be conceived of by the American mind. Five of them together had been sixty-three times in

jail, and one no less than twenty-one times.   Yet, though they were all " under special surveillance," they had come here without let or hindrance within a year. When I recall that, I want to shut the door quick.   I sent the exhibit to Washington at the time.

Dr. Jane Elizabeth Robbins, the "Woman Doctor."

But then, again, when I think of Mrs. Michelangelo, in her poor mourning for one child run over and killed, wiping her tears away and going bravely to work to keep the home together for the other five until the oldest shall be old enough to take her father's place; and when, as now, there strays into my hand the letter from my good friend, the "woman doctor" in the slum, in which she wrote, when her father lay dead: "The little scamps of the street have been positively pathetic; they have made such shy, boyish attempts at friendliness; one little chap offered to let me hold his top while it was spinning, in token of affection," — when I read that, I have not the heart to shut anybody out.

Except, of course, the unfit, the criminal, and the pauper, cast off by their own, and the man brought over here merely to put money into the pockets of the steamship agent, the padrone, and the mine owner. We have laws to bar these out. Suppose we begin by being honest with ourselves and the immigrant, and respecting our own laws. The door that is to be shut is over yonder, at the port where they take ship. There is where the scrutiny is to be made, to be effective. When the door has been shut and locked against the man who left his country for his country's good, whether by its "assistance" or not, and when trafficking in the immigrant for private profit has been stopped, then, perhaps, we shall be better able to decide what degree of ignorance in him constitutes unfitness for citizenship and cause for shutting him out. Perchance then, also, we shall hear less of the cant about his being a peril to the republic. Doubtless ignorance is a peril, but the selfishness that trades upon ignorance is a much greater. He came to us without a country, ready to adopt such a standard of patriotism as he found, at its face value, and we gave him the rear tenement and slum politics. If he accepted the standard, whose fault was it? His being in such a hurry to vote that he could not wait till the law made him a citizen was no worse, to my mind, than the treachery of the "upper class" native, who refuses to go to the polls for fear he may rub up against him there. This last let us settle with first, and see what remains of our problem. We can approach it honestly, then, at all events.

I came into town on the Pennsylvania Railroad the other day just when the emigrant lighter had tied up at the wharf to discharge its west-bound cargo. For a full hour I stood watching the stream of them, thousands upon thousands, carrying knapsacks and trunks, odd in speech and ways, but all of them with hopeful faces set toward the great country where they were to win their own way. So they answered the query of the eagle at the island gate. Scarce an hour within the gate, they were no longer a problem. The country needs these men of strong arms and strong courage. It is in the city the shoe pinches. What can we do to relieve it?

Much could be done with effective inspection on the other side, to discourage the blind immigration that stops short in the city's slums. They come to better themselves, and it is largely a question of making it clear to them that they do not better themselves and make us to be worse off by staying there, whereas their going farther would benefit both. But I repeat that that lever must be applied over there, to move this load. Once they are here, we might have a land and labor bureau that would take in the whole country, and serve as a great directory and distributing agency, instead of leaving it to private initiative to take up the crowds, — something much more comprehensive than anything now existing. There would still be a surplus; but at least it would be less by so many as we sent away. And in the nature of things the congestion would be lessened as more went out. Immigrants go where they have friends, and if those friends lived in Michigan we should not be troubled with them long in New York. If the immigration came all from one country, we should, because of that, have no problem at all, or not much of one at all events, except perhaps in the Jews, who have lived in Ghettos since time out of mind. The others would speedily be found making only a way station of New York. It is the constant kaleidoscopic change I spoke of that brings us hordes every few years who have to break entirely new ground. It seems to have been always so. Forty years after the settlement of Manhattan Island, says Theodore Roosevelt in his history of New York, eighteen different languages and dialects were spoken in its streets, though the future metropolis was then but a small village. "No sooner," says he, "has one set of varying elements been fused together, than another stream has been poured into the crucible." What was true of New York two hundred years ago is true to-day of the country of which it is the gateway.

In dealing with the surplus that remains, we shall have to rely first and foremost on the public school. Of that I shall speak hereafter. It can do more and better work than it is doing, for the old as for the young, when it becomes the real neighborhood centre, especially in the slums. The flag flies over it, that is one thing, and not such a little thing as some imagine. I think we are beginning to see it, with our Flag Day and our putting it out when we never thought of it five or six years ago. And by the way, when last I was in Denmark, my native land, I noticed they had a way of flying the flag on Sunday, — whether in honor of the day, or because they loved it, or because they felt the need of flying it in the face of their big and greedy German neighbor, I shall not say. But it was all right. Why can we not do the same ? It would not hurt the flag, and it would not hurt the day. They would both be better for it — we would all be.

You cannot have too much of the flag in the right way, and there would be nothing wrong about that. Just go into one of the Children's Aid Society's ragged schools, where the children are practically all from abroad, and see how they take to it. Watch an Italian parade, in which it is always

One Way of bringing the Children into Camp: Basket-weaving in Vacation School.

borne side by side with the standard of United Italy, and if you had any doubts about what it stands for you will change your mind quickly. The sight of it is worth a whole course in the school, for education in citizenship.

And then it looks fine in the landscape always. It always makes me think there that I added to the red and white of my fathers' flag only the blue of heaven, where wrongs are righted, and I feel better for it. Why should it not have the same effect on others? I know it has.

The school might be made the means, as the house to which all the life of the neighborhood turned, of enrolling the immigrants in the perilous years when they are not yet citizens. I know what they mean; I have gone through them, seen most of the mischief they hold for the unattached. That *is* the mischief, that they are unattached. A way must be found of claiming them, if they are not to be lost to the cause of good citizenship where they might so easily have been saved. I spoke of it in " The Making of an American." They want to belong, they are waiting to be claimed by some one, and the some one that comes is Tammany with its slum politics. The mere enrolling of them, with leave to march behind a band of music, suffices with the young. They belong then. The old are used to enrolment. Where they came from they were enrolled in the church, in the army, by the official vaccinator, by the tax-collector — oh, yes, the tax-collector — and here, set all of a sudden adrift, it seems like a piece of home to have some one come along and claim them, write them down, and tell them that they are to do so and so. Childish, is it? Not at all. It is just human nature, the kind we are working with.

The mere fact that the schoolhouse is there, inviting them in, is something. When it comes to seek them out, to invite them to their own hall for discussion, for play, it will be a good deal, particularly if the women go along. And the enrolment of the schoolhouse could be counted as being for decency.

It makes all the difference what the start is like. " Excellency," wrote an Italian to his consul in New York, " I arrived from Italy last week. As soon as I landed a policeman clubbed me. I am going to write to Victor Emmanuel how things are done here. Viva l' Italia! Abbasso l' America!" I should not be surprised to find that man plotting anarchy in Paterson as soon as he got his bearings, and neither need you be.

There is still another alternative to either keeping them out or keeping them in the city, namely, to ship them away after they have reached the slum and been stranded there, individually or in squads. The latter way was tried when the great Jewish immigration first poured in, in the early eighties. Five colonies of refugee Jews were started in southern New Jersey, but they failed. The soil was sandy and poor, and the work unfamiliar. Thrown upon his own resources, in a strange and unfriendly neighborhood, the man grew discouraged and gave up in despair. The colonies were in a state of collapse when the New York managers of the Baron de Hirsch Fund took them under the arms and gave them a start on a new plan. They themselves had located a partly industrial, partly farming, community in the neighborhood. They persuaded several large clothing contractors to move their plants out to the villages, where they would be assured of steady hands, with much less chance of disturbing strikes; while on the other hand their workers would have steadier work and could never starve in dull seasons, for they could work their farms and gardens. And, indeed, a perfect frenzy for spading and hoeing seized them when the crops appeared, with promise of unlimited potatoes for the digging of them. The experiment is still in progress. It is an experiment, because as yet the Hirsch Fund millions back the colonies up, and there is no passing of reasonable judgment upon them till they have stood alone awhile. To all appearances they are prospering, Woodbine, the Hirsch colony, especially so, with its agricultural school that has set out upon the mission of turning the Jew back to the soil from which he has been barred so long. Its pupils came out of the sweat shops and the tenement barracks of the Ghetto, and a likelier lot it would not be easy to find. One can but wish that the hopes of their friends may be realized in fullest measure. They have put their hands to a task that seems like turning back the finger of time, and snags of various kinds beset their way.

I remember the President of the Board coming into my office one day with despair written all over him: of a hundred families, carefully picked to go into the country where homes and work awaited them, when it came to the actual departure only seven wanted to go. It was the old story of objection to "the society of the stump." They wanted the crowds, the bands, the kosher butcher shops, the fake auction stores, and the synagogues they were used to. They have learned a lesson from that in the Jersey colonies, and are building entertainment halls for the social life that is to keep them together. Only a year or so ago an attempt at home-building, much nearer New York, at New Orange, just over the hills in Jersey, came to an abrupt end. It left out the farming end, aiming merely at the removal of needle workers from the city with their factory. A building was put up for a large New York tailoring firm, and it moved over bodily with its men — that is, with such as were willing to go. Work was plentiful in the city, and they were not all ready to surrender the tenement for the sake of a home upon the land, though a very attractive little cottage awaited them on singularly easy terms. However that was almost got over when the firm suddenly threw up the contract. It proved to be costlier for them to manufacture away from the city, and they could not compete.

If there is yet an element of doubt about the Jew as a colonist, there is none about his ability to make ends meet as an individual farmer, given a fair chance. More than a thousand such are now scattered through the New England states and the dairy counties of New York. The Jewish Agricultural Aid Societies of New York and Chicago gave them their start, and report decided progress. The farmers are paying their debts and laying away money. As a dairy farmer or poultry raiser the Jew has more of an immediate commercial grip on the situation and works with more courage than if he has to wait for long, uncertain crops. In Sullivan and Ulster counties, New York, a hundred Jewish farmers keep summer boarders besides, and are on the highroad to success. Very recently the New York society has broken new paths upon an individual "removal plan," started by the B'nai B'rith in 1900. Agents are sent throughout the country to make arrangements with Jewish communities for the reception of workers from the Ghetto; and so successful have been these efforts that at this writing some five thousand have been moved singly and scattered over the country from the Atlantic to the Pacific — that is, in not yet three years since the beginning. They are carefully looked after, and the reports show that over eighty per cent of all do well in their new surroundings. This result has been wrought at a per capita expense of twelve dollars, not a very great sum for such a work.

In its bold outline the movement contemplates nothing less than the draining of the Ghetto by the indirect process of which I spoke. "The importance of it," says the Removal Committee in its report for 1901, "is found, not in the numbers removed, but in the inauguration of the movement, which should and must be greatly extended, and which is declared to be of far-reaching significance. The experience of past years has proven that almost every family removed becomes a centre around which immediately and with ever increasing force others congregate. The committee in charge of the Russian immigration in 1890, 1891, etc., has evidence that cities and towns, to which but a very small number of newly arrived immigrants were sent, have become the centres of large Russian-Jewish communities. No argument is needed to emphasize this statement."

It is pleasing to be told that the office of the Removal Committee has been besieged by eager applicants from the beginning. So light is breaking also in that dark corner.

There is enough of it everywhere, if one will only look away from the slum to those it holds fast.

"The people are all right," was the unvarying report of the early Tenement House Committees, "if we only give them half a chance." When the country was in the throes of the silver campaign, the newspapers told the story of an old laborer who went to the sub-treasury and demanded to see the "boss." He undid the strings of an old leathern purse with fumbling fingers, and counted out more than two hundred dollars in gold eagles, the hoard of a lifetime of toil and self-denial. They were for the government, he said. He had not the head to understand all the talk that was going on, but he gathered from what he heard that the government was in trouble, and that somehow it was about not having gold enough. So he had brought what he had. He owed it all to the country, and now that she needed it he had come to give it back.

The man was an Irishman. Very likely he was enrolled in Tammany and voted its ticket. I remember a tenement at the bottom of a back alley, over on the East Side, where I once went visiting with the pastor of a mission chapel. Up in the attic there was a family of father and daughter in two rooms that had been made out of one by dividing off the deep dormer window. It was midwinter, and they had no fire. He was a pedler, but the snow had stalled his push-cart, and robbed them of their only other source of income, a lodger who hired cot room in the attic for a few cents a night. The daughter was not able to work. But she said, cheerfully, that they were "getting along." When it came out that she had not tasted solid food for many days, was starving in fact, — indeed, she died within a year, of the slow starvation of the tenements that parades in the mortality returns under a variety of scientific names which all mean the same thing, — she met her pastor's gentle chiding with the excuse: "Oh, your church has many that are poorer than I. I don't want to take your money."

These were Germans, ordinarily held to be close-fisted; but I found that in their dire distress they had taken in a poor old man who was past working, and kept him all winter, sharing with him what they had. He was none of theirs; they hardly even knew him, as it appeared. It was enough that he was "poorer than they," and lonely and hungry and cold.

It was over here that the children of Mr. Elsing's Sunday-school gave out of the depth of their poverty fifty-four dollars in pennies to be hung on the Christmas tree as their offering to the persecuted Armenians. One of their teachers told me of a Bohemian family that let the holiday dinner she brought them stand and wait, while they sent out to bid to the feast four little ragamuffins of the neighborhood who else would have gone hungry. And here it was in "the hard winter" when no one had work, that the nurse from the Henry Street settlement found her cobbler patient entertaining

The Children's Christmas Tree.

a lodger, with barely bread in the house for himself and his boy. He introduced the stranger with some embarrassment, and when they were alone, excused himself for doing it. The man was just from prison — a man with "a history."

"But," said the nurse, doubtfully, "is it a good thing for your boy to have that man in the house?"

There was a passing glimpse of uneasiness in the cobbler's glance, but it went as quickly as it had come. He laid his hand upon the nurse's. "This," he said, "ain't no winter to let a fellow from Sing Sing be on the street."

I might keep on, and fill many pages with instances of such kind, which simply go to prove that our poor human nature is at least as robust on Avenue A as up on Fifth Avenue, if it has half a chance, and often enough with no chance at all; and I might set over against it the product of sordid and mean environment which one has never far to seek. Good and evil go together in the tenements as in the fine houses, and the evil sticks out sometimes merely because it lies nearer the surface. The point is that the good does outweigh the bad, and that the virtues that turn the balance are after all those that make for manhood and good citizenship anywhere; while the faults are oftenest the accidents of ignorance and lack of training, which it is the business of society to correct. I recall my discouragement when I looked over the examination papers of a batch of candidates for police appointment, — young men largely the product of our public schools in this

city and elsewhere, — and read in them that five of
the original New England states were "England,
Ireland, Scotland, Belfast, and Cork"; that the
Fire Department ruled New York in the absence
of the mayor, — I have sometimes wished it did,
and that he would stay away awhile, while they
turned the hose on at the City Hall to make a clean
job of it, — and that Lincoln was murdered by
Ballington Booth.   But we shall agree, no doubt,
that the indictment of those papers was not of the
men who wrote them, but of the school that stuffed
its pupils with useless trash, and did not teach them
to think.   Neither have I forgotten that it was one
of these very men who, having failed and afterward
got a job as a bridge policeman, on his first pay day
went straight from his post, half frozen as he was,
to the settlement worker who had befriended him
and his sick father, and gave him five dollars for
"some one who was poorer than they."   Poorer
than they !   What worker among the poor has not
heard it ?   It is the charity of the tenement that
covers a multitude of sins.   There were thirteen
in this policeman's family, and his wages were the
biggest item of income in the house.

Jealousy, envy, and meanness wear no fine
clothes and masquerade under no smooth speeches
in the slums.   Often enough it is the very naked-
ness of the virtues that makes us stumble in our

judgment.   I have in mind the "difficult case " that
confronted some philanthropic friends of mine in
a rear tenement on Twelfth Street, in the person
of an aged widow, quite seventy I should think,
who worked uncomplainingly for a sweater all day
and far into the night, pinching and saving and
stinting herself, with black bread and chickory
coffee as her only fare, in order that she might
carry her pitiful earnings to her big, lazy lout of a
son in Brooklyn.   He never worked.   My friends'
difficulty was a very real one, for absolutely every
attempt to relieve the widow was wrecked upon her
mother heart.   It all went over the river.   Yet
would you have had her different ?

Sometimes it is only the unfamiliar setting that
shocks.   When an East Side midnight burglar, discovered and pursued, killed a tenant who blocked
his way of escape, not long ago, his "girl" gave
him up to the police.   But it was not because he
had taken human life.   " He was good to me," she
explained to the captain whom she told where to
find him, "but since he robbed the church I had
no use for him."   He had stolen, it seems, the com-
munion service in a Staten Island church.   The
thoughtless laughed.   But in her ignorant way she
was only trying to apply the ethical standards she
knew.   Our servant, pondering if the fortune
she was told is "real good" at fifteen cents, when

it should have cost her twenty-five by right, only she told the fortune-teller she had only fifteen, and lied in telling, is doing the same after her fashion. Stunted, bemuddled, as their standards were, I think I should prefer to take my chances with either rather than with the woman of wealth and luxury who gave a Christmas party to her lap-dog, as on the whole the sounder and by far the more hopeful.

All of which is merely saying that the country is all right, and the people are to be trusted with the old faith in spite of the slum. And it is true, if we remember to put it that way, — in spite of the slum. There is nothing in the slum to warrant that faith save human nature as yet uncorrupted. How long it is to remain so is altogether a question of the sacrifices we are willing to make in our fight with the slum. As yet, we are told by the officials having to do with the enforcement of the health ordinances, which come closer to the life of the individual than any other kind, that the poor in the tenements are " more amenable to the law than the better class." It is of the first importance, then, that we should have laws deserving of their respect, and that these laws should be enforced, lest they conclude that the whole thing is a sham. Respect for law is a very powerful bar against the slum. But what, for instance, must the poor Jew understand, who is permitted to buy a live hen at the market, but neither to kill nor keep it in his tenement, and who on his feast day finds a whole squad of policemen detailed to follow him around and see that he does not do any of the things with his fowl for which he must have bought it? Or the day laborer, who drinks his beer in a " Raines law hotel," where brick sandwiches, consisting of two pieces of bread with a brick between, are set out on the counter, in derision of the state law which forbids the serving of drinks without "meals"? [1] The Stanton Street saloon keeper who did that was solemnly acquitted by a jury. Or the boy, who may buy fireworks on the Fourth of July, but not set them off? These are only ridiculous instances of an abuse that pervades our community life to an extent which constitutes one of its gravest perils. Insincerity of that kind is not lost on our fellow-citizen by adoption, who is only anxious to fall

[1] The following is from the New York *Herald* of April 8, 1902: One of the strangest sandwich complications so far recorded occurred in a saloon in Columbia Street, Brooklyn, on Sunday. A boy rushed into the Amity Street police station at noon, declaring that two men in the saloon were killing each other. Two policemen ran to the place, and found the bartender and a customer pummelling each other on the floor. When the men had been separated the police learned that the trouble had arisen from the attempt of the customer to eat the sandwich which had been served with his drink. The barkeeper objected, and, finding remonstrance in vain, resorted to physical force to rescue the sandwich from the clutches of the hungry stranger. The police restored the sandwich to the bartender and made no arrests.

in with the ways of the country; and especially is it not lost on his boy.

We shall see how it affects him. He is the one for whom we are waging the battle with the slum. He is the to-morrow that sits to-day drinking in the lesson of the prosperity of the big boss who declared with pride upon the witness stand that he rules New York, that judges pay him tribute, and that only when *he* says so a thing "goes"; and that he is "working for his own pocket all the time just the same as everybody else." He sees corporations pay blackmail and rob the people in return, quite according to the schedule of Hester Street. Only there it is the police who charge the pedler twenty cents, while here it is the politicians taking toll of the franchises, twenty per cent. Wall Street is not ordinarily reckoned in the slum, because of certain physical advantages; but, upon the evidence of the day, I think we shall have to conclude that the advantage ends there. The boy who is learning such lessons, — how is it with him?

The president of the Society for the Prevention of Cruelty to Children says that children's crime is increasing, and he ought to know. The managers of the Children's Aid Society, after nearly fifty years of wrestling with the slum for the boy, in which they have lately seemed to get the upper hand, said recently, that on the East Side children are growing up in certain districts "entirely neglected," and that the number of such children "increases beyond the power of philanthropic and religious bodies to cope properly with their needs." In the Tompkins Square Lodging House the evening classes were thinning out, and the keeper wailed, "Those with whom we have dealt of late have not been inclined to accept this privilege; how to make night school attractive to shiftless, indifferent street boys is a difficult problem to solve."

Perhaps it was only that he had lost the key. Across the square, the Boys' Club of St. Mark's Place, that began with a handful, counts seven thousand members to-day, and is building a house of its own. The school census man announces that no boy in that old stronghold of the "bread or blood" brigade need henceforth loiter in the street because of there not being room in the public school, and the brigade has disbanded for want of recruits. The factory is being more and more firmly shut against the boy, and the bars let down at the playground. From Tompkins Square, nevertheless, came Jacob Beresheim, whose story let me stop here to tell you.

CHAPTER IX

THE GENESIS OF THE GANG

JACOB BERESHEIM was fifteen when he was charged with murder. It is now more than six years ago, but the touch of his hand is cold upon mine, with mortal fear, as I write. Every few minutes, during our long talk on the night of his arrest and confession, he would spring to his feet, and, clutching my arm as a drowning man catches at a rope, demand with shaking voice, " Will they give me the chair? " The assurance that boys were not executed quieted him only for the moment. Then the dread and the horror were upon him again.

Of his crime the less said the better. It was the climax of a career of depravity that differed from other such chiefly in the opportunities afforded by an environment which led up to and helped shape it. My business is with that environment. The man is dead, the boy in jail. But unless I am to be my brother's jail keeper merely, the iron bars do not square the account of Jacob with society. Society exists for the purpose of securing justice to its members, appearances to the contrary notwithstanding.

When it fails in this, the item is carried on the ledger with interest and compound interest toward a day of reckoning that comes surely with the pay-master. We have heard the chink of his coin on the counter, these days, in the unblushing revela-tions before legislative investigating committees of degraded citizenship, of the murder of the civic conscience, and in the applause that hailed them from the unthinking crowd. And we have begun to understand that these are the interest on Jacob's account, older, much older, than himself. He is just an item carried on the ledger. But with that knowledge the account is at last in the way of get-ting squared. Let us see how it stands.

We shall take Jacob as a type of the street boy on the East Side, where he belonged. What does not apply to him in the review applies to his class. But there was very little of it indeed that he missed or that missed him.

He was born in a tenement in that section where the Gilder Tenement House Commission found 324,000 persons living out of sight and reach of green spot of any kind, and where sometimes the buildings — front, middle, and rear — took up ninety-three per cent of all the space in the block. Such a home as he had was there, and of the things that belonged to it he was the heir. The sunlight was not among them. It "never entered" there. Dark

ness and discouragement did, and dirt.   Later on,
when he took to the dirt as his natural weapon in
his battles with society, it was said of him that it
was the only friend that stuck to him, and it was
true.   Very early the tenement gave him up to the
street.   The thing he took with him as the one
legacy of home was the instinct for the crowd,
which meant that the tene-
ment had wrought its worst
mischief upon him; it had
smothered that in him around
which character is built.   The
more readily did he fall in
with the street and its ways.
Character implies depth, a
soil, and growth.   The street
is all surface.   Nothing grows
there; it hides only a sewer.

It taught him gambling as
its first lesson, and stealing   Jacob Beresheim.
as the next.   The two are never far apart.   From
shooting craps behind the " cop's " back to filching
from the grocer's stock or plundering a defenceless pedler is only a step.   There is in both the
spice of law-breaking that appeals to the shallow
ambition of the street as heroic.   At the very time
when the adventurous spirit is growing in the boy,
and his games are all of daring, of chasing and

being chased, the policeman looms up to take a hand, and is hailed with joyful awe. Occasionally the raids have a comic tinge. A German grocer wandered into police headquarters with an appeal for protection against the boys.

" Vat means dot 'cheese it'? " he asked, rubbing his bald head in helpless bewilderment. " Efery dime dey says 'cheese it,' somedings vas gone."

To the lawlessness of the street the home opposes no obstacle, as we have seen. Within the memory of most of us the school did not. It might have more to offer even now. But we have gone such a long way since the day I am thinking of that I am not going to find fault. I used to think that some of them needed to be made over, until they were fit to turn out whole, sound boys, instead of queer manikins stuffed with information for which they have no use, and which is none of their business anyhow. It seemed to me, sometimes, when watching the process of cramming the school course with the sum of human knowledge and conceit, as if it all meant that we distrusted Nature's way of growing a man from a boy, and had set out to show her a shorter cut. A common result was the kind of mental befogment that had Abraham Lincoln murdered by Ballington Booth,[†] and a superficiality, a hopeless slurring of tasks, that hitched perfectly with the spirit of the street, and left nothing to

[†]Ballington Booth, with Maud Booth, founded the Volunteers of America in New York City in 1896, after breaking with the Salvation Army. Riis is referring to the fact that some students confused his name with that of John Wilkes Booth, the assassin of Abraham Lincoln.

be explained in the verdict of the reformatory,
" No moral sense." There was no moral sense to
be got out of the thing, for there was little sense of
any kind in it. The boy was not given a chance
to be honest with himself by thinking a thing
through ; he came naturally to accept as his mental
horizon the headlines in his penny paper and the
literature of the Dare-Devil-Dan-the-Death-Dealing-
Monster-of-Dakota order, which comprise the ordinary æsthetic equipment of the slum. The mystery
of his further development into the tough need not
perplex anybody.

But Jacob Beresheim had not even the benefit of
such schooling as there was to be had. He did not
go to school, and nobody cared. There was indeed
a law directing that every child should go, and a
corps of truant officers to catch him if he did not ;
but the law had been a dead letter for a quarter of a
century. There was no census to tell which children ought to be in school, and no place but a jail
to put those in who shirked. Jacob was allowed to
drift. From the time he was twelve till he was fifteen, he told me, he might have gone to school three
weeks, — no more.

Church and Sunday-school missed him. I was
going to say that they passed by on the other side,
remembering the migration of the churches up-town
as the wealthy moved out of and the poor into the
region south of Fourteenth Street. But that would
hardly be fair. They moved after their congrega-

tions; but they left nothing behind.   In the twenty
years that followed the war, while enough to people
a large city moved in down-town, the number of
churches there was reduced from 141 to 127.
Fourteen Protestant churches moved out.   Only
two Roman Catholic churches and a synagogue
moved in.   I am not aware that there has been any
large increase of churches in the district since, but
we have seen that the crowding has not slackened
pace.   Jacob had no trouble in escaping the Sunday-school, as he had escaped the public school.
His tribe will have none until the responsibility
incurred in the severance of Church and State sits
less lightly on a Christian community, and the
Church, from a mob, shall have become an army,
with von Moltke's plan of campaign,[†] "March apart,
fight together."   The Christian Church is not alone
in its failure.   The Jew's boy is breaking away from
safe moorings rather faster than his brother of the
new dispensation.   The Church looks on, but it has
no cause for congratulation.   He is getting nothing
in place of that which he lost, and the result is bad.
There is no occasion for profound theories about it.
The facts are plain enough.   The new freedom has
something to do with it; but neglect to look after
the young has quite as much.   Apart from its religious aspect, seen from the angle of the community's
interest wholly, the matter is of the gravest import.

[†]Helmuth von Moltke (1800–1891) was chief of the Prussian and
German general staffs; his innovative command tactics and logistical
methods enabled military victories that resulted in the formation of the
German Empire.

What the boy's play has to do with building character in him Froebel has told us. Through it, he showed us, the child "first perceives moral relations," and he made that the basis of the kindergarten and all common-sense education. That prop was knocked out. New York never had a children's playground till within the last three years. Truly it seemed, as Abram S. Hewitt[†] said, as if in the early plan of our city the children had not been thought of at all. Such moral relations as Jacob was able to make out ran parallel with the gutter always, and counter to law and order as represented by the policeman and the landlord. The landlord had his windows to mind, and the policeman his lamps and the city ordinances which prohibit even kite-flying below Fourteenth Street where the crowds are. The ball had no chance at all. We have seen in New York a boy shot down by a policeman for the heinous offence of playing football in the street on Thanksgiving Day. But a boy who cannot kick a ball around has no chance of growing up a decent and orderly citizen. He must have his childhood, so that he may be fitted to give to the community his manhood. The average boy is just like a little steam-engine with steam always up. The play is his safety-valve. With the landlord in the yard and

†Abram S. Hewitt (1822–1903), a millionaire industrialist, son-in-law of the industrialist and philanthropist Peter Cooper, served in the U.S. Congress (1874–1887) and was the successful Tammany-supported Democratic candidate for mayor of New York City in 1886, defeating Theodore Roosevelt (Republican) and Henry George (Independent), a radical socialist who was supported by the Central Labor Union.

the policeman on the street sitting on his safety-valve and holding it down, he is bound to explode. When he does, when he throws mud and stones, and shows us the side of him which the gutter developed, we are shocked, and marvel much what our boys are coming to, as if we had any right to expect better treatment of them. I doubt if Jacob, in the whole course of his wizened little life, had ever a hand in an honest game that was not haunted by the spectre of the avenging policeman. That he was not "doing anything" was no defence. The mere claim was proof that he was up to mischief of some sort. Besides, the policeman was usually right. Play in such a setting becomes a direct incentive to mischief in a healthy boy. Jacob was a healthy enough little animal.

Such fun as he had he got out of law-breaking in a small way. In this he was merely following the ruling fashion. Laws were apparently made for no other purpose that he could see. Such a view as he enjoyed of their makers and executors at election seasons inspired him with seasonable enthusiasm, but hardly with awe. A slogan, now, like that raised by Tammany's late candidate for district attorney,[†] — "To hell with reform!" — was something he could grasp. Of what reform meant he had only the vaguest notion, but this

[†] In the first Greater New York election, held in November 1897 and won by the Tammany candidates.

thing had the right ring to it. Roosevelt preaching enforcement of law was from the first a "lob-
ster" to him, not to be taken seriously. It is not
among the least of the merits of the man that,
by his sturdy personality, as well as by his unyielding persistence, he won the boy over to the
passive admission that there might be something
in it. It had not been his experience.

There was the law which sternly commanded
him to go to school, and which he laughed at
every day. Then there was the law to prevent
child labor. It cost twenty-five cents for a false
age certificate to break that, and Jacob, if he
thought of it at all, probably thought of perjury
as rather an expensive thing. A quarter was a
good deal to pay for the right to lock a child up
in a factory, when he ought to have been at play.
The excise law was everybody's game. The sign
that hung in every saloon, saying that nothing
was sold there to minors, never yet barred out his
"growler" when he had the price. There was
another such sign in the tobacco shop, forbidding
the sale of cigarettes to boys of his age. Jacob
thought that when he had the money he smoked
as many as fifteen packs a day, and he laughed
when he told me. He laughed, too, when he
remembered how the boys of the East Side took
to carrying balls of cord in their pockets, on the

wave of the Lexow reform, on purpose to measure the distance from the school door to the nearest saloon. They had been told that it should be two hundred feet, according to law. There were schools that had as many as a dozen within the tabooed limits. It was in the papers how, when the highest courts said that the law was good, the saloon keepers attacked *the schools* as a nuisance and detrimental to property. In a general way Jacob sided with the saloon keeper; not because he had any opinion about it, but because it seemed natural. Such opinions as he ordinarily had he got from that quarter.

When, later on, he came to be tried, his counsel said to me, " He is an amazing liar." No, hardly amazing. It would have been amazing if he had been anything else. Lying and mockery were all around him, and he adjusted himself to the things that were. He lied in self-defence.

Jacob's story ends here, as far as he is personally concerned. The story of the gang begins. So trained for the responsibility of citizenship, robbed of home and of childhood, with every prop knocked from under him, all the elements that make for strength and character trodden out in the making of the boy, all the high ambition of youth caricatured by the slum and become base passions, — so equipped he comes to the business of life. As a " kid " he

hunted with the pack in the street. As a young
man he trains with the gang, because it furnishes the
means of gratifying his inordinate vanity; that is the
slum's counterfeit of self-esteem.   Upon the Jacobs
of other days there was a last hold, — the father's
authority.   Changed conditions have loosened that

Heading off the Gang.   Vacation Playground near Old Frog Hollow.

also.   There is a time in every young man's life
when he knows more than his father.   It is like the
measles or the mumps, and he gets over it, with
a little judicious firmness in the hand that guides.
It is the misfortune of the slum boy of to-day that
it is really so, and that he knows it.   His father is
an Italian or a Jew, and cannot even speak the lan-

guage to which the boy is born.   He has to depend
on him in much, in the new order of things.   The
old man is "slow," he is "Dutch."   He may be
an Irishman with some advantages; he is still a
"foreigner."   He loses his grip on the boy.

Ethical standards of which he has no conception
clash.   Watch the meeting of two currents in river
or bay, and see the line of drift that tells of the
struggle.   So in the city's life strive the currents of
the old and the new, and in the churning the boy
goes adrift.   The last hold upon him is gone.   That
is why the gang appears in the second generation,
the first born upon the soil, — a fighting gang if the
Irishman is there with his ready fist, a thievish gang
if it is the East Side Jew, — and disappears in the
third.   The second boy's father is not "slow."   He
has had experience.   He was clubbed into decency
in his own day, and the night stick wore off the
glamour of the thing.   His grip on the boy is good,
and it holds.

It depends now upon chance what is to become
of the lad.   But the slum has stacked the cards
against him.   There arises in the lawless crowd
a leader, who rules with his stronger fists or his
readier wit.   Around him the gang crystallizes,
and what he is it becomes.   He may be a thief,
like David Meyer, a report of whose doings I have
before me.   He was just a bully, and, being the

biggest in his gang, made the others steal for him and surrender the "swag," or take a licking. But that was unusual. Ordinarily the risk and the "swag" are distributed on more democratic principles. Or he may be of the temper of Mike of Poverty Gap, who was hanged for murder at nineteen. While he sat in his cell at police headquarters, he told with grim humor of the raids of his gang on Saturday nights when they stocked up at "the club." They used to "hook" a butcher's cart or other light wagon, wherever found, and drive like mad up and down the avenue, stopping at saloon or grocery to throw in what they wanted. His job was to sit at the tail of the cart with a six-shooter and pop at any chance pursuer. He chuckled at the recollection of how men fell over one another to get out of his way. "It was great to see them run," he said. Mike was a tough, but with a better chance he might have been a hero. The thought came to him, too, when it was all over and the end in sight. He put it all in one sober, retrospective sigh, that had in it no craven shirking of the responsibility which was properly his: "I never had no bringing up."

There was a meeting some time after his death to boom a scheme for "getting the boys off the street," and I happened to speak of Mike's case. In the audience was a gentleman of means and position, and his daughter, who manifested great interest and joined heartily in the proposed movement. A week later, I was thunderstruck at reading of the arrest of my sympathetic friend's son for train-wrecking up the state. The fellow was of the same age as Mike. It appeared that he was supposed to be attending school, but had been reading dime novels instead, until he arrived at the point where he "had to kill some one before the end of the month." To that end he organized a gang of admiring but less resourceful comrades. After all, the planes of fellowship of Poverty Gap and Madison Avenue lie nearer than we often suppose. I set the incident down in justice to the memory of my friend Mike. If this one went astray with so much to pull him the right way and but the single strand broken, what then of the other?

Mike's was the day of Irish heroics. Since their scene was shifted from the East Side, there has come over there an epidemic of child crime of meaner sort, but following the same principle of gang organization. It is difficult to ascertain the exact extent of it, because of the well-meant but, I am inclined to think, mistaken effort on the part of the children's societies to suppress the record of it for the sake of the boy. Enough testimony comes from the police and the courts, however, to make it clear that thieving is largely on the in-

crease among the East Side boys. And it is amazing at what an early age it begins. When, in the
fight for a truant school, I had occasion to gather
statistics upon this subject, to meet the sneer of the
educational authorities that the "crimes" of street
boys compassed at worst the theft of a top or
a marble, I found among 278 prisoners, of whom I
had kept the run for ten months, two boys, of four
and eight years respectively, arrested for breaking
into a grocery, not to get candy or prunes, but
to rob the till. The little one was useful to
"crawl through a small hole." There were "burglars" of six and seven years; and five in a bunch,
the whole gang apparently, at the age of eight.
"Wild" boys began to appear in court at that
age. At eleven, I had seven thieves, two of whom
had a record on the police blotter, and an "habit-
ual liar"; at twelve, I had four burglars, three ordinary thieves, two arrested for drunkenness, three
for assault, and three incendiaries; at thirteen, five
burglars, one with a "record," as many thieves, one
"drunk," five charged with assault and one with
forgery; at fourteen, eleven thieves and house-
breakers, six highway robbers, — the gang on its
unlucky day, perhaps, — and ten arrested for fighting, not counting one who had assaulted a policeman, in a state of drunken frenzy. One of the
gangs made a specialty of stealing baby carriages,

when they were left unattended in front of stores. They "drapped the kids in the hallway" and "sneaked" the carriages. And so on. The recital was not a pleasant one, but it was effective. We got our truant school, and one way that led to the jail was blocked.

Craps.

It may be that the leader is neither thief nor thug, but ambitious. In that case the gang is headed for politics by the shortest route. Likewise, sometimes, when he is both. In either case it carries the situation by assault. When the gang wants a thing, the easiest way seems to it always to take it. There was an explosion in a Fifth Street tenement, one winter's night, that threw twenty families into a wild panic, and injured two of the tenants badly. There was much mystery about it, until it came out that the housekeeper had had a "run in" with the gang in the block. It wanted club room in the house, and she would not let it in. Beaten, it avenged itself in characteristic fashion by leaving a package of gunpowder on the stairs, where she would be sure to find it when she went the rounds with her candle to close up. That was a gang of the kind I have reference to, headed straight for Albany. And what is more, it will get there, unless things change greatly. The gunpowder was just a "bluff" to frighten the housekeeper, an instalment of the kind of politics it meant to play when it got its chance.

There was "nothing against" this gang except a probable row with the saloon keeper, since it applied elsewhere for house room. Not every gang has a police record of theft and "slugging" beyond the early encounters of the street. "Our honorable leader" is not always the captain of a band of cutthroats. He is the honorary president of the "social club" that bears his name, and he counts for something in the ward. But the ethical standards do not differ. "Do others, or they will do you," felicitously adapted from Holy Writ for the use of the slum, and the classic war-cry, "To the victor the spoils," made over locally to read, "I am not in politics for my health," still interpret the creed of the political as of the "slugging" gang. They draw their inspiration from the same source. Of what gang politics mean every large city in our country has had its experience. New York is no exception. History on the subject is being made yet, in sight of us all.

Our business with the gang, however, is in the making of it. Take now the showing of the reformatory,[1] to which I have before made reference, and see what light it throws upon the matter: 77.80 per cent of prisoners with no moral sense, or next to none, yet more than that proportion possessed of "good natural mental capacity," which is to say that they had the means of absorbing it from their environment, if there had been any to absorb. Bad homes sent half (47.79) of all prisoners there; bad company 97.60 per cent. The reformatory repeats the prison chaplain's verdict, "weakness, not wickedness," in its own way: "Malevolence does not characterize the criminal, but aversion to continuous

---

[1] "Year-Book of Elmira State Reformatory," 1901. The statistics deal with 10,538 prisoners received there in twenty-seven years. The social stratum whence they came is sufficiently indicated by the statement that 15.96 per cent were illiterates, and 47.59 per cent were able to read and write with difficulty; 32.39 per cent had an ordinary common school education; 4.06 per cent came out of high schools or colleges.

labor." If "the street" had been written across it in capital letters, it could not have been made plainer. Less than 15 per cent of the prisoners came from good homes, and one in sixty-six (1.51) had kept good company; evidently he was not of the mentally capable. They will tell you at the prison that, under its discipline, eighty odd per cent are set upon their feet and make a fresh start. With due allowance for a friendly critic, there is still room for the three-fourths labelled normal, of "natu-
ral mental capacity."
They came to their own
with half a chance, even
the chance of a prison.
The Children's Aid So-
ciety will give you still
better news of the boys
rescued from the slum
before it had branded
them for its own. Scarce
five per cent are lost,
though they leave such
a black mark that they

Children's Playground. Good Citizenship at the Bottom of this Barrel.

make trouble for all the good boys that are sent out from New York. Better than these was the kindergarten record in San Francisco. New York has no monopoly of the slum. Of nine thousand children from the slummiest quarters of that city who had gone through the Golden Gate Association's kindergartens, just one was found to have got into jail. The merchants who looked coldly on the experiment before, brought their gold to pay for keeping it up. They were hard-headed men of business, and the demonstration that schools were better than jails any day appealed to them as eminently sane and practical.

And well it might. The gang is a distemper of the slum that writes upon the generation it plagues the receipt for its own corrective. It is not the night stick, though in the acute stage that is not to be dispensed with. Neither is it the jail. To put the gang behind iron bars affords passing relief, but it is like treating a symptom without getting at the root of the disease. Prophylactic treatment is clearly indicated. The boy who flings mud and stones is entering his protest in his own way against the purblind policy that gave him jails for schools and the gutter for a playground; that gave him dummies for laws and the tenement for a home. He is demanding his rights, of which he has been cheated, — the right to his childhood, the right to know the true dignity of labor that makes a self-respecting manhood. The gang, rightly understood, is our ally, not our enemy. Like any ailment of the body, it is a friend come to tell us of something that has gone amiss. The thing for us to do is to find out what it is, and set it right.

That is the story of the gang. That we have read and grasped its lesson at last, many things bear witness. Here is the League for Political Educa- tion providing a playground for the children up on the West Side, near the model tenements which I described. Just so! With a decent home and a chance for the boy to grow into a healthy man, his political education can proceed without much fur- ther hindrance. Now let the League for Political Education trade off the policeman's club for a boys' club, and it may consider its course fairly organized.

I spoke of the instinct for the crowd in the man as evidence that the slum had got its grip on him. And it is true of the boy. The experience that the helpless poor will not leave their slum when a chance of better things is offered is wearily familiar to most of us. One has to have resources to face the lone- liness of the woods and the fields. We have seen what resources the slum has at its command. In the boy it laid hold of the instinct for organization, the desire to fall in and march in line that belongs to all boys, and is not here, as abroad, cloyed with military service in the young years, — and anyhow is stronger in the American boy than in his Euro- pean brother, — and perverted it to its own use. That is the simple secret of the success of the club,

the brigade, in winning back the boy.   It is fighting
the street with its own weapon.   The gang is the
club run wild.

How readily it owns the kinship was never better
shown than by the experience of the college settlement girls, when they first went to make friends in
the East Side tenements.   I have told it before, but
it will bear telling again, for it holds the key to the
whole business.   They gathered in the drift, all the
little embryo gangs that were tuning up in the district, and made them into clubs, — Young Heroes,
Knights of the Round Table, and such like; all
except one, the oldest, that had begun to make a
name for itself with the police.   That one held
aloof, observing coldly what went on, to make sure it
was "straight."   They let it be, keeping the while
an anxious eye upon it; until one day there came a
delegation with this olive branch: " If you will let
us in, we will change and have your kind of a gang."
Needless to say it was let in.   And within a year,
when, through a false rumor that the concern was
moving away, there was a run on the settlement's
penny provident bank, the converted gang proved
itself its stanchest friend by doing actually what
John Halifax did in Miss Mulock's story: it
brought all the pennies it could raise in the neighborhood by hook or by crook and deposited them as
fast as the regular patrons — the gang had not yet

risen to the dignity of a bank account — drew them out, until the run ceased. This same gang which, the year before, was training for trouble with the police!

The cry, " Get the boys off the street," that has been raised in our cities, as the real gravity of the situation has been made clear, has led to the adoption of curfew ordinances in many places. Any attempt to fit such a scheme to metropolitan life would result only in adding one more dead-letter law, more dangerous than all the rest, to those we have. New York is New York, and one look at the crowds in the streets and the tenements will convince anybody. Besides, the curfew rings at nine o'clock. The dangerous hours, when the gang is made, are from seven to nine, between supper and bedtime. This is the gap the club fills out. The boys take to the street because the home has nothing to keep them there. To lock them up in the house would only make them hate it more. The club follows the line of least resistance. It has only to keep also on the line of common sense. It must be a real club, not a reformatory. Its proper function is to head off the jail. The gang must not run it. But rather that than have it help train up a band of wretched young cads. The signs are not hard to make out. When a boy has had his head swelled by his importance as a member of the Junior

Street-cleaning Band to the point of reproving his mother for throwing a banana peel in the street, the thing to be done is to take him out and spank him, if it *is* reverting to "the savagery" of the street. Better a savage than a cad. The boys have the making of both in them. Their vanity furnishes abundant material for the cad, but only when unduly pampered. Left to itself, the gang can be trusted not to develop that kink.

It comes down in the end to the personal influence that is always most potent in dealing with these problems. We had a gang start up once when my boys were of that age, out in the village on Long Island where we lived. It had its headquarters in our barn, where it planned divers raids that aimed at killing the cat and other like outrages; the central fact being that the boys had an air rifle, with which it was necessary to murder something. My wife discovered the conspiracy, and, with woman's wit, defeated it by joining the gang. She "gave in wood" to the election bonfires, and pulled the safety valve upon all the other plots by entering into the true spirit of them,— which was adventure rather than mischief,— and so keeping them within safe lines. She was elected an honorary member, and became the counsellor of the gang in all its little scrapes. I can yet see her dear brow wrinkled in the study of some knotty gang problem, which we discussed when the boys had been long asleep. They did not dream of it, and the village never knew what small tragedies it escaped, nor who it was that so skilfully averted them.

It is always the women who do those things. They are the law and the gospel to the boy, both in one. It is the mother heart, I suppose, and there is nothing better in all the world. I am reminded of the conversion of "the Kid" by one who was in a very real sense the mother of a social settlement up-town, in the latitude of Battle Row. The Kid was driftwood. He had been cast off by a drunken father and mother, and was living on what he could scrape out of ash barrels, and an occasional dime for kindling-wood which he sold from a wheelbarrow, when the gang found and adopted him. My friend adopted the gang in her turn, and civilized it by slow stages. Easter Sunday came, when she was to redeem her promise to take the boys to witness the services in a neighboring church, where the liturgy was especially impressive. It found the larger part of the gang at her door, — a minority, it was announced, were out stealing potatoes, hence were excusable, — in a state of high indignation.

"The Kid's been cussin' awful," explained the leader. The Kid showed in the turbulent distance, red-eyed and raging.

" But why ? " asked my friend, in amazement.

" 'Cause he can't go to church ! "

It appeared that the gang had shut him out, with
a sense of what was due to the occasion, because of
his rags.   Restored to grace, and choking down
reminiscent sobs, the Kid sat through the Easter
service, surrounded by the twenty-seven "proper"
members of the gang.   Civilization had achieved
a victory, and no doubt my friend remembered it in
her prayers with thanksgiving.   The manner was
of less account.   Battle Row has its own ways,
even in its acceptance of means of grace.

I walked home from the office in the early gloam-
ing.   The street wore its normal aspect of mingled
dulness and the kind of expectancy that is always
waiting to turn any excitement, from a fallen horse
to a fire, to instant account.   The early June heat
had driven the multitudes from the tenements into
the street for a breath of air.   The boys of the
block were holding a meeting at the hydrant.   In
some way they had turned the water on, and were
splashing in it with bare feet, revelling in the sense
that they were doing something that " went against "
their enemy, the policeman.   Upon the quiet of the
evening broke a bugle note and the tramp of many
feet keeping time.   A military band came around
the corner, stepping briskly to the tune of " The
Stars and Stripes Forever."   Their white duck

"The gang fell in with joyous shouts."

trousers glimmered in the twilight, as the hundred legs moved as one. Stoops and hydrant were deserted with a rush. The gang fell in with joyous shouts. The young fellow linked arms with his sweetheart and fell in too. The tired mother hurried with the baby carriage to catch up. The butcher came, hot and wiping his hands on his apron, to the door to see them pass.

"Yes," said my companion, guessing my thoughts, — we had been speaking of the boys, — "but look at the other side. There is the military spirit. Do you not fear danger from it in this country?"

No, my anxious friend, I do not. Let them march; and if with a gun, better still. Often enough it is the choice of the gun on the shoulder, or, by and by, the stripes on the back in the lockstep gang.

CHAPTER X

JIM

I USED to think that it would have been better for Jim if he had never been born. What the good bishop said of some children — that they were not so much born into the world as they were damned into it — seemed true of Jim, if ever it was true of any one. He had had a father, once, who was kind to him, but it was long since. The one he called by that name last had been sent to Sing Sing, to the lad's great relief, for a midnight burglary, shortly after he married Jim's mother. His back hurt yet when he thought of the evil days when he was around. If any one had thought it worth while to teach Jim to pray, he would have prayed with all his might that his father might never come out. But no one did, so that he was spared that sin. I suppose that was what it would have been called. I am free to confess that I would have joined Jim in sinning with a right good will, even to the extent of speeding the benevolent intentions of Providence in that direction — anyhow, until Jim should be able to take care of himself. I mean with his fists. He was in a way of learning that without long delay, for ever since he was a little shaver he had had to fight his own way, and sometimes his mother's. He was thirteen when I met him, and most of his time had been put in around the Rag Gang's quarters, along First Avenue and the river front, where that kind of learning was abundant and came cheap.

His mother drank. I do not know what made her do it — whether it was the loss of the first husband, or getting the second, or both. It did not seem important when she stood there, weak and wretched and humble, with Jim. And as for my preaching to her, sitting in my easy-chair, well fed and respectable, that would come near to being impertinence. So it always struck me. Perhaps I was wrong. Anyway, it would have done her no good. Too much harm had been done her already. She would disappear for days, sometimes for weeks at a time, on her frequent sprees. Jim never made any inquiries. On those occasions he kept aloof from us, and paddled his own canoe, lest we should ask questions. It was when she had come home sobered that we saw them always together. Now it was the rent, and then again a few groceries. With such lifts as she got, sandwiched in with much good advice, and by the aid of an odd job now and then, Mrs. Kelly managed to keep a bit

of a roof over her boy and herself, down in the
"village" on the river front.   At least, Jim had a
place to sleep.   Until, one day, our visitor reported
that she was gone for good — she and the boy.
They were both gone, — nobody in the neighborhood knew or cared where, — and the room was
vacant.   Except that they had not been dispossessed, we could learn nothing.   Jim was not found,
and in the press of many things the Kellys were
forgotten.   Once or twice his patient, watchful
eyes, that seemed to be always trying to understand
something to which he had not found the key,
haunted me at my office ; but at last I forgot about
them too.

Some months passed.   It was winter.   A girl,
who had been one of our cares, had been taken to
the city hospital to die, and our visitor went there
to see and comfort her.   She was hastening down
the long aisle between the two rows of beds, when
she felt something tugging feebly at the sleeve of
her coat.   Looking round, she saw on the pillow
of the bed she had just passed the face of Jim's
mother.

"Why, Mrs. Kelly!" she exclaimed, and went
to her.   "Where — ?"   But the question that rose
to her lips was never spoken.   One glance was
enough to show that her time was very short, and
she was not deceived.   The nurse supplied the

facts briefly in a whisper. She had been picked up in the street, drunk or sick — the diagnosis was not clearly made out at the time, but her record was against her. She lay a day or two in a police cell, and by the time it was clear that it was not rum this time, the mischief was done. Probably it would have been done anyhow. The woman was worn out. What now lay on the hospital cot was a mere wreck of her, powerless to move or speak. She could only plead with her large, sad eyes. As she tried to make them say that which was in her soul, two big tears rolled slowly down the wan cheeks and fell on the coarse sheet. The visitor understood. What woman would not?

"Jim?" she said, and the light of joy and understanding came into the yearning eyes. She nodded ever so feebly, and the hand that rested in her friend's twitched and trembled in the effort to grasp hers.

"I will find him. It is all right. Now, you be quite happy. I will bring him here."

The white face settled back on the pillow, and the weary eyes closed with a little sigh of contentment very strange in that place. When the visitor passed her cot ten minutes later, she was asleep, with a smile on her lips.

It proved not so easy a matter to find Jim. We came upon his track in his old haunts after a while, only to lose it again and again. It was clear that he was around, but it seemed almost as if he were purposely dodging us; and in fact that proved to have been the case when at last, after a hunt of weary days and nights through the neighborhood, he was brought in. Ragged, pale, and pinched by hunger, we saw him with a shock of remorse for having let him drift so long. His story was simple enough. When his mother failed to come back, and, the rent coming due, the door of what had been home to him, even such as it was, was closed upon him, he took to the street. He slept in hallways and with the gang among the docks, never going far from the "village" lest he should miss news of his mother coming back. The cold nights came, and he shivered often in his burrows; but he never relaxed his watch. All the time his mother lay dying less than half a dozen blocks away, but there was no one to tell him. Had any one done so, it is not likely that the guard would have let him through the gate, as he looked. Seven weeks he had spent in the streets when he heard that he was wanted. The other boys told him that it was the "cruelty" man sure; and then began the game of hide-and-seek that tried our patience and wore on his mother, sinking rapidly now, but that eventually turned up Jim.

We took him up to the hospital, and into the

"'Oh, mother! You were gone so long!'"

ward where his mother lay. Away off at the farther end of the room, he knew her, the last in the row, and ran straight to her before we could stop him, and fell on her neck.

"Mother!" we heard him say, while he hugged her, with his head on her pillow. "Mother, why don't you speak to me? I am all right — I am."

He raised his head and looked at her. Happy tears ran down the thin face turned to his. He took her in his arms again.

"I am all right, mother; honest, I am. Don't you cry. I couldn't keep the rooms, mother! They took everything, only the deed to father's grave. I kept that."

He dug in the pocket of his old jacket, and brought out a piece of paper, carefully wrapped in many layers of rags and newspaper that hung in dirty tatters.

"Here it is. Everything else is gone. But it is all right. I've got you, and I am here. Oh, mother! You were gone so long!"

Longer — poor Jim — the parting that was even then adding another to the mysteries that had vexed my soul concerning you. Happiness at last had broken the weary heart. But if it added one, it dispelled another: I knew then that I erred, Jim, when I thought it were better if you had never been born!

CHAPTER XI

LETTING IN THE LIGHT

I HAD been out of town and my way had not fallen through the Mulberry Bend in weeks until that morning when I came suddenly upon the park that had been made there in my absence. Sod had been laid, and men were going over the lawn cutting the grass after the rain. The sun shone upon flowers and the tender leaves of young shrubs, and the smell of new-mown hay was in the air. Crowds of little Italian children shouted with delight over the "garden," while their elders sat around upon the benches with a look of contentment such as I had not seen before in that place. I stood and looked at it all, and a lump came in my throat as I thought of what it had been, and of all the weary years of battling for this. It had been such a hard fight, and now at last it was won. To me the whole battle with the slum had summed itself up in the struggle with this dark spot. The whir of the lawn-mower was as sweet a song in my ear as that which the skylark sang when I was a boy, in Danish fields, and which gray hairs do not make the man forget.

264

"Keep off the grass!"

In my delight I walked upon the grass. It seemed as if I should never be satisfied till I had felt the sod under my feet, — sod in the Mulberry Bend! I did not see the gray-coated policeman hastening my way, nor the wide-eyed youngsters awaiting with shuddering delight the catastrophe that was coming, until I felt his cane laid smartly across my back and heard his angry command:

"Hey! Come off the grass! D'ye think it is made to walk on?"

So that was what I got for it. It is the way of the world. But it was all right. The park was there, that was the thing. And I had my revenge. I had just had a hand in marking five blocks of tenements for destruction to let in more light, and in driving the slum from two other strongholds. Where they were, parks are being made to-day in which the sign "Keep off the grass!" will never be seen. The children may walk in them from morning till night, and I too, if I want to, with no policeman to drive us off. I tried to tell the policeman something about it. But he was of the old dispensation. All the answer I got was a gruff:

"G'wan now! I don't want none o' yer guff!"

It was all "guff" to the politicians, I suppose, from the day the trouble began about the Mulberry Bend, but toward the end they woke up nobly. When the park was finally dedicated to the people's use, they took charge of the celebration with immense unction, and invited themselves to sit in the high seats and glory in the achievement which they had done little but hamper and delay from the first. They had not reckoned with Colonel Waring,[†] however. When they had had their say, the colonel arose, and, curtly reminding them that they had really had no hand in the business, proposed three cheers for the citizen effort that had struck the slum this staggering blow. There was rather a feeble response on the platform, but rousing cheers from the crowd, with whom the colonel was a prime favorite, and no wonder. Two years later he laid down his life in the fight which he so valiantly and successfully waged. It is the simple truth that he was killed by politics. The services which he had rendered the city would have entitled him in any reputable business to be retained in the employment that was his life and his pride. Had he been so retained, he would not have gone to Cuba, and would in all human probability be now alive. But Tammany is not "in politics for its health" and had no use for him, though no more grievous charge could be laid at his door, even in the heat of the campaign, than that he was a "foreigner," being from Rhode Island. Spoils politics never craved a heavier sacrifice of any community.

It was Colonel Waring's broom that first let light

†George E. Waring (1833–1898), a sanitary engineer who served in the Civil War, was appointed Street Cleaning Commissioner by Mayor William L. Strong, and served 1895–97. He died of yellow fever in 1898, soon after he visited Havana, Cuba, to prepare a report on how to improve sanitary conditions there and thus eliminate the disease.

into the slum. That which had come to be considered an impossible task he did by the simple
formula of "putting a man instead of a voter behind
every broom." The words are his own. The man,
from a political dummy who loathed his job and

himself in it with
cause, became a self-
respecting citizen,
and the streets that
had deen dirty were
swept. The ash bar-
rels which had be-
fouled the sidewalks
disappeared, almost
without any one know-
ing it till they were
gone. The trucks that
obstructed the chil-
dren's only play-
ground, the street,
went with the dirt,

Colonel George E. Waring, Jr.

despite the opposition of the truckman who had
traded off his vote to Tammany in the past for stall
room at the curbstone. They did not go without a
struggle. When appeal to the alderman proved
useless, the truckman resorted to strategy. He
took a wheel off, or kept a perishing nag, that could
not walk, hitched to the truck over night to make

it appear that it was there for business. But sub-
terfuge availed as little as resistànce. In the Mulberry Bend he made his last stand. The old houses
had been torn down, leaving a three-acre lot full
of dirt mounds and cellar holes. Into this the
truckmen of the Sixth Ward hauled their carts,
and defied the street cleaners. They were no
longer in their way, and they were on the Park Department's domain, where no Colonel Waring was
in control. But while their owners were triumph-
ing, the children playing among the trucks set one
of them rolling down into a cellar, and three or four
of the little ones were crushed. That was the end.
The trucks disappeared. Even Tammany has not
ventured to put them back, so great was the relief
of their going. They were not only a hindrance to
the sweeper and the skulking-places of all manner
of mischief at night, but I have repeatedly seen the
firemen baffled in their efforts to reach a burning
house, where they stood four and six deep in the
wide " slips " at the river.

Colonel Waring did more for the cause of labor
than all the walking delegates of the town together,
by investing a despised but highly important task
with a dignity which won the hearty plaudits of a
grateful city. When he uniformed his men and
announced that he was going to parade with them
so that we might all see what they were like, the

town laughed and poked fun at the "white wings";
but no one went to see them who did not come
away converted to an enthusiastic belief in the man
and his work.   Public sentiment, that had been half
reluctantly suspending judgment, expecting every
day to see the colonel "knuckle down to politics"
like his predecessors, turned in an hour, and after
that there was little trouble.   The tenement house
children organized street cleaning bands to help
along the work, and Colonel Waring enlisted them
as regular auxiliaries and made them useful.

They had no better friend.   When the unhappy
plight of the persecuted push-cart men — all immigrant Jews, who were blackmailed, robbed, and driven
from pillar to post as a nuisance after they had bought
a license to trade in the street — appealed vainly
for a remedy, Colonel Waring found a way out in
a great morning market in Hester Street that
should be turned over to the children for a playground in the afternoon.   But though he proved
that it would pay interest on the investment in
market fees, and many times in the children's happiness, it was never built.   It would have been a most
fitting monument to the man's memory.   His broom
saved more lives in the crowded tenements than a
squad of doctors.   It did more: it swept the cob-
webs out of our civic brain and conscience, and set
up a standard of a citizen's duty which, however we

A Tammany-swept East Side Street before Colonel Waring's Day.

may for the moment forget, will be ours until we
have dragged other things than our pavements out
of the mud.

Even the colonel's broom would have been powerless to do that for "the Bend." That was hopeless
and had to go. There was no question of children
or playground involved. The worst of all the gangs,
the Whyós, had its headquarters in the darkest
of its dark alleys; but it was left to the police.
We had not begun to understand that the gangs
meant something to us beyond murder and ven-

The Same Street when Colonel Waring wielded the Broom.

geance, in those days. No one suspected that they
had any such roots in the soil that they could be
killed by merely destroying the slum. The cholera
was rapping on our door, and, with the Bend there,
we felt about it as a man with stolen goods in his
house must feel when the policeman comes up the
street. Back in the seventies we began discussing
what ought to be done. By 1884 the first Tenement House Commission had summoned up
courage to propose that a street be cut through
the bad block. In the following year a bill was

brought in to destroy it bodily, and then began the long fight that resulted in the defeat of the slum a dozen years later.

It was a bitter fight, in which every position of the enemy had to be carried by assault. The enemy was the deadly official inertia that was the outcome of political corruption born of the slum plus the indifference of the mass of our citizens, who probably had never seen the Bend. If I made it my own concern to the exclusion of all else, it was only because I knew it. I had been part of it. Homeless and alone, I had sought its shelter, not for long, — that was not to be endured, — but long enough to taste of its poison, and I hated it. I knew that the blow must be struck there, to kill. Looking back now over those years, I can see that it was all as it should be. We were learning the alphabet of our lesson then. We could have learned it in no other way so thoroughly. Before we had been at it more than two or three years, it was no longer a question of the Bend merely. The Small Parks law,[†] that gave us a million dollars a year to force light and air into the slum, to its destruction, grew out of it. The whole sentiment which in its day, groping blindly and angrily, had wiped out the disgrace of the Five Points, just around the corner, crystallized and took shape in its fight. It waited merely for the issue of that, to attack the slum in its other

[†]Riis was secretary of the Small Parks Committee, which lobbied for the passage of a law providing for the development of public parks in the tenement districts.

strongholds; and no sooner was the Bend gone than the rest surrendered. Time was up.

But it was not so easy campaigning at the start. In 1888 plans were filed for the demolition of the block. It took four years to get a report of what it would cost to tear it down. About once in two months during all that time the authorities had to be prodded into a spasm of activity, or we would probably have been yet where we were then. Once, when I appealed to the corporation counsel to give a good reason for the delay, I got the truth out of him without evasion.

"Well, I tell you," he said blandly, "no one here is taking any interest in that business. That is good enough reason for you, isn't it?"

It was. That Tammany reason became the slogan of an assault upon official incompetence and treachery that hurried things up considerably. The property was condemned at a total cost to the city of a million and a half, in round numbers, including the assessment of half a million for park benefit which the property owners were quick enough, with the aid of the politicians, to get saddled on the city at large. In 1894 the city took possession and became the landlord of the old barracks. For a whole year it complacently collected the rents and did nothing. When it was shamed out of that rut, too, and the tenements were at last torn down, the square lay as the wreckers had left it for another year, until it became such a plague spot that, as a last resort, with a citizen's privilege, I arraigned the municipality before the Board of Health for maintaining a nuisance upon its premises. I can see the shocked look of the official now, as he studied the complaint.

" But, my dear sir," he coughed diplomatically, "isn't it rather unusual? I never heard of such a thing."

" Neither did I," I replied, " but then there never was such a thing before."

That night, while they were debating the " unusual thing," happened the accident to the children of which I spoke, emphasizing the charge that the nuisance was " dangerous to life," and there was an end. In the morning the Bend was taken in hand, and the following spring the Mulberry Bend Park was opened.

I told the story of that in " The Making of an American," and how the red tape of the comptroller's office pointed the way out, after all, with its check for three cents that had gone astray in the purchase of a school site. Of that sort of thing we had enough. But the Gilder Tenement House Commission had been sitting, the Committee of Seventy had been at work, and a law was on the statute books authorizing the expenditure of three

The Mulberry Bend.

million dollars for two open spaces in the parkless district on the East Side, where Jacob Beresheim was born. It had been shown that while the proportion of park area inside the limits of the old city was equal to one-thirteenth of all, below Fourteenth Street, where one-third of the people lived, it was barely one-fortieth. It took a citizen's committee appointed by the mayor just three weeks to seize the two park sites for the children's use, and it took the Good Government Clubs with their allies at Albany less than two months to get warrant of law for the tearing down of the houses ahead of final condemnation, lest any mischance befall through delay or otherwise, — a precaution which subsequent events proved to be eminently wise. I believe the legal proceedings are going on yet.

The playground part of it was a provision of the Gilder law that showed what apt scholars we had been. I was a member of that committee, and I fed fat my grudge against the slum tenement, knowing that I might not again have such a chance. Bone Alley went. I shall not soon get the picture of it, as I saw it last, out of my mind. I had wandered to the top floor of one of the ramshackle tenements in the heart of the block, to a door that stood ajar, and pushed it open. On the floor lay three women rag-pickers with their burdens, asleep, overcome by the heat and beer, the stale stench of

which filled the place. Swarms of flies covered
them. The room — no! let it go. Thank God, we
shall not again hear of Bone Alley. Where it

Bone Alley.

cursed the earth with its gloom and its poverty,
the sun shines to-day on children at play. If we
are slow to understand the meaning of it all, they
will not be. We shall have light from that quarter

when they grow up, on what is truly " educational "
in the bringing up of young citizens. The children
will teach us something for a change that will do
us lasting good.

Half a dozen blocks away, in Rivington Street,
the city's first public bath-house has at last been
built, after many delays, and godliness will have a
chance to move in with cleanliness. The two are
neighbors everywhere, but in the slum the last
must come first. Glasgow has half a dozen public
baths. Rome, two thousand years ago, washed its
people most sedulously, and in heathen Japan
to-day, I am told, there are baths, as we have
saloons, on every corner. Christian New York
never had an all-year bath-house until now. In a
tenement population of 255,033 the Gilder Commission found only 306 who had access to bath-
rooms in the houses where they lived, and they
would have found the same thing wherever they
went. The Church Federation canvass of the
Fifteenth Assembly District over on the West Side,
where they did not go, counted three bath-tubs to
1321 families. Nor was that because they so elected.
The People's Baths took in 121,386 half dimes
last year (1901) for as many baths, and more than
forty per cent of their customers were Italians. In
the first five months of the present year the Rivington Street baths accommodate 224,876 bathers, of

whom 66,256 were women and girls. And this in winter. The free river baths have registered five and six millions of bathers in one brief season. The "great unwashed" were not so from choice, it would appear.

The river baths were only for summer, and their time is past. As the sewers that empty into the river multiply, it is getting less and less a place fit to bathe in, though the boys find no fault. Sixteen public bath-houses on shore are to take the place of the swimming baths. They are all to be in the crowded tenement districts. The sites for the first three are being chosen now. And a wise woman [1] offers to build and equip one all complete at her own expense, as her gift to the city.

Pull up now a minute, if you think, with some good folks, that the world is not advancing, but just marking time, and look back half a century. I said that New York never had a public bath till now. I meant a free bath. As long ago as 1852, just fifty years ago, the Association for improving the Condition of the Poor built one in Mott Street near Grand Street, and spent $42,000 in doing it. It ran eight years, and was then closed for want of patronage. Forty years passed, and it was again the Association for improving the Condition of the Poor that built the People's Baths in the same neighbor-

[1] Mrs. A. A. Anderson.

hood. That time they succeeded at once. And now here we are, planning a great system of municipal baths as the people's right, not as a favor to any one, and the old lie that the poor prefer to steep in their squalor is no longer believed by any person with sense. This month contracts will be given out for the fitting of nine public schools with shower-baths where we had one before, and notice is given that that one will be open to the people on Sunday mornings. No, we are not marking time; we are forging ahead. Every park, every playground, every bath-house, is a nail in the coffin of the slum, and every big, beautiful schoolhouse, built for the people's use, not merely to lock the children up in during certain hours for which the teachers collect pay, is a pole rammed right through the heart of it so that even its ghost shall never walk again. For ever so much of it we thank that association of men of splendid courage and public spirit. They fight to win because they believe in the people. They fight *with* the people and so they are bound to win.

Every once in a while these days a false note in it all jars upon me — a note of dread lest those we are trying to help get tired of the word "reform" and balk. Reform such as we have occasionally had is to blame for some of that. Certainly you do not want to reform men by main strength, drag them into righteousness by the hair of the head, as it were.   And let it be freely admitted that the man on Fifth Avenue needs to be reformed quite as much as his neighbor in Mulberry Street whom he forgot, — more, since it is his will to mend things that has to be righted, while it is the other's power to do it that is lacking.   But right there stop.   Let us have no pretending that there is nothing to mend. There is a good deal, and it is not going to be mended by stuffing the one you would help with conceit and ingratitude.   Ingratitude does not naturally inhabit the slums, but it is a crop that is easily grown there, and where it does grow there is an end of efforts to mend things in that generation.   You do not want to come *down* to your work for your fellows, when you go from the brown-stone front to the tenement; but neither do you want to make him believe that you feel you are coming up to him, for you know you do not feel that way.   And moreover, it is not true, if you are coming at all.   You want to come right *over*, to help him reform conditions of his life with which he cannot grapple alone, and it is as good for him, as it is for you to know that you are doing it.   For that is the brotherhood.   And now you can see how that is the only thing that really helps.   Charity may corrupt, correction may harden and estrange, — in the family they do neither.   There you can give and take without offence. Children of one Father! Spin all the fine theories you like, build up systems of profound philosophy, of social ethics, of philanthropic endeavor; back to that you get — if you get anywhere at all.

I did not mean to preach. I was just thinking that the Association for Improving the Condition of the Poor, in its fifty years of battling with all that makes the slum, has come nearer that ideal than any and all the rest of us. And the president of it these ten years, the same who with his brother[†] tried to reform Gotham Court, is the head, too, of the citizens' union which is the whole reform programme in a nutshell. All of which is as it ought to be.

To return to the East Side where the light was let in. Bone Alley brought thirty-seven dollars under the auctioneer's hammer. Thieves' Alley, in the other park down at Rutgers Square, where the police clubbed the Jewish cloakmakers a few years ago for the offence of gathering to assert their right to " being men, live the life of men," as some one who knew summed up the labor movement, brought only seven dollars, and the old Helvetia House, where Boss Tweed and his gang met at night to plan their plundering raids on the city's treasury, was knocked down for five. Kerosene Row, in the same block, did not bring enough to have bought kindling wood with which to start one of the nu-

†The president of the Association was Robert Fulton Cutting (1852–1934), who also was the first chairman of the Citizens Union (founded in 1897); his brother was William Bayard Cutting (1850–1912), a lawyer who served as U.S. Civil Service Commissioner (1896–97) and was a trustee of Columbia University.

merous fires that gave it its bad name.   It was in
Thieves' Alley that the owner in the days long gone
by hung out the sign, " No Jews need apply."
I stood and watched the opening of the first municipal playground upon the site of the old alley, and
in the thousands that thronged street and tenements
from curb to roof with thunder of applause, there
were not twoscore who could have found lodging
with the old Jew-baiter.   He had to go with his
alley, before the better day could bring light and
hope to the Tenth Ward.

What became of the people who were dispossessed?   The answer to that is the reply, too, to
the wail that goes up from the speculative builder
every time we put the screws on the tenement
house law.   It does not pay him to build any more,
he says.   But when the multitudes of Mulberry
Bend, of Hester Street, and of the Bone Alley Park
were put out, there was more than room enough
for them in new houses ready for their use.   In the
Seventh, Tenth, Eleventh, Thirteenth, and Seven-
teenth wards, where they would naturally go if they
wanted to be near home, there were 4268 vacant
apartments with room for over 18,000 tenants at
our New York average of four and a half to the
family.   Including the Bend, the whole number
of the dispossessed was not 12,000.   On Manhattan Island there were at that time more than

37,000 vacant flats, so that it seems those builders were either "talking through their hats," or else they were philanthropists pure and simple.   And I know they were not that.   The whole question of re-housing the population that had been so carefully considered abroad made us no trouble, though it gave a few well-meaning people unnecessary concern. The unhoused were scattered some, which was one of the things we hoped for, but hardly dared believe would come to pass.   Many of them, as it appeared, had remained in their old slum more from force of habit and association than because of necessity.

"Everything takes ten years," said Abram S. Hewitt, when, exactly ten years after he had as mayor championed the Small Parks Act, he took his seat as chairman of the Advisory Committee on Small Parks.   The ten years had wrought a great change.   It was no longer the slum of to-day, but that of to-morrow, that challenged attention. The committee took the point of view of the chil-dren from the first.   It had a large map prepared, showing where in the city there was room to play and where there was none.   Then it called in the police and asked them to point out where there was trouble with the boys; and in every instance the policeman put his finger upon a treeless slum.

" They have no other playground than the street,"

was the explanation given in each case. " They smash lamps and break windows. The storekeepers kick and there is trouble. That is how it begins." " Many complaints are received daily of boys annoying pedestrians, storekeepers, and tenants by their continually playing baseball in some parts of almost every street. The damage is not slight. Arrests are frequent, much more frequent than when they had open lots to play in. " This last was the report of an up-town captain. He remembered the days when there were open lots there. " But those lots are now built upon," he said, "and for every new house there are more boys and less chance for them to play."

The committee put a red daub on the map to indicate trouble. Then it asked those police captains who had not spoken to show them where their precincts were, and why they had no trouble. Every one of them put his finger on a green spot that marked a park.

" My people are quiet and orderly," said the captain of the Tompkins Square precinct.[†]

The police took the square from a mob by storm twice in my recollection, and the commander of the precinct was hit on the head with a hammer by " his people " and laid out for dead.

" The Hook Gang is gone," said he of Corlears Hook. The professional pursuit of that gang was

[†] Tompkins Square Park, which had playgrounds added to its grass and trees in 1905, covers the square blocks between Avenues A and B from E. Seventh to E. Tenth Streets.

to rob and murder inoffensive citizens by night and throw them into the river, and it achieved a bad eminence at its calling.

"The whole neighborhood has taken a change, and decidedly for the better," said the captain of

Mulberry Bend Park.

Mulberry Street; and the committee rose and said that it had heard enough.

The map was hung on the wall, and in it were stuck pins to mark the site of present and projected schools as showing where the census had found the children crowding. The moment that was done the committee sent the map and a copy of chapter 338 of the laws of 1895 to the mayor, and reported that its task was finished. This is the law and all there is of it : —

"The people of the State of New York, represented in Senate and Assembly, do enact as follows : —

"Section 1. Hereafter no schoolhouse shall be constructed in the city of New York without an open-air playground attached to or used in connection with the same.

"Section 2. This act shall take effect immediately."

Where the map was daubed with red the school pins crowded one another. On the lower East Side, where child crime was growing fast, and no less than three storm centres were marked down by the police, nine new schools were going up or planned, and in the up-town precinct whence came the wail about the ball players there were seven. It was common sense, then, to hitch the school playground and the children together. It seemed a happy combination, for the new law had been a stumbling-block to the school commissioners, who were in a quandary over the needful size of an "open-air playground." The roof garden idea, which was at the start a measure of simple economy to save large expenditure for land, had suggested a way out. But there was the long vacation, when schools are closed and children most in need of

Roof Playground on a Public School.

a chance to play. To get the playground on the roof of the schoolhouse recognized as the *public playground* seemed a long step toward turning it into a general neighborhood evening resort, that should be always open, and so towards bringing school and people, and especially the school and the boy, together in a bond of mutual sympathy good for them both.

That was the burden of the committee's report. It made thirteen recommendations besides, as to the location of parks and detached playgrounds, only two of which have been adopted to date. But that is of less account — as also was the

information imparted to me as secretary of the
committee by our late Tammany mayor — and
may he be the last — that we had "as much
authority as a committee of bootblacks in his
office" — it is all of less account than the fact that
the field has at last been studied and its needs
been made known. The rest will follow, with or
without the politician's authority. One of the
two suggestions carried out was for a riverside park
in the region up-town, on the West Side, where
the Federation of Churches and Christian Workers
found "saloon social ideals minting themselves upon
the minds of the people at the rate of seven saloon
thoughts to one educational thought." "Hudsonbank" (it is at the foot of West Fifty-third Street)
has been a playground these three years, in the
charge of the Outdoor Recreation League, and it
is recorded with pride by the directors, that not
a board was stolen from the long fence that en-
closes it in all that time, while fences all about
were ripped to pieces. Boards have a market
value in that neighborhood and private property
was not always highly regarded. But this is "the
children's"; that is why, within a year now, the
bluff upon which the playground is will have been
laid out as a beautiful park, and a bar set to the
slum in that quarter, where it already had got a
firm grip. Hard by there is a recreation pier, and

on summer evenings the young men of the neighborhood may be seen trooping riverward with their
girls to hear the music. The gang that "laid out"
two policemen, to my knowledge, has gone out of
business.

The best-laid plans are sometimes upset by
surprising snags. We had planned for two municipal playgrounds on the East Side, where the
need is greatest, and our plans were eagerly
accepted by the city authorities. But they were
never put into practice. A negligent attorney
killed one, a lazy clerk the other. And both served
under the reform government. The first of the two
playgrounds was to have been in Rivington Street,
adjoining the new public bath, where the boys, for
want of something better to do, were fighting daily
battles with stones, to the great damage of windows
and the worse aggravation of the householders.
Four hundred children in that neighborhood pe-
titioned the committee for a place of their own,
where there were no windows to break; and we
found one. It was only after the proceedings had
been started that we discovered that they had been
taken under the wrong law and the money spent in
advertising had been wasted. It was then too late.
The daily assaults upon the windows were resumed.

The other case was an attempt to establish a
model school park in a block where more than four

thousand children attended day and night school. The public school and the Pro-Cathedral,[†] which divided the children between them, were to be allowed to stand, at opposite ends of the block. The surrounding tenements were to be torn down to make room for a park and playground which should embody the ideal of what such a place ought to be, in the opinion of the committee. For the roof garden was not in the original plan except as an alternative of the street-level playground, where land came too high. The plentiful supply of light and air, the safety from fire, to be obtained by putting the school in a park, beside the fact that it could thus be "built beautiful," were considerations of weight. Plans were made, and there was great rejoicing in Essex Street, until it came out that this scheme had gone the way of the other. The clerk who should have filed the plans in the register's office left that duty to some one else, and it took just twenty-one days to make the journey, a distance of five hundred feet or less. The Greater New York had come then with Tammany, and the thing was not heard of again. When I traced the failure down to the clerk in question, and told him that he had killed the park, he yawned and said: —

"Yes, and I think it is just as well it is dead. We haven't any money for those things. It is very nice to have small parks, and very nice to have a horse and wagon, if you can afford it. But we can't. Why, there isn't enough to run the city government."

†The Pro-Cathedral was the seat of the Episcopal Church bishop of New York City.

So the labor of weary weeks and months in the children's behalf was all undone by a third-rate clerk in an executive office; but he saved the one thing he had in mind: the city government is "run" to date, and his pay is secure.

It is a pity to have to confess it, but it was not the only time reform in office gave its cause a black eye in the sight of the people. The Hamilton Fish Park[†] that took the place of Bone Alley was laid out with such lack of sense that it will have to be worked all over again. The gymnasium and bath in it that cost, I am told, $90,000, was never of any use for either purpose and was never opened. A policeman sat in the door and turned people away, while around the corner clamoring crowds besieged the new public bath I spoke of. There were more people waiting, sitting on the steps and strung out halfway through the block, when I went over to see, one July day, than could have found room in three buildings like it. So, also, after seven years, the promised park down by the Schiff Fountain called Seward Park[††] lies still, an unlovely waste, waiting to be made beautiful. Tammany let its heelers build shanties in it to sell fish and dry-goods and such in. Reform just let things be, no matter how bad they were, and broke its promises to the people.

†Hamilton Fish Park, named after Hamilton Fish (1849–1936), New York State Assembly Speaker 1895–96, is south of E. Houston Street between Pitt and Columbia Streets, to the Samuel Gompers Houses.

††Seward Park, named after William H. Seward, Abraham Lincoln's Secretary of State, extends from the Seward Houses to East Broadway, between Essex and Hester Streets.

No, that is not fair. There was enough to do besides, to straighten up things. Tammany had seen to
that. This very day[1] the contractor's men are beginning work in Seward Park, which shall give that
most crowded spot on earth its pleasure-ground, and
I have warrant for promising that within a year not
only will the " Ham-Fish " Park be restored, but
Hudsonbank and the Thomas Jefferson Park in
Little Italy, which are still dreary wastes, be opened
to the people; while from the Civic Club in Richard
Croker's old home ward comes the broad hint that
unless condemnation proceedings in the case of the
park and playground, to take the place of the old
tenements at East Thirty-fifth Street and Second
Avenue, are hurried by the Tammany Commission,
the club will take a hand and move to have the
commission cashiered. There is to be no repetition
of the Mulberry Bend scandal.

It is all right. Neither stupidity, spite, nor cold-
blooded neglect will be able much longer to cheat
the child out of his rights. The playground is here
to wrestle with the gang for the boy, and it will win.
It came so quietly that we hardly knew of it till we
heard the shouts. It took us seven years to make up
our minds to build a play pier, — recreation pier is
its municipal title, — and it took just about seven
weeks to build it when we got so far; but then we

[1] June 26, 1901.

Kindergarten on the Recreation Pier, at the Foot of E. 24th Stree.

learned more in one day than we had dreamed of in the seven years. Half the East Side swarmed over it with shrieks of delight, and carried the mayor and the city government, who had come to see the show, fairly off their feet. And now that pier has more than seven comrades — great, handsome structures, seven hundred feet long, some of them, with music every night for mother and the babies, and for papa, who can smoke his pipe there in peace. The moon shines upon the quiet river, and the steamers go by with their lights. The street is far away with its noise. The young people go sparking in all honor, as it is their right to do. The councilman who spoke of "pernicious influences" lying in wait for them there made the mistake of his life, unless he has made up his mind to go out of politics. That is just a question of effective superintendence, as is true of model tenements, and everything else in this world. You have got to keep the devil out of everything, yourself included. He will get in if he can, as he got into the Garden of Eden. The play piers have taken a hold of the people which no crabbed old bachelor can loosen with trumped-up charges. Their civilizing influence upon the children is already felt in a reported demand for more soap in the neighborhood where they are, and even the grocer smiles approval.

The play pier is the kindergarten in the educational campaign against the gang. It gives the little ones a chance. Often enough it is a chance for life. The street as a playground is a heavy contributor to the undertaker's bank account in more than one way. Distinguished doctors said at the tuberculosis congress this spring that it is to blame with its dust for sowing the seeds of that fatal disease in the half-developed bodies. I kept the police slips of a single day in May two years ago, when four little ones were killed and three crushed under the wheels of trucks in tenement streets. That was unusual, but no day has passed in my recollection that has not had its record of accidents, which bring grief as deep and lasting to the humblest home as if it were the pet of some mansion on Fifth Avenue that was slain. In the Hudson Guild[†] on the West Side they have the reports of ten children that were killed in the street immediately around there. The kindergarten teaching has borne fruit. Private initiative set the pace, but the playground idea has at last been engrafted upon the municipal plan. The Outdoor Recreation League was organized by public-spirited citizens, including many amateur athletes and enthusiastic women, with the object of " obtaining recognition of the necessity for recreation and physical exercise as fundamental to the moral and physical welfare of the people." Together with the School Reform Club and the Federation of Churches

†The Hudson Guild settlement house was founded by Dr. John Lovejoy Elliott on W. Twenty-sixth Street, between Ninth and Tenth Avenues. It continues to operate there, in the midst of the Chelsea-Elliott Houses, a New York City Housing Authority project.

and Christian Workers, it maintained a playground
on the up-town West Side where the ball came into
play for the first time as a recognized factor in civic
progress.   The day might well be kept for all time

The East River Park.

among those that mark human emancipation, for it
was social reform and Christian work in one, of the
kind that tells.

Only the year before, the athletic clubs had
vainly craved the privilege of establishing a gymnasium in the East River Park, where the children
wistfully eyed the sacred grass, and cowered under
the withering gaze of the policeman.   A friend
whose house stands opposite the park found them

one day swarming over her stoop in such shoals that she could not enter, and asked them why they did not play tag under the trees instead. The instant shout came back, " 'Cause the cop won't let us." And now even Poverty Gap is to have its playground — Poverty Gap, that was partly transformed by its one brief season's experience with its Holy Terror Park,[1] a dreary sand lot upon the site of the old tenements in which the Alley Gang murdered the one good boy in the block, for the offence of supporting his aged parents by his work as a baker's apprentice. And who knows but the Mulberry Bend and " Paradise Park" at the Five Points may yet know the climbing pole and the vaulting buck. So the world moves. For years the city's only playground that had any claim upon the name — and that was only a little asphalted strip behind a public school in First Street — was an old graveyard. We struggled vainly to get possession of another, long abandoned. But the dead were of more account than the living.

But now at last it is their turn. I watched the crowds at their play where Seward Park is to be. The Outdoor Recreation League had put up gymnastic apparatus, and the dusty square was jammed with a mighty multitude. It was not an

[1] The name bestowed upon it by the older toughs before the fact, not after.

ideal spot, for it had not rained in weeks, and
powdered sand and cinders had taken wing and
floated like a pall over the perspiring crowd. But
it was heaven to them. A hundred men and
boys stood in line, waiting their turn upon the
bridge ladder and the travelling rings, that hung
full of struggling and squirming humanity, groping
madly for the next grip. No failure, no rebuff, discouraged them. Seven boys and girls rode with
looks of deep concern — it is their way — upon
each end of the seesaw, and two squeezed into
each of the forty swings that had room for one,
while a hundred counted time and saw that none

The Seward Park.

had too much. It is an article of faith with these
children that nothing that is "going" for their
benefit is to be missed. Sometimes the result pro-
vokes a smile, as when a band of young Jews, start-
ing up a club, called themselves the Christian
Heroes. It was meant partly as a compliment, I
suppose, to the ladies that gave them club room;

but at the same time, if there was anything in a
name, they were bound to have it. It is rather to
cry over than to laugh at, if one but understands
it. The sight of these little ones swarming over a
sand heap until scarcely an inch of it was in sight,
and gazing in rapt admiration at the poor show of
a dozen geraniums and English ivy plants on the
window-sill of the overseer's cottage, was pathetic
in the extreme. They stood for ten minutes at a
time, resting their eyes upon them. In the crowd
were aged women and bearded men with the inevitable Sabbath silk hat, who it seemed could
never get enough of it. They moved slowly, when
crowded out, looking back many times at the en-
chanted spot, as long as it was in sight.

Perhaps there was in it, on the part of the children at least, just a little bit of the comforting sense
of proprietorship. They had contributed of their
scant pennies more than a hundred dollars toward
the opening of the playground, and they felt that
it was their very own. All the better. Two
policemen watched the passing show, grinning;
their clubs hung idly from their belts. The words
of a little woman whom I met once in Chicago
kept echoing in my ear. She was the "happiest
woman alive," for she had striven long for a playground for her poor children, and had got it.

"The police like it," she said. "They say that
it will do more good than all the Sunday-schools
in Chicago. The mothers say, 'This is good busi-

The Seward Park on Opening Day.

ness.' The carpenters that put up the swings and things worked with a will; everybody was glad. The police lieutenant has had a tree called after him. The boys that did that used to be terrors. Now they take care of the trees. They plead for a low limb that is in the way, that no one may cut it off."

The twilight deepens and the gates of the playground are closed. The crowds disperse slowly. In the roof garden on the Hebrew Institute[†] across East Broadway lights are twinkling and the band is tuning up. Little groups are settling down to a quiet game of checkers or love-making. Pater-

[†]Founded in 1889, it was supported by wealthy "uptown" German Jews such as Jacob H. Schiff, whose families arrived in New York two generations before the East European Jews. The Hebrew Institute became the Educational Alliance in 1891, moving to East Broadway opposite Seward Park (opened in 1900) and across from where the Seward Park Branch of The New York Public Library was built in 1910.

familias leans back against the parapet where palms
wave luxuriously in the summer breeze.   The newspaper drops from his hand; he closes his eyes and
is in dreamland, where strikes come not.   Mother
knits contentedly in her seat, with a smile on her
face that was not born of the Ludlow Street tenement.   Over yonder a knot of black-browed men

In the Roof Garden of the Hebrew Educational Alliance.

talk with serious mien.   They might be met any
night in the anarchist café, half a dozen doors away,
holding forth against empires.   Here wealth does
not excite their wrath, nor power their plotting.
In the roof garden anarchy is harmless, even though
a policeman typifies its government.   They laugh
pleasantly to one another as he passes, and he gives
them a match to light their cigars.   It is Thursday,
and smoking is permitted.   On Friday it is dis-

couraged because it offends the orthodox, to whom
the lighting of a fire, even the holding of a candle,
is anathema on the Sabbath eve.

The band plays on. One after another, tired
heads droop upon babes slumbering peacefully at
the breast. Ludlow Street — the tenement — are
forgotten; eleven o'clock is not yet. Down along
the silver gleam of the river a mighty city slumbers.
The great bridge has hung out its string of shining
pearls from shore to shore. "Sweet land of liberty!"
Overhead the dark sky, the stars that twinkled
their message to the shepherds on Judæan hills, that
lighted their sons through ages of slavery, and the
flag of freedom borne upon the breeze, — down
there the tenement, the — Ah, well! let us forget
as do these.

Now if you ask me: " And what of it all? What
does it avail?" let me take you once more back to
the Mulberry Bend, and to the policeman's verdict
add the police reporter's story of what has taken
place there. In fifteen years I never knew a week
to pass without a murder there, rarely a Sunday.
It was the wickedest, as it was the foulest, spot in
all the city. In the slum the two are interchange-
able terms for reasons that are clear enough for me.
But I shall not speculate about it, only state the
facts. The old houses fairly reeked with outrage
and violence. When they were torn down, I

counted seventeen deeds of blood in that place
which I myself remembered, and those I had forgotten probably numbered seven times seventeen.
The district attorney connected more than a score
of murders of his own recollection with Bottle

Bottle Alley, Whyo Gang's Headquarters.

This picture was evidence at a murder trial.   The X marks the place where the murderer
stood when he shot his victim on the stairs.

Alley, the Whyó Gang's headquarters. Five years
have passed since it was made into a park, and
scarce a knife had been drawn or a shot fired in
all that neighborhood.   Only twice have I been
called as a police reporter to the spot.   It is not
that the murder has moved to another neighbor-

hood, for there has been no increase of violence in Little Italy or wherever else the crowd went that moved out. It is that the light has come in and made crime hideous. It is being let in wherever the slum has bred murder and robbery, bred the gang, in the past. Wait, now, another ten years, and let us see what a story there will be to tell.

Avail? Why, it was only the other day that Tammany was actually caught applauding[1] Comptroller Coler's[†] words in Plymouth Church, " Whenever the city builds a schoolhouse upon the site of a dive and creates a park, a distinct and permanent mental, moral, and physical improvement has been made, and public opinion will sustain such a policy, even if a dive-keeper is driven out of business and somebody's ground rent is reduced." And Tammany's press agent, in his enthusiasm, sent forth this pæan: " In the light of such events how absurd it is for the enemies of the organization to contend that Tammany is not the greatest moral force in the community." Tammany a moral force! The park and the playground have availed, then, to bring back the day of miracles.

[1] To be sure, it did nothing else. When the people asked for $5000 to fit up one playground, Mayor Van Wyck replied with a sneer that " Vaudeville destroyed Rome."

[†] Bird S. Coler (1867–1941) was New York City Comptroller during the 1898–1901 administration of Tammany-supported Mayor Robert A. Van Wyck, which came in with the much-enlarged Greater New York. Among other books, he published *The Financial Effects of Consolidation*.

CHAPTER XII

THE PASSING OF CAT ALLEY

WHEN Santa Claus comes around to New York this Christmas he will look in vain for some of the slum alleys he used to know. They are gone. Where some of them were, there are shrubs and trees and greensward; the sites of others are holes and hillocks yet, that by and by, when all the official red tape is unwound, — and what a lot of it there is to plague mankind! — will be levelled out and made into playgrounds for little feet that have been aching for them too long. Perhaps it will surprise some good people to hear that Santa Claus knew the old alleys; but he did. I have been there with him, and I knew that, much as some things which he saw there grieved him, — the starved childhood, the pinching poverty, and the slovenly indifference that cut deeper than the rest because it spoke of hope that was dead, — yet by nothing was his gentle spirit so grieved and shocked as by the show that proposed to turn his holiday into a battalion drill of the children from the alleys and the courts for patricians, young and old, to review. It was well meant, but it was not Christmas. That belongs to the home, and in the darkest slums Santa Claus found homes where his blessed tree took root and shed its mild radiance about, dispelling the darkness, and bringing back hope and courage and trust.

They are gone, the old alleys. Reform wiped them out. It is well. Santa Claus will not have harder work finding the doors that opened to him gladly, because the light has been let in. And others will stand ajar that before were closed. The chimneys in tenement-house alleys were never built on a plan generous enough to let him in in the orthodox way. The cost of coal had to be considered in putting them up. Bottle Alley and Bandits' Roost are gone with their bad memories. Bone Alley is gone, and Gotham Court. I well remember the Christmas tree in the court, under which a hundred dolls stood in line, craving partners among the girls in its tenements. That was the kind of battalion drill that they understood. The ceiling of the room was so low that the tree had to be cut almost in half; but it was beautiful, and it lives yet, I know, in the hearts of the little ones, as it lives in mine. The "Barracks" are gone, Nibsey's Alley is gone, where the first Christmas tree was lighted the night poor Nibsey lay dead in his coffin. And Cat Alley is gone.

Cat Alley was my alley. It was mine by right of long acquaintance. We were neighbors for twenty years. Yet I never knew why it was called Cat Alley. There was the usual number of cats, gaunt and voracious, which foraged in its ash-barrels; but beyond the family of three-legged cats, that pre-

The First Christmas Tree in Gotham Court.

sented its own problem of heredity, — the kittens took it from the mother, who had lost one leg under the wheels of a dray, — there was nothing specially remarkable about them. It was not an alley, either, when it comes to that, but rather a row of four or five old tenements in a back yard that was reached by a passageway somewhat less than three feet wide between the sheer walls of the front houses. These had once had pretensions to some style. One of them had been the parsonage of the church next door that had by turns been an old-style Methodist tabernacle, a fashionable negroes' temple, and an Italian mission church, thus marking time, as it were, to the upward movement of the immigration that came in at the bottom, down in the Fourth Ward, fought its way through the Bloody Sixth, and by the time it had travelled the length of Mulberry Street had acquired a local standing and the right to be counted and rounded up by the political bosses. Now the old houses were filled with newspaper offices and given over to perpetual insomnia. Week-days and Sundays, night or day, they never slept. Police headquarters was right across the way, and kept the reporters awake. From his window the chief looked down the narrow passageway to the bottom of the alley, and the alley looked back at him, nothing daunted. No man is a hero to his valet, and the chief was not an autocrat to Cat Alley. It knew all his human weaknesses, could tell when his time was up generally before he could, and winked the other eye with the captains when the newspapers spoke of his having read them a severe lecture on gambling or Sunday beer-selling. Byrnes[†]it worshipped, but for the others who were

†Thomas F. Byrnes became Chief of Detectives (1880), Chief Inspector (1888), and Superintendent (1892) of the New York City Police Department. He was credited with cleaning up street crime in Lower Manhattan, but was implicated by the 1895 Lexow Commission on police corruption, and Theodore Roosevelt, president of the (civilian) police commission, forced him to resign in 1895.

before him and followed after, it cherished a neighborly sort of contempt.

In the character of its population Cat Alley was
properly cosmopolitan. The only element that was
missing was the native American, and in this also
it was representative of the tenement districts in
America's chief city. The substratum was Irish, of
volcanic properties. Upon this were imposed layers
of German, French, Jewish, and Italian, or, as the
alley would have put it, Dutch, Sabé, Sheeny, and
Dago; but to this last it did not take kindly. With
the experience of the rest of Mulberry Street before
it, it foresaw its doom if the Dago got a footing
there, and within a month of the moving in of the
Gio family there was an eruption of the basement
volcano, reënforced by the sanitary policeman, to
whom complaint had been made that there were too
many "Ginnies" in the Gio flat. There were four
— about half as many as there were in some of the
other flats when the item of house rent was lessened
for economic reasons; but it covered the ground:
the flat was too small for the Gios. The appeal of
the signora was unavailing. "You got-a three bam-
bino," she said to the housekeeper, "all four, lika
me," counting the number on her fingers. "I no
putta me broder-in-law and me sister in the street-a.
Italian lika to be together."

The housekeeper was unmoved. "Humph!" she

said, "to liken my kids to them Dagos! Out they go." And they went.

Up on the third floor there was the French couple. It was another of the contradictions of the alley that of this pair the man should have been a typical, stolid German, she a mercurial Parisian, who at seventy sang the " Marseillaise " with all the spirit of the Commune in her cracked voice, and hated from the bottom of her patriotic soul the enemy with whom the irony of fate had yoked her. However, she improved the opportunity in truly French fashion. He was rheumatic, and most of the time was tied to his chair. He had not worked for seven years. " He no goode," she said, with a grimace, as her nimble fingers fashioned the wares by the sale of which, from a basket, she supported them both. The wares were dancing girls with tremendous limbs and very brief skirts of tricolor gauze, — " ballerinas," in her vocabulary, — and monkeys with tin hats, cunningly made to look like German soldiers. For these she taught him to supply the decorations. It was his department, she reasoned ; the ballerinas were of her country and hers. *Parbleu !* must one not work ? What then ? Starve ? Before her look and gesture the cripple quailed, and twisted and rolled and pasted all day long, to his country's shame, fuming with impotent rage.

" I wish the devil had you," he growled.

She regarded him maliciously, with head tilted on
one side, as a bird eyes a caterpillar it has speared.

"Hein!" she scoffed.   "Du den, vat?"

He scowled.   She was right; without her he was
helpless.   The judgment of the alley was unim-
peachable.   They were and remained "the French
couple."

Cat Alley's reception of Madame Klotz at first
was not cordial.   It was disposed to regard as a
hostile act the circumstance that she kept a special
holiday, of which nothing was known except from
her statement that it referred to the fall of somebody
or other whom she called the Bastille, in suspicious
proximity to the detested battle of the Boyne; but
when it was observed that she did nothing worse
than dance upon the flags "*avec ze leetle bébé*" of the
tenant in the basement, and torture her "Dootch"
husband with extra monkeys and gibes in honor of
the day, unfavorable judgment was suspended, and
it was agreed that without a doubt the "bastard"
fell for cause; wherein the alley showed its sound
historical judgment.   By such moral pressure when
it could, by force when it must, the original Irish
stock preserved the alley for its own quarrels, free
from "foreign" embroilments.   These quarrels were
many and involved.   When Mrs. M'Carthy was to
be dispossessed, and insisted, in her cups, on killing the housekeeper as a necessary preliminary, a

The Mouth of the Alley.

By permission of the Century Company.

study of the causes that led to the feud developed the following normal condition: Mrs. M'Carthy had the housekeeper's place when Mrs. Gehegan was poor, and fed her "kids." As a reward, Mrs. Gehegan worked around and got the job away from her. Now that it was Mrs. M'Carthy's turn to be poor, Mrs. Gehegan insisted upon putting her out. Whereat, with righteous wrath, Mrs. M'Carthy proclaimed from the stoop: "Many is the time Mrs. Gehegan had a load on, an' she went upstairs an' slept it off. I didn't. I used to show meself, I did, as a lady. I know ye're in there, Mrs. Gehegan. Come out an' show yerself, an' l'ave the alley to judge betwixt us." To which Mrs. Gehegan prudently vouchsafed no answer.

Mrs. M'Carthy had succeeded to the office of housekeeper upon the death of Miss Mahoney, an ancient spinster who had collected the rents since the days of "the riot," meaning the Orange riot — an event from which the alley reckoned its time, as the ancients did from the Olympian games. Miss Mahoney was a most exemplary and worthy old lady, thrifty to a fault. Indeed, it was said when she was gone that she had literally starved herself to death to lay by money for the rainy day she was keeping a lookout for to the last. In this she was obeying her instincts; but they went counter to those of the alley, and the result was

very bad. As an example, Miss Mahoney's life was
a failure. When at her death it was discovered
that she had bank-books representing a total of two
thousand dollars, her nephew and only heir promptly
knocked off work and proceeded to celebrate, which
he did with such fervor that in two months he had
run through it all and killed himself by his ex-
cesses. Miss Mahoney's was the first bank account
in the alley, and, so far as I know, the last.

From what I have said, it must not be supposed
that fighting was the normal occupation of Cat
Alley. It was rather its relaxation from unceasing
toil and care, from which no to-morrow held promise of relief. There was a deal of good humor in
it at most times. "Scrapping" came naturally to
the alley. When, as was sometimes the case, it
was the complement of a wake, it was as the mirth
of children who laugh in the dark because they are
afraid. But once an occurrence of that sort scandalized the tenants. It was because of the violation
of the Monroe Doctrine, to which, as I have said,
the alley held most firmly, with severely local appli-
cation. To Mulberry Street Mott Street was a
foreign foe from which no interference was desired
or long endured. A tenant in "the back" had died
in the hospital of rheumatism, a term which in the
slums sums up all of poverty's hardships, scant and
poor food, damp rooms, and hard work, and the

family had come home for the funeral. It was not
a pleasant home-coming. The father in his day
had been strict, and his severity had driven his
girls to the street. They had landed in Chinatown,[†]
with all that implies, one at a time; first the older
and then the younger, whom the sister took under
her wing and coached. She was very handsome,
was the younger sister, with an innocent look in
her blue eyes that her language belied, and smart,
as her marriage-ring bore witness to. The alley,
where the proprieties were held to tenaciously,
observed it and forgave all the rest, even her
" Chink " husband. While her father was lying
ill, she had spent a brief vacation in the alley.
Now that he was dead, her less successful sister
came home, and with her a delegation of girls from
Chinatown. In their tawdry finery they walked
in, sallow and bold, with Mott Street and the ac-
cursed pipe written all over them, defiant of public
opinion, yet afraid to enter except in a body. The
alley considered them from behind closed blinds,
while the children stood by silently to see them
pass. When one of them offered one of the "kids"
a penny, he let it fall on the pavement, as if it were
unclean. It was a sore thrust, and it hurt cruelly;
but no one saw it in her face as she went in where
the dead lay, with scorn and hatred as her offering.
  The alley had withheld audible comment with

†By the 1870s, a small Chinatown had developed in Lower
Manhattan, with its nucleus at Doyer, Pell, and Mott Streets. The
Chinese Exclusion Act of 1882 prevented new immigration from China,
but new residents migrated from California and the western states, to
escape often-violent racists.

a tact that did it credit; but when at night Mott Street added its contingent of "fellows" to the mourners properly concerned in the wake, and they started a fight among themselves that was unauthorized by local sanction, its wrath was aroused, and it arose and bundled the whole concern out into the street with scant ceremony. There was never an invasion of the alley after that night. It enjoyed home rule undisturbed.

Withal, there was as much kindness of heart and neighborly charity in Cat Alley as in any little community up-town or down-town, or out of town, for that matter. It had its standards and its customs, which were to be observed; but underneath it all, and not very far down either, was a human fellowship that was capable of any sacrifice to help a friend in need. Many was the widow with whom and with whose children the alley shared its daily bread, which was scanty enough, God knows, when death or other disaster had brought her to the jumping-off place. In twenty years I do not recall a suicide in the alley, or a case of suffering demanding the interference of the authorities, unless with such help as the hospital could give. The alley took care of its own, and tided them over the worst when it came to that. And death was not always the worst. I remember yet with a shudder a tragedy which I was just in time with the police to prevent. A laborer, who lived in the attic, had gone mad, poisoned by the stenches of the sewers in which he worked. For two nights he had been pacing the hallway, muttering incoherent things, and then fell to sharpening an axe, with his six children playing about — beautiful, brown-eyed girls they were, sweet and innocent little tots. In five minutes we should have been too late, for it appeared that the man's madness had taken on the homicidal tinge. They were better out of the world, he told us, as we carried him off to the hospital. When he was gone, the children came upon the alley, and loyally did it stand by them until a job was found for the mother by the local political boss. He got her appointed scrub-woman at the City Hall, and the alley, always faithful, was solid for him ever after. Organized charity might, and indeed did, provide groceries on the instalment plan. The Tammany captain provided the means of pulling the family through and of bringing up the children, although there was not a vote in the family. It was not the first time I had met him and observed his plan of "keeping close" to the people. Against it not the most carping reform critic could have found just ground of complaint.

The charity of the alley was contagious. With the reporters' messenger boys, a harum-scarum lot, in "the front," the alley was not on good terms for

any long stretch at a time. They made a racket at
night, and had sport with "old man Quinn," who
was a victim of dropsy. He was "walking on
dough," they asseverated, and paid no attention to the
explanation of the alley that he had "kidney feet."
But when the old man died and his wife was left
penniless, I found some of them secretly contribut-
ing to her keep. It was not so long after that that
another old pensioner of the alley, suddenly drawn
into their cyclonic sport in the narrow passageway,
fell and broke her arm. Apparently no one in the
lot was individually to blame. It was an unfortu-
nate accident, and it deprived her of her poor means
of earning the few pennies with which she eked out
the charity of the alley. Worse than that, it took
from her hope after death, as it were. For years
she had pinched and saved and denied herself to
keep up a payment of twenty-five cents a week
which insured her decent burial in consecrated
ground. Now that she could no longer work, the
dreaded trench in the Potter's Field yawned to
receive her. That was the blow that broke her
down. She was put out by the landlord soon after
the accident, as a hopeless tenant, and I thought
that she had gone to the almshouse, when by chance
I came upon her living quite happily in a tenement
on the next block. "Living" is hardly the word;
she was really waiting to die, but waiting with a

cheerful content that amazed me until she herself betrayed the secret of it. Every week one of the messenger boys brought her out of his scanty wages the quarter that alike insured her peace of mind and the undisturbed rest of her body in its long sleep, which a life of toil had pictured to her as the greatest of earth's boons.

Death came to Cat Alley in varying forms, often enough as a welcome relief to those for whom it called, rarely without its dark riddle for those whom it left behind, to be answered without delay or long guessing. There were at one time three widows with little children in the alley, none of them over twenty-five. They had been married at fifteen or sixteen, and when they were called upon to face the world and fight its battles alone were yet young and inexperienced girls themselves. Improvidence! Yes. Early marriages are at the bottom of much mischief among the poor. And yet perhaps these, and others like them, might have offered the homes from which they went out, as a valid defence. To their credit be it said that they accepted their lot bravely, and, with the help of the alley, pulled through. Two of them married again, and made a bad job of it. Second marriages seldom turned out well in the alley. They were a refuge of the women from work that was wearing their lives out, and gave them in exchange usually a tyrant who

hastened the process. There never was any sentiment about it. "I don't know what I shall do,"
said one of the widows to me, when at last it was
decreed that the tenements were to be pulled down,
"unless I can find a man to take care of me. Might
get one that drinks? I would hammer him half to
death." She did find her "man," only to have him
on her hands too. It was the last straw. Before
the wreckers came around she was dead. The
amazed indignation of the alley at the discovery of
her second marriage, which till then had been kept
secret, was beyond bounds. The supposed widow's
neighbor across the hall, whom we knew in the front
generally as "the Fat One," was so stunned by the
revelation that she did not recover in season to go
to the funeral. She was never afterward the same.

In the good old days when the world was right,
the Fat One had enjoyed the distinction of being
the one tenant in Cat Alley whose growler never
ran dry. It made no difference how strictly the
Sunday law was observed toward the rest of the
world, the Fat One would set out from the alley with
her growler in a basket, — this as a concession to
the unnatural prejudices of a misguided community,
not as an evasion, for she made a point of showing
it to the policeman on the corner, — and return
with it filled. Her look of scornful triumph as
she marched through the alley, and the backward

The Wrecking of Cat Alley.

By permission of the Century Company.

toss of her head toward police headquarters, which said plainly: " Ha! you thought you could! But you didn't, did you? " were the admiration of the alley. It allowed that she had met and downed Roosevelt in a fair fight. But after the last funeral the Fat One never again carried the growler. Her spirit was broken. All things were coming to an end, the alley itself with them.

One funeral I recall with a pleasure which the years have in no way dimmed. It was at a time before the King's Daughters' Tenement House Committee was organized, when out-of-town friends used to send flowers to my office for the poor. The first notice I had of a death in the alley was when a delegation of children from the rear knocked and asked for daisies. There was something unnaturally solemn about them that prompted me to make inquiries, and then it came out that old Mrs. Walsh was dead and going on her long ride up to Hart's Island; for she was quite friendless, and the purse-strings of the alley were not long enough to save her from the Potter's Field. The city hearse was even then at the door, and they were carrying in the rough pine coffin. With the children the crippled old woman had been a favorite; she had always a kind word for them, and they paid her back in the way they knew she would have loved best. Not even the coffin of the police sergeant

who was a brother of the district leader was so
gloriously decked out as old Mrs. Walsh's when
she started on her last journey.   The children
stood in the passageway with their arms full of
daisies, and gave the old soul a departing cheer;
and though it was quite irregular, it was all right,
for it was well meant, and Cat Alley knew it.

They were much like other children, those of the
alley.   It was only in their later years that the alley
and the growler set their stamp upon them.   While
they were small, they loved, like others of their
kind, to play in the gutter, to splash in the
sink about the hydrant, and to dance to the hand-
organ that came regularly into the block, even
though they sadly missed the monkey that was its
chief attraction till the aldermen banished it in a
cranky fit.   Dancing came naturally to them, too;
certainly no one took the trouble to teach them.   It
was a pretty sight to see them stepping to the time
on the broad flags at the mouth of the alley.   Not
rarely they had for an appreciative audience the
big chief himself, who looked down from his window, and the uniformed policeman at the door.
Even the commissioners deigned to smile upon the
impromptu show in breathing-spells between their
heavy labors in the cause of politics and pull.   But
the children took little notice of them; they were
too happy in their play.   They loved my flowers,

too, with a genuine love that did not spring from
the desire to get something for nothing, and the
parades on Italian feast-days that always came
through the street. They took a fearsome delight
in watching for the big dime museum giant, who
lived around in Elizabeth Street, and who in his last
days looked quite lean and hungry enough to send

Trilby.
By permission of the Century Company.

a thrill to any little boy's heart, though he had
never cooked one and eaten him in his whole life,
being quite a harmless and peaceable giant. And
they loved Trilby.

Trilby was the dog. As far back as my memory
reaches there was never another in Cat Alley. She
arrived in the block one winter morning on a dead
run, with a tin can tied to her stump of a tail, and

with the Mott Street gang in hot pursuit. In her
extremity she saw the mouth of the alley, dodged
in, and was safe. The Mott Streeters would as soon
have thought of following her into police headquarters as there. Ever after she stayed. She
took possession of the alley and of headquarters,
where the reporters had their daily walk, as if they
were hers by right of conquest, which in fact they
were. With her whimsically grave countenance, in
which all the cares of the vast domain she made it
her daily duty to oversee were visibly reflected, she
made herself a favorite with every one except the
"beanery-man" on the corner, who denounced her
angrily, when none of her friends were near, for
coming in with his customers at lunch-time on purpose to have them feed her with his sugar, which
was true. At regular hours, beginning with the opening of the department offices, she would make the
round of the police building and call on all the officials, forgetting none. She rode up in the elevator
and left it at the proper floors, waited in the ante-
rooms with the rest when there was a crowd, and
paid stated visits to the chief and the commissioners, who never omitted to receive her with a nod
and a "Hello, Trilby!" no matter how pressing
the business in hand. The gravity with which
she listened to what went on, and wrinkled up her
brow in an evident effort to understand, was comi-

cal to the last degree. She knew the fire alarm signals and when anything momentous was afoot. On the quiet days, when nothing was stirring, she would flock with the reporters on the stoop and sing.

There never was such singing as Trilby's. That was how she got her name. I tried a score of times to find out, but to this day I do not know whether it was pain or pleasure that was in her note. She had only one, but it made up in volume for what it lacked in range. Standing in the circle of her friends, she would raise her head until her nose pointed straight toward the sky, and pour forth her melody with a look of such unutterable woe on her face that peals of laughter always wound up the performance; whereupon Trilby would march off with an injured air, and hide herself in one of the offices, refusing to come out. Poor Trilby! with the passing away of the alley she seemed to lose her grip. She did not understand it. After wandering about aimlessly for a while, vainly seeking a home in the world, she finally moved over on the East Side with one of the dispossessed tenants. But on all Sundays and holidays, and once in a while in the middle of the week, she comes yet to inspect the old block in Mulberry Street and to join in a quartette with old friends.

Trilby and Old Barney were the two who stuck

to the alley longest.   Barney was the star boarder.
As everything about the place was misnamed, the
alley itself included, so was he.   His real name was
Michael, but the children called him Barney, and

Old Barney.

the name stuck.   When they were at odds, as they
usually were, they shouted " Barney Bluebeard!"
after him, and ran away and hid in trembling delight as he shook his key-ring at them, and showed
his teeth with the evil leer which he reserved specially for them.   It was reported in the alley that

he was a woman-hater; hence the name. Certain it is that he never would let one of the detested sex cross the threshold of his attic room on any pretext. If he caught one pointing for his aerie, he would block the way and bid her sternly begone. She seldom tarried long, for Barney was not a pleasing object when he was in an ugly mood. As the years passed, and cobweb and dirt accumulated in his room, stories were told of fabulous wealth which he had concealed in the chinks of the wall and in broken crocks; and as he grew constantly shabbier and more crabbed, they were readily believed. Barney carried his ring and filed keys all day, coining money, so the reasoning ran, and spent none; so he must be hiding it away. The alley hugged itself in the joyful sensation that it had a miser and his hoard in the cockloft. Next to a ghost, for which the environment was too matter-of-fact, that was the thing for an alley to have.

Curiously enough, the fact that, summer and winter, the old man never missed early mass and always put a silver quarter — even a silver dollar, it was breathlessly whispered in the alley — in the contribution box, merely served to strengthen this belief. The fact was, I suspect, that the key-ring was the biggest end of the business Old Barney cultivated so assiduously. There were keys enough on it, and they rattled most persistently as he sent forth the strange whoop which no one ever was able to make out, but which was assumed to mean "Keys! keys!" But he was far too feeble and tremulous to wield a file with effect. In his younger days he had wielded a bayonet in his country's defence. On the rare occasions when he could be made to talk, he would tell, with a smouldering gleam in his sunken eyes, how the Twenty-third Illinois Volunteers had battled with the Rebs weary nights and days without giving way a foot. The old man's bent back would straighten, and he would step firmly and proudly, at the recollection of how he and his comrades earned the name of the "heroes of Lexington" in that memorable fight. But only for the moment. The dark looks that frightened the children returned soon to his face. It was all for nothing, he said. While he was fighting at the front he was robbed. His lieutenant, to whom he gave his money to send home, stole it and ran away. When he returned after three years there was nothing, nothing! At this point the old man always became incoherent. He spoke of money the government owed him and withheld. It was impossible to make out whether his grievance was real or imagined.

When Colonel Grant came to Mulberry Street as a police commissioner, Barney brightened up under

a sudden idea.   He might get justice now.   Once
a week, through those two years, he washed himself,
to the mute astonishment of the alley, and brushed
up carefully, to go across and call on " the general's
son " in order to lay his case before him.   But he
never got farther than the Mulberry Street door.
On the steps he was regularly awestruck, and the
old hero, who had never turned his back to the
enemy, faltered and retreated.   In the middle of
the street he halted, faced front, and saluted the
building with all the solemnity of a grenadier on
parade, then went slowly back to his attic and to
his unrighted grievance.

It had been the talk of the neighborhood for
years that the alley would have to go in the Elm
Street widening which was to cut a swath through
the block, right over the site upon which it stood ;
and at last notice was given about Christmas time
that the wreckers were coming.   The alley was
sold,— thirty dollars was all it brought, — and the
old tenants moved away, and were scattered to the
four winds.   Barney alone stayed.   He flatly refused to budge.   They tore down the church next
door and the buildings on Houston Street, and filled
what had been the yard, or court, of the tenements
with débris that reached halfway to the roof, so
that the old locksmith, if he wished to go out or in,
must do so by way of the third-story window, over

a perilous path of shaky timbers and sliding brick. He evidently considered it a kind of siege, and shut himself in his attic, bolting and barring the door, and making secret sorties by night for provisions. When the chimney fell down or was blown over, he punched a hole in the rear wall and stuck the stove-pipe through that, where it blew defiance to the new houses springing up almost within arm's-reach of it. It suggested guns pointing from a fort, and perhaps it pleased the old man's soldier fancy. It certainly made smoke enough in his room, where he was fighting his battles over with himself, and occasionally with the janitor from the front, who climbed over the pile of bricks and in through the window to bring him water. When I visited him there one day, and, after giving the password, got behind the bolted door, I found him, the room, and everything else absolutely covered with soot, coal-black from roof to rafters. The password was "Lettér!" yelled out loud at the foot of the stairs. That would always bring him out, in the belief that the government had finally sent him the long-due money. Barney was stubbornly defiant, he would stand by his guns to the end; but he was weakening physically under the combined effect of short rations and nightly alarms. It was clear that he could not stand it much longer.

The wreckers cut it short one morning by ripping

off the roof over his head before he was up.   Then,
and only then, did he retreat.   His exit was characterized by rather more haste than dignity.   There
had been a heavy fall of snow overnight, and Barney slid down the jagged slope from his window,
dragging his trunk with him, in imminent peril of
breaking his aged bones.   That day he disappeared
from Mulberry Street.   I thought he was gone for
good, and through the Grand Army of the Republic
had set inquiries on foot to find what had become
of him, when one day I saw him from my window,
standing on the opposite side of the street, key-ring
in hand, and looking fixedly at what had once been
the passageway to the alley, but was now a barred
gap between the houses, leading nowhere.   He
stood there long, gazing sadly at the gateway, at the
children dancing to the Italian's hand-organ, at
Trilby trying to look unconcerned on the stoop,
and then went his way silently, a poor castaway, and
I saw him no more.

So Cat Alley, with all that belonged to it, passed
out of my life.   It had its faults, but it can at least
be said of it, in extenuation, that it was very human.
With them all it had a rude sense of justice that did
not distinguish its early builders.   When the work
of tearing down had begun, I watched, one day, a
troop of children having fun with a see-saw they
had made of a plank laid across a lime barrel.

The whole Irish contingent rode the plank, all at once, with screams of delight. A ragged little girl from the despised " Dago " colony watched them from the corner with hungry eyes. Big Jane, who was the leader by virtue of her thirteen years and her long reach, saw her and stopped the show.

" Here, Mame," she said, pushing one of the smaller girls from the plank, " you get off an' let her ride. Her mother was stabbed yesterday."

And the little Dago rode, and was made happy.

CHAPTER XIII

JUSTICE TO THE BOY

SOMETIMES, when I see my little boy hugging himself with delight at the near prospect of the kindergarten, I go back in memory forty years and more to the day when I was dragged, a howling captive, to school, as a punishment for being bad at home. I remember, as though it were yesterday, my progress up the street in the vengeful grasp of an exasperated servant, and my reception by the aged monster — most fitly named Madame Bruin — who kept the school. She asked no questions, but led me straightway to the cellar, where she plunged me into an empty barrel and put the lid on over me. Applying her horn goggles to the bunghole, to my abject terror, she informed me, in a sepulchral voice, that that was the way bad boys were dealt with in school. When I ceased howling from sheer fright, she took me out and conducted me to the yard, where a big hog had a corner to itself. She bade me observe that one of its ears had been slit half its length. It was because the hog was lazy, and little boys who were that way minded — zip! she clipped a pair of tailor's shears close to my ear.   It was my first lesson in school.   I hated it from that hour.

The barrel and the hog were never part of the curriculum in any American boy's school, I suppose ; they seem too freakish to be credited to any but the demoniac ingenuity of my home ogre.   But they stood for a comprehension of the office of school and teacher which was not patented by any day or land.   It is not so long since the notion yet prevailed that the schools were principally to lock children up in for the convenience of their parents, that we should have entirely forgotten it.   Only the other day a clergyman from up the state came into my office to tell of a fine reform school they had in his town.   They were very proud of it.

" And how about the schools for the good boys in your town ? " I asked, when I had heard him out. " Are they anything to be proud of ? "

He stared.   He guessed they were all right, he said, after some hesitation.   But it was clear that he did not know.

It is not necessary to go back forty years to find us in the metropolis upon the clergyman's platform, if not upon Madame Bruin's.   A dozen or fifteen will do.   They will bring us to the day when roof playgrounds were contemptuously left out of the estimates for an East Side school, as "frills" that had nothing to do with education ; when the Board

The Old.

The New.

of Health found but a single public school in more than sixscore that was so ventilated as to keep the children from being poisoned by foul air; when the authority of the Talmud had to be invoked by the Superintendent of School Buildings to convince the president of the Board of Education, who happened to be a Jew, that seventy-five or eighty pupils were far too many for one class-room; when a man who had been dead a year was appointed a school trustee of the Third Ward, under the mouldy old law surviving from the day when New York was a big village, and filled the office as well as if he had been alive, because there were no schools in his ward — it was the wholesale grocery district; when manual training and the kindergarten were yet the fads of yesterday, looked at askance; when fifty thousand children roamed the streets for whom there was no room in the schools, and the only defence of the School Commissioners was that they "didn't know" there were so many; and when we mixed truants and thieves in a jail with entire unconcern. Indeed, the jail filled the title rôle in the educational cast of that day. Its inmates were well lodged and cared for, while the sanitary authorities twice condemned the Essex Market school across the way as wholly unfit for children to be in, but failed to catch the ear of the politician who ran things unhindered. When (in 1894) I denounced the "system" of enforcing — or not enforcing — the compulsory education law as a device to make thieves out of our children by turning over their training to the street, he protested angrily; but the experts of the Tenement House Commission found the charge fully borne out by the facts. They were certainly plain enough in the sight of us all, had we chosen to see.

When at last we saw, we gave the politician a vacation for a season. To say that he was to blame for all the mischief would not be fair. We were to blame for leaving him in possession. He was only a link in the chain which our indifference had forged; but he was always and everywhere an obstruction to betterment, — sometimes, illogically, in spite of himself. Successive Tammany mayors had taken a stand for the public schools when it was clear that reform could not be delayed much longer; but they were helpless against a system of selfishness and stupidity of which they were the creatures, though they posed as its masters. They had to go with it as unfit, and upon the wave that swept out the last of the rubbish came reform. The Committee of Seventy took hold, the Good Government Clubs, the Tenement House Commission, and the women of New York. Five years we strove with the powers of darkness, and look now at the change! The New York school system is not yet the ideal one, — it may never be ; but the jail, at least, has been cast out of the firm. We have a compulsory education law under which it is possible to punish the parent for the boy's truancy, as he ought to be if there was room in the school for the lad, and he let him drift. And the day cannot be delayed much longer now when every child shall find the latchstring out on the school door. We have had to put our hands deep into our pockets to get so far, and we shall have to put them in deeper yet a long way. But it is all right. We are beginning to see the true bearing of things. Last week the Board of Estimate and Apportionment appropriated six millions of dollars for new schools — exactly what the battleship *Massachusetts* cost all complete with guns and fittings, so they told me on board. Battleships are all right when we need them, but even then it is the man behind the gun who tells, and that means the schoolmaster. The Board of Education asked for sixteen millions. They will get the other ten when we have caught our breath. Since the beginning of 1895 [1] we have built sixty-nine new public schools in Manhattan and the Bronx, at a cost of $12,038,764, exclusive of cost of sites, furnishings, heating, lighting, and ventilating the buildings, which would add two-thirds at least of that amount, making it a round

[1] Up to June, 1902.

twenty millions of dollars. And every one of the
sixty-nine has its playground, which will by and by
be free to all the neighborhood. The idea is at last
working through that the schools belong to the
people, and are primarily for the children and their
parents; not mere vehicles of ward patronage, or for
keeping an army of teachers in office and pay.

Public School No. 177, Manhattan.

The silly old régime is dead. The ward trustee
is gone with his friend the alderman, loudly pro-
claiming the collapse of our liberties in the day
that saw the schools taken from "the people's"
control. They were "the people." Experts manage our children's education, which was supposed,

in the old plan, to be the only thing that did not require any training. To superintend a brickyard demanded some knowledge, but anybody could run the public schools. It cost us an election to take that step. One of the Tammany district leaders, who knew what he was talking about, said to me after it was all over: "I knew we would win. Your bringing those foreigners here did the business. Our people believe in home rule. We kept account of the teachers you brought from out of town, and who spent the money they made here out of town, and it got to be the talk among the tenement people in my ward that their daughters would have no more show to get to be teachers. That did the business. We figured the school vote in the city at forty-two thousand, and I knew we could not lose." The "foreigners" were teachers from Massachusetts and other states, who had achieved a national reputation at their work.

There lies upon my table a copy of the minutes of the Board of Education of January 9, 1895, in which is underscored a report on a primary school in the Bronx. "It is a wooden shanty," is the inspector's account, "heated by stoves, and is a regular tinder box; cellar wet, and under one classroom only. This building was erected in order, I believe, to determine whether or not there was a school population in the neighborhood to warrant the purchase of property to erect a school on."

That was the way then of taking a school census, and the result was the utter failure of the compulsory education law to compel anything. To-day we have a biennial census, ordained by law, which, when at last it gets into the hands of some one who can count,[1] will tell us how many Jacob Beresheims are drifting upon the shoals of the street. And we have a truant school to keep them safe in. To it, says the law, no thief shall be committed. It is not yet five years since the burglar and the truant — which latter, having been refused admission to the school because there was not room for him, inconsequently was locked up for contracting idle ways — were herded in the Juvenile Asylum, and classified there in squads of those who were four feet, four feet seven, and over four feet seven! I am afraid I scandalized some good people during the fight for decency in this matter, by insisting that it ought to be considered a good mark for Jacob that he despised such schools as

[1] After two attempts that were not shining successes, the politicians at Albany and New York calmly dropped the matter, and for four years ignored the law. The Superintendent of Schools is at this writing (June, 1902) preparing to have the police take the child census, without which it is hard to see how he can know the extent of the problem he is wrestling with. Half-day classes are a fair index of the number of those anxious to get in; but they tell us nothing of the dangerous class who shun the schools.

were provided for him. But it was true. Except
for the risk of the burglar, the jail was preferable
by far. The woman into whose hands the management of the truant school fell, made out, after little
more than a year's experience, that of twenty-five
hundred so-called incorrigibles, the barest handful
— scarce sixty — were rightly so named, and even
these a little longer and tighter grip might probably
win over. For such a farm school is yet to be provided. The rest responded promptly to an appeal
to their pride. She "made it a personal matter"
with each of them, and the truant vanished; the
boy was restored. The burglar, too, made it a
personal matter in the old contact, and the result
was two burglars for one. I have yet to find any
one who has paid attention to this matter and is
not of the opinion that the truant school strikes
at the root of the problem of juvenile crime. After
thirty years of close acquaintance with the child
population of London, Mr. Andrew Drew, chairman of the Industrial Committee of the School
Board, declared his conviction that "truancy is to
be credited with nearly the whole of our juvenile
criminality." But for years there seemed to be no
way of convincing the New York School Board
that the two had anything to do with one another.
Even now it seems to be a case of one convinced
against his will being "of the same opinion still,"

Letter H Plan of Public School No. 165, showing Front on West 109th Street.

for, though the Superintendent of Schools speaks of that bar to the jail as preposterously inadequate, nothing is done to strengthen it.

Nothing on that tack. But there is a long leg and a short leg on the course, and I fancy Superintendent Snyder does the tacking on the long leg. Mr. Snyder builds New York's schools, and he does that which no other architect before his time ever did or tried; he "builds them beautiful." In him New York has one of those rare men who open windows for the soul of their time. Literally, he found barracks where he is leaving palaces to the people. If any one thinks this is overmeasure of praise, let him look at the "Letter H" school, now become a type, and see what he thinks of it. The idea suggested itself to him as meeting the demands of a site in the middle of a block, while he was poking about old Paris on a much-needed vacation, and now it stands embodied in a dozen beautiful schools on Manhattan Island, copies, every one, of the handsomest of French palaces, the Hôtel de Cluny. I cannot see how it is possible to come nearer perfection in the building of a public school. There is not a dark corner in the whole structure, from the splendid gymnasium under the red-tiled roof to the indoor playground on the street floor, which, when thrown into one with the two yards that lie enclosed in the arms of the H, give the children nearly an

acre of asphalted floor to romp on from street to
street; for the building sets right through the block,
with just such a front on the other street as it shows
on this one. If there be those yet upon whom the
notion grates that play and the looks of the school
should be counted in as educational factors, why,
let them hurry up and catch on. They are way
behind. The play through which the child "first
perceives moral relations" comes near being the
biggest and strongest factor in it all to-day; and as
for the five or ten thousand dollars put in for "the
looks" of things where the slum had trodden every
ideal and every atom of beauty into the dirt, I expect to live to see that prove the best investment a
city ever made.

We are getting the interest now in the new pride
of the boy in "his school," and no wonder. When
I think of the old Allen Street school, with its hard
and ugly lines, where the gas had to be kept burning even on the brightest days, recitations suspended every half-hour, and the children made to
practice calisthenics so that they should not catch
cold while the windows were opened to let in fresh
air; of the dark playground downstairs, with the
rats keeping up such a racket that one could hardly
hear himself speak at times; or of that other East
Side "playground" where the boys "weren't allowed to speak above a whisper," so as not to dis-

turb those studying overhead, I fancy that I can make out both the cause and the cure of the boy's desperation. "We try to make our schools pleasant enough to hold the children," wrote the Superintendent of Schools in Indianapolis to me once, and added that they had no truant problem worth bothering about. With the kindergarten and manual training firmly ingrafted upon the school course, as they are at last, and with it reaching out to enlist also the boy's play through playground and vacation schools, I shall be willing to turn the boy who will not come in over to the reformatory. They will not need to build a new wing to the jail for his safekeeping.

All ways lead to Rome. The reform in school building dates back, as does every other reform in New York, to the Mulberry Bend. It began there. The first school that departed from the soulless old tradition, to set beautiful pictures before the child's mind as well as dry figures on the slate, was built there. At the time I wanted it to stand in the park, hoping so to hasten the laying out of that; but although the Small Parks law expressly permitted the erection on park property of buildings for "the instruction of the people," the officials upon whom I pressed my scheme could not be made to understand that as including schools. Perhaps they were right. I catechised thirty-one Fourth Ward girls in a sewing school, about that time, twenty-six of whom had attended the public schools of the district more than a year. One wore a badge earned for excellence in her studies. In those days every street corner was placarded with big posters of Napoleon on a white horse riding through fire and

Public School No. 153, the Bronx.

smoke. There was one right across the street. Yet only one of the thirty-one knew who Napoleon was. She "thought she had heard of the gentleman before." It came out that the one impression she retained of what she had heard was that "the gentleman" had two wives, both at one time probably. They knew of Washington that he was the first

President of the United States, and cut down a cherry tree. They were sitting and sewing at the time almost on the identical spot on Cherry Hill[†] where he lived when he held the office. To the question who ruled before Washington the answer came promptly: no one; he was the first. They agreed reluctantly, upon further consideration, that there was probably "a king of America" before his day, and the Irish damsels turned up their noses at the idea. The people of Canada, they thought, were copper-colored. The same winter I was indignantly bidden to depart from a school in the Fourth Ward by a trustee who had heard that I had written a book about the slum and spoken of "his people" in it.

Those early steps in the reform path stumbled sadly over obstacles that showed what a hard pull we had ahead. I told in "The Making of an American" how I fared when I complained that the Allen Street school was overrun with rats, and how I went out to catch one of them to prove to the City Hall folk that I was not a liar, as they said. We won the fight for the medical inspection of the schools that has proved such a boon, against much opposition within the profession, from which we should have had only support. And this in face of evidence of a kind to convince anybody. I remember one of the exhibits. There had been a

†In 1789, George Washington lived in a four-story mansion on Cherry Hill (now Cherry Street, which runs parallel to the East River, between the Brooklyn and Manhattan Bridges, one block west of Water Street).

scarlet-fever epidemic on the lower West Side,
which the health inspectors finally traced to the
public school of the district. A boy with the disease had been turned loose before the "peeling"
was over, and had achieved phenomenal popularity
in the classroom by a trick he had of pulling the
skin from his fingers as one would skin a cat. The
pieces he distributed as souvenirs among his comrades, who carried them proudly home to show to
their admiring playmates who were not so lucky as
to sit on the bench with the clever lad. The epidemic followed as a matter of course. But though
the Health Department put through that reform,
when it came to inspecting the eyes of the children,
we lost. The cry that it would "interfere with
private practice" defeated us. The fact was easily
demonstrated that not only was ophthalmia rampant
in the schools with its contagion, but that the pupils
were made both near-sighted and stupid by the want
of proper arrangement of their seats and of themselves in their classrooms. But self-interest prevailed.
However, nothing is ever settled till it is settled
right. I have before me the results of an examination of thirty-six public schools containing 55,470 pupils. It was made by order of the Board of Health
this month (August, 1902), and ought to settle that
matter for good. Of the 55,470, not less than
6670 had contagious eye-disease; 2328 were cases of

operative trachoma, 3243 simple trachoma, and 1099
conjunctivitis. In one school in the most crowded
district of the East Side 22.2 per cent were so
afflicted. No wonder the doctors "were horrified"
at the showing. So was the President of the Board
of Health, who told me to-day that he would leave
no stone unturned until effective inspection of the
school children by eye-specialists had been assured.
So we go, step by step, ever forward.

Speaking of that reminds me of a mishap I had
in the Hester Street school, — the one with the
"frills" which the Board of Education cut off. I
happened to pass it after school hours, and went in
to see what sort of a playground the roof would
have made. I met no one on the way, and, finding
the scuttle open, climbed out and up the slant of
the roof to the peak, where I sat musing over our
lost chance, when the janitor came to close up. He
must have thought I was a crazy man, and my
explanation did not make it any better. He haled
me down, and but for the fortunate chance that the
policeman on the beat knew me, I should have been
taken to the lockup as a dangerous lunatic — all for
dreaming of a playground on the roof of a schoolhouse.

Janitor and Board of Commissioners to the contrary notwithstanding, the dream became real.
There stands another school in Hester Street to-

day within easy call, that has a roof playground where two thousand children dance under the harvest moon to the music of a brass band, as I shall tell you about hereafter — the joy of it to have that story to tell! — and all about are others like it, with

Girls' Playground on the Roof.

more coming every year. To the indignant amazement of my captor, the janitor, his school has been thrown open to the children in the summer vacation, and in the winter they put a boys' club in to worry him. What further indignities there are in store for him, in this day of "frills," there is no telling. The Superintendent of Schools told me only yesterday that he was going to Boston to look into new sources of worriment they have invented there. The world does move in spite of janitors. In two short years our school authorities advanced from the cautious proposition that it "was the sense" of the Board of Superintendents that the schoolhouses might well be used in the cause of education as neighborhood centres, etc., (1897), to the flat declaration that "every rational system of education should make provisions for play" (1899). And to cut off all chance of relapse into the old doubt whether "such things are educational," that laid so many of our hopes on the dusty shelf of the circumlocution office, the state legislature has expressly declared that the commonwealth will take the chance, which Boards of Education shunned, of a little amusement creeping in. The schools may be used for "purposes of recreation." To the janitor it must seem that the end of all things is at hand.

So the schools and their playgrounds were thrown open to the children during the long vacation, with kindergarten teachers to amuse them, and vacation schools tempted the little ones from the street into the cool shade of the classrooms. They wrought in wood and iron, they sang and they played and studied nature, — out of a barrel, to be sure, that came twice a week from Long Island filled with

" specimens "; but later on we took a hint from Chicago, and let the children gather their own specimens on excursions around the bay and suburbs of the city. That was a tremendous success. And there is better still coming, as I shall show presently. It sometimes seems to me as if we were here face to face with the very thing we are seeking and know not how to find. The mere hint that money might be lacking to pay for the excursions set the St. Andrew's Brotherhood men on Long Island to devising schemes for inviting the school children out on trolley and shore trips. What if they all, the Christian Endeavor, the Epworth League, and the other expressions of the same human desire to find the lost brother, who are looking about for something to try their young strength and enthusiasm on — what if they were to hitch on here and help pull the load that may get mired else? They need men and women in that work. Mere paid teaching will never do it. If they can only get them, I think we may be standing upon the threshold of something which shall bring us nearer to a universal brotherhood than all the consecration and all the badges yet devised. I am thinking of the children and of the chance to take them at once out of the slum and into our hearts, while making of the public school the door to a house of citizenship in which we shall all dwell together in full understanding. With-

The New Idea: a Stairway of Public School No. 170.

out that door the house will never be what we planned. And there is the key, all ready-made, in the children.

The mere contact with nature, even out of a barrel, brought something to those starved child lives that struck a new note. Sometimes it rang with a sharp and jarring sound. The boys in the Hester Street school could not be made to take an interest in the lesson on wheat until the teacher came to the effect of drought and a bad year on the farmer's pocket. Then they understood. They knew the process. Strikes cut into the earnings of Hester Street, small enough at the best of times, at frequent intervals, and the boys need not be told what a bad year means. No other kind ever occurs there. They learned the lesson on wheat in no time, after that. Oftener it was a gentler note that piped timidly in the strange place. A barrel of wild roses came one day, instead of the expected "specimens," and these were given to the children. They took them greedily. "I wondered," said the teacher, "if it was more love of the flower, or of getting something for nothing, no matter what." But even if it were largely the latter, there was still the rose. Nothing like it had come that way before, and without a doubt it taught its own lesson. The Italian child might have jumped for it more eagerly, but its beauty was not wasted in Jew-town, either. The baby kissed it, and it lay upon more than one wan cheek, and whispered, who knows what thought of hope and courage that were nearly gone. Even in Hester Street the wild rose from the hedge was not wasted.

The result of it all was wholesome and good, because it was common sense. The way to fight the slum in the children's lives is with sunlight and flowers and play, which their child hearts crave, if their eyes have never seen them. The teachers reported that the boys were easier to manage, more quiet, and played more fairly than before. The police reports showed that fewer were arrested or run over in the streets than in other years. A worse enemy was attacked than the trolley car or the truck. In the kindergarten at the Hull House in Chicago there hangs a picture of a harvest scene, with the man wiping his brow, and a woman resting at his feet. Miss Addams[†] told me that a little girl with an old face picked it out among all the rest, and considered it long and gravely. " Well," she said, when her inspection was finished, " he knocked her down, didn't he ? " A two hours' argument for kindergartens or vacation schools could not have put it stronger or better.

It is five seasons since the Board of Education took over the work begun by the Association for Improving the Condition of the Poor as an object lesson for us all, and I have before me the schedule for this summer's work, just begun. It embraces seventeen vacation schools in which the boys are taught basketry, weaving, chair-caning, sloyd, fret-sawing, and how to work in leather and iron, while the girls learn sewing, millinery, embroidering, knitting, and the domestic arts, besides sharing in the boys' work where they can. There are thirty-five school playgrounds with kindergarten and gymnasiums and games, and half a dozen of the play piers are used for the same purpose. In twelve open-air playgrounds and parks, teachers sent by the Board of Education lead the children's

†Jane Addams (1836–1935) founded Hull House, a social settlement, in Chicago in 1899. In 1910 Ms. Addams was elected the first woman president of the National Conference of Social Work. A feminist and a pacifist, she founded the National Federation of Settlements in 1911, was president of the Women's International League for Peace and Freedom (1919–1935), and shared the Nobel Peace Prize in 1931.

play, and in as many more public baths teach boys and girls to swim on alternate days. In Crotona Park, up in the Bronx, under big spreading oaks and maples, athletic meets are held of boys from down-town and up-town schools in friendly rivalry, and the Frog Hollow Gang, that wrecked railroad trains there in my recollection, is a bad memory. Over at Hudsonbank on the site of the park that is coming there, teams hired by the Board of Education are ploughing up the site of Stryker's Lane, and the young toughs of the West Side who held that the world owed them a living and collected it as they could, are turning truck farmers. They are planting potatoes, and gardening, and learning the secret of life that the living is his who can earn it. The world "do move." No argument is needed now to persuade those who hold the purse strings that all this is "good business." Instead, the mayor of the city is asking the Board of Education to tell him of more and better ways of putting the machinery to use. The city will foot the bill, if we will show them how. And we will show them how.

The last four years have set us fifty years ahead, and there is no doubling on that track now. Where we had one kindergarten when I was put out of the Fourth Ward school by a trustee for daring to intrude there to find out what they were teaching, we have a hundred and fifteen at this writing in Manhattan alone, and soon we shall have as many as five hundred that are part of the public school in the greater city. "The greatest blessing which the nineteenth century bequeathed to little

Truck Farming on the Site of Stryker's Lane.

children," Superintendent Maxwell calls the kindergarten, and since the children are our own to-morrow, he might have said to all of us, to the state. The kindergarten touch is upon the whole system of teaching. Cooking, the only kind of temperance preaching that counts for anything in a school course, is taught in the girls' classes. A minister of justice declared in the Belgian Chamber that the nation was reverting to a new form of barbarism, which he described by the term "alcoholic barbarism," and pointed out as its first cause the "insufficiency of the food procurable by the working classes." He referred to the quality, not the quantity. The United States experts, who lately made a study of the living habits of the poor in New York, spoke of it as a common observation that "a not inconsiderable amount of the prevalent intemperance can be traced to poor food and unattractive home tables." The toasting-fork in Jacob's sister's hand beats preaching in the campaign against the saloon, just as the boys' club beats the police club in fighting the gang.

The cram and the jam are being crowded out as common-sense teaching steps in and takes their place, and the "three H's," the head, the heart, and the hand, — a whole boy, — are taking the place too long monopolized by the "three R's." There was need of it. It had seemed sometimes as if, in our anxiety lest he should not get enough, we were in danger of stuffing the boy to the point of making a hopeless dunce of him. It is a higher function of the school to teach principles than to impart facts merely. Teaching the boy municipal politics and a thousand other things to make a good citizen of him, instead of so filling him with love of his country and pride in its traditions that he is bound to take the right stand when the time comes, is as though one were to attempt to put all the law of the state into its constitution to make it more binding. The result would be hopeless congestion and general uselessness.

It comes down to the teacher in the end, and there are ten thousand of them in our big city.[1] To them, too, a day of deliverance has come. Half the machine teaching, the wooden output of our public schools in the past, I believe was due to the practical isolation of the teachers between the tyranny of politics and the distrust of those who had good cause to fear the politician and his work. There was never a more saddening sight than that of the teachers standing together in an almost solid body to resist reform of the school system as an attack upon them. There was no pretence on their part that the schools did not need reform. They knew better. They fought for their places. Throughout the fight no word came from them of the children's rights. They imagined that theirs were in danger, and they had no thought for anything else. We gathered then the ripe fruit of politics, and it will be a long while, I suppose, before we get the taste out of our mouths. But the grip of politics on

[1] On May 31, 1902, there were 10,036 class teachers in elementary schools in the Greater New York, exclusive of principals and the non-teaching staffs, and of the high school teachers. With these, the total number was 11,570, with a register of 445,964 pupils.

our schools has been loosened, if not shaken off altogether, and the teacher's slavery is at an end, if
she herself so wills it.   Once hardly thought worthy
of a day laborer's hire, she ranks to-day with a
policeman in pay and privilege.   The day that sees

Doorway of Public School No. 165.

her welcomed as an honored guest in every home
with a child in school will break the last of her
bonds, and do more for the schools and for us than
any one thing I can think of.   Until that day comes
the teachers, as a class apart, will have interests
apart, or feel that they have, and will be bound to

stand together to defend them; and they will work for pay. But for the real work of a teacher no one can ever pay her.

The day is coming. The windows of the school-house have been thrown open, and life let in with the sunlight. The time may be not far distant when ours shall be schools "for discovering aptitude," in Professor Felix Adler's wise plan. The problem is a vast one, even in its bulk; every year seats must be found on the school benches for twenty thousand additional children. In spite of all we have done, there are to-day in the greater city nearly thirty thousand children in half-day or part-time classes, waiting their chance. But that it can and will be solved no one can doubt. We have just *got* to, that is all.

In the solution the women of New York will have had no mean share. In the struggle for school reform they struck the telling blows, and the credit of the victory was justly theirs. The Public Education Association, originally a woman's auxiliary to Good Government Club E, has worked as energetically with the school authorities in the new plan as it fought to break down the old and secure decency. It has opened many windows for little souls by hanging schoolrooms with beautiful casts and pictures, and forged at the same time new and strong links in the chain that bound the

boy all too feebly to the school. At a time when
the demand of the boys of the East Side for club
room, which was in itself one of the healthiest signs
of the day, had reached an exceedingly dangerous
pass, the Public Education Association broke ground
that will yet prove the most fertile field of all. The
Raines law saloon, quick to discern in the new demand the gap that would divorce it by and by from
the man, attempted to bridge it by inviting the boy
in under its roof. Occasionally the girl went along.
A typical instance of how the scheme worked was
brought to my attention at the time by the head
worker of the college settlement. The back room
of the saloon was given to the club free of charge,
with the understanding that the boy members
should " treat." As a means of raising the needed
funds, the club hit upon the plan of fining members
ten cents when they " got funny."

To defeat this device of the devil some way
must be found; but club room was scarce among
the tenements. The Good Government Clubs
proposed to the Board of Education that it open
the empty classrooms at night for the children's
use. It was my privilege to plead their cause
before the School Board, and to obtain from it
the necessary permission, after some hesitation
and doubt as to whether " it was educational."
The Public Education Association assumed the

responsibility for "the property," and the Hester
Street school was opened. The property was not
molested; only one window was broken that winter
by a stray ball, and that was promptly paid for
by those who broke it. But the boys who met
there under Miss Winifred Buck's management
learned many a lesson of self-control and practical
wisdom that proved "educational" in the highest
degree. Her plan is simplicity itself. Through
their play,— the meeting usually begins with a
romp,— in quarters where there is not too much
elbow-room, the boys learn the first lesson of
respecting one another's rights. The subsequent
business meeting puts them upon the fundamentals
of civilized society, as it were. Out of the debate
of the question, Do we want boys who swear,
steal, gamble, and smoke cigarettes? grow convic-
tions as to why these vices are wrong that put
"the gang" in its proper light. Punishment comes
to appear, when administered by the boys themselves, a natural consequence of law-breaking, in
defence of society; and the boy is won. He can
thenceforward be trusted to work out his own
salvation. If he does it occasionally with excessive
unction, remember how recent was his conversion.
"*Resolved*, that wisdom is better than wealth," was
rejected as a topic for discussion by one of the
clubs, because "everybody knows it is." This was

in the Tenth Ward.   If temptation had come that
way in the shape of a push-cart with pineapples
— we are all human!   Anyway, they had learned
the right.

That was the beginning of a work of which we
shall, I hope, hear a good deal more hereafter.   It is
all in its infancy yet, this attempt on the part of
the municipality to get the boys off the street and
out of the reach of the saloon.   A number of
schools were thrown open, where the crowds were
greatest, for evening play and for clubs, and sometimes they laid hold of the youngster and sometimes not.   It was a question again of the man
or the woman who was at the helm.   One school
I found that surged with a happy crowd.   It was
over at Rivington and Suffolk streets, No. 160.
Oh, how I wish they would soon stop this hopeless
numbering of our schools, and call them after our
great and good men, as Superintendent Maxwell
pleads, so that " the name of every school may in
itself be made a lesson in patriotism and good citizenship to its pupils."   There they would be in
their right place.   One alderman got the idea during the Strong reform administration, but they
hitched the names to the new parks instead of the
schools, and that turned out wrong.   So they have
the Ham Fish Park for Hamilton Fish, the "Sewer"
Park for William H. Seward, the Thomas Jefferson

Park up-town which no one will ever call anything
but the Little Italy Park, and the good name of
De Witt Clinton put to the bad use of spoiling
beautiful " Hudsonbank." Only, the effort will be
wasted. The old name will stick. How different

Main Entrance of Public School No. 153.

if the new schools had been called after these states-
men! And what a chance to get their pupils interested! In the " Alexander Hamilton School," for
instance, where " the Grange " and his thirteen
trees abide yet.

But that is another story. I was thinking of the
Jackson Pleasure Club of boys from eleven to thir-

teen which I found in session in No. 160, and of its very instructive constitution. I am going to print it here entire for the instruction of some good people who don't understand. The boys got it all up themselves with the help of a copy of the United States Constitution and the famous " Stamp Act."

CONSTITUTION OF THE JACKSON PLEASURE CLUB

EVENING RECREATION CENTRE P. S. No. 160, NEW YORK
CITY

We the boys of the J. P. C. in order to form a perfect club, we establish justice insure domestic tranquillity provide for the common defence. We promote the general welfare and secure the blessing of liberty to ourselves and our descendants to establish the Constitution for the J. P. C.

No boys can be members who are less than thirteen years and must be from the 7th Grammar on.

No member can be President or Vice President unless 6 months in club.

All officers will keep their term six months.

The officers can not commit a law until it is passed by the members. If it is an important one it will be passed by votes. By this I mean that if $\frac{5}{8}$ of the members pass it is passed if $\frac{1}{2}$ is passed it is not passed.

Several committees are appointed to look over these rules which seldom happen on the streets.

If any member or officer is seen gambling, smoking or fighting a fine of $0.02 will be asked and must be paid the next meeting.

Special meetings will be held each month. Meetings will be held at 8 o'clock P.M. to 9 P.M.

No secrets or slang language or nicknames allowed or a fine of $.03 is asked.

If any body receites a recitation and makes a mistake he is not to be laughed at or a fine of $.02 must be paid.

If any member takes the laws into his own hands and interferes with the president or any other officers or walks up and down the meeting room or draws pictures on the boards a fine of $.02 will be paid.

Any one who is spoken to 3 times about order will be put out for that meeting.

Amendment 1. No member will be allowed to go on a stranger's roof, or a fine of $.03 will be asked.

Why not on a stranger's roof? Because flying kites, up there the boys run across and interfere with the neighbor's pigeons, which is apt to make him wroth. So you see it is all in the interests of "domestic tranquillity and the common defence." They are not meaningless phrases, those big words, they are the boy's ideas of self-government, of a real democracy, struggling through in our sight. And suppose he does walk on rhetorical stilts, he has precedent and will show it to you. A nation learned to walk on them. Who shall say they are not good enough for him?

But to return to what I was speaking about: with the women to lead, the school has even turned the tables on the jail and invaded it bodily. For now

nearly five years the Public Education Association
has kept school in the Tombs, for the boys locked
up their awaiting trial.   Of thirty-one pupils on this
school register, when I examined it one day, twelve
were charged with burglary, four with highway robbery, and three with murder.   That was the gang
run to earth at last.   Better late than never.   The
windows of their prison overlooked the spot where
the gallows used to stand that cut short many a
career such as they pursued.   They were soberly
attentive to their studies, which were of a severely
practical turn.   Their teacher, Mr. David Willard,
who was a resident of the university settlement in
its old Delancey Street home has his own sound
view of how to head off the hangman.   Daily and
nightly he gathers about him, in the house on
Chrystie Street where he makes his home, half
the boys and girls of the neighborhood, whom he
meets as their friend, on equal terms.   Mr. Willard,
though a young man, is one of the most unique per-
sonages in the city.   He is now one of the proba-
tion officers, under the new law which seeks to save
the young offender rather than to wreak vengeance
upon him, and his influence for good is great.   The
house in Chrystie Street is known far and wide as
"the Children's House."   They have their clubs
there, and their games, of which Willard is the
heart and soul.   "I never saw anything remarkable

in him," said one of his old college professors to
me; "if anything, he was rather a dull student."
It seems, then, that even colleges are not always
institutions for "discovering aptitude." It was reserved for Chrystie Street in Willard's case.

Once a week another teacher comes to the Tombs[†]
school, and tells the boys of our city's history, its
famous buildings and great men, trying so to
arouse their interest as a first step toward a citizen's
pride. This one also is sent by a club of women,
the City History Club, which in five years has done
strange things among the children. It sprang from
the proposition of Mrs. Robert Abbe that the man
and the citizen has his birth in the boy, and that to
love a thing one must know it first. The half-dozen
classes that were started for the study of our city's
history have swelled into many scores of times that
number, with a small army of pupils. The pregnant fact was noted early by the teachers, that the
immigrant boy easily outstrips in interest for his
adopted home the native, who perchance turns up
his nose at him, and later very likely complains of
the "unscrupulousness" of the Jew, who forged
ahead of him in business as well.

The classes meet in settlement, school, or church
to hear about the deeds of the fathers, and, when they
have listened and read, go with their teachers and see
for themselves the church where Washington wor-

†The prison commonly known as the Tombs officially was the
Manhattan House of Detention for Men.

shipped, the graves where the great dead lie, the fields where they fought and bled. And when the little Italian asks, with shining eyes, " Which side were *we* on?" who can doubt that the lesson has sunk into a heart that will thenceforward beat more loyally for the city of his home? We have not any too much pride in our city, the best of us, and that is why we let it be run by every scalawag boss who comes along to rob us. In all the land there is no more historic building than Fraunces' Tavern, where Washington bade good-by to his officers; but though the very Chamber of Commerce was organized there, the appeal of patriotic women has not availed to save it to the people as a great relic of the past. The last time I was in it a waiter, busy with a lot of 'longshoremen who were eating their lunch and drinking their beer in the " Long Room," had hung his dirty apron on a plaster bust of the Father of his Country that stood upon the counter about where he probably sat at the historic feast. My angry remonstrance brought only an uncomprehending stare for reply.

But in spite of the dullards, the new life I spoke of, the new sense of responsibility of our citizenship, is stirring. The People's Institute draws nightly audiences to the great hall of the Cooper Institute for the discussion of present problems and social topics — audiences largely made up of workingmen

more or less connected with the labor movement.
The " People's Club," an outgrowth of the Institute,
offers a home for the lonely wage-earner, man or
woman, and more accept its offer every year. It
has now nearly four hundred members, one fourth
of them women. Every night its rooms at 241

Superintendent C. B. J. Snyder, who builds our Beautiful Schools.

East Fourteenth Street are filled. Classes for
study and recreation are organized right along.
The People's University Extension Society invades
the home, the nursery, the kindergarten, the club,
wherever it can, with help and counsel to mothers
with little children, to young men and to old. In

a hundred ways those who but yesterday neither knew nor cared how the other half lived are reaching out and touching the people's life. The social settlements labor unceasingly, and where there was one a dozen years ago there are forty. Down on the lower East Side, the Educational Alliance conducts from the Hebrew Institute an energetic campaign among the Jewish immigrants that reaches many thousands of souls, two-thirds of them children, every day in the week. More than threescore clubs hold meetings in the building on Saturday and Sunday. Under the same roof the Baron Hirsch Fund teaches the children of refugee Jews the first elements of American citizenship, love for our language and our flag, and passes them on to the public schools within six months of their landing, the best material they receive from anywhere.

So the boy is being got ready for dealing, in the years that are to come, with the other but not more difficult problems of setting his house to rights, and ridding it of the political gang which now misrepresents him and us. And justice to Jacob is being evolved. Not yet without obstruction and dragging of feet. The excellent home library plan that proved so wholesome in the poor quarters of Boston has only lately caught on in New York, because of difficulty in securing the visitors upon whom the plan depends for its success.[1] The same want has kept the boys' club from reaching the development that would apply the real test to it as a barrier against the slum. There are fifteen clubs for every Winifred Buck that is in sight. From the City History Club, the Charity Organization Society, from everywhere, comes the same complaint. The hardest thing in the world to give is still one's self. But it is all the time getting to be easier. There are daily more women and men who, thinking of the boy, can say, and do, with my friend of the college settlement, when an opportunity to enter a larger field was offered her, "No, I am content to stay here, to be ready for Johnnie when he wants me."

Justice for the boy, and for his father. An itin-

---

[1] The managers of the New York Public Library have found a way, and have maintained twenty-seven home libraries during the past year (1901): little cases of from fifteen to forty books entrusted to the care of some family in the tenement. Miss Adeline E. Brown, who is in charge of the work, reports a growing enthusiasm for it. The librarian calls weekly. "We come very near to the needs of these families," she writes, "the visit meaning more to them than the books. In nearly every case we allow the books to be given out at any time by the child who glories in the honor of being librarian. In one wretched tenement, on the far East Side, we are told that the case of books is taken down into the yard on Sunday afternoon, and neighbors and lodgers have the use of them." It is satisfactory to know that the biggest of the home libraries is within stone's throw of Corlear's Hook, which the "Hook Gang" terrorized with rapine and murder within my recollection.

Miss Brown adds that "the girls prefer bookcases with doors of glass, as they like to scrub it with sapolio, but the boys are more interested in the lock and key."

erant Jewish glazier, crying his wares, was beckoned into a stable by the foreman, and bidden to replace a lot of broken panes, enough nearly to exhaust his stock. When, after working half the day, he asked for his pay, he was driven from the place with jeers and vile words. Raging and impotent, he went back to his poor tenement, cursing a world in which there was no justice for a poor man. If he had next been found ranting with anarchists against the social order, would you have blamed him? He found instead, in the Legal Aid Society, a champion that pleaded his cause and compelled the stableman to pay him his wages. For a hundred thousand such — more shame to us — this society has meant all that freedom promised: justice to the poor man. It too has earned a place among the forces that are working out through the new education the brighter day, for it has taught the lesson which all the citizens of a free state need most to learn — respect for law.

CHAPTER XIV

THE BAND BEGINS TO PLAY

" Nothing in this world of ours is settled until it is settled right." From the moment we began the fight for the children's play there was but one ending to that battle; but it did seem sometimes a long way off, never farther than when, just four months ago, the particular phase of it that had seemed to promise most was officially stamped as nonsense. The playgrounds on top of the big schoolhouses, which were to be the neighborhood roof-gardens of our fond imaginings, were " of little use," said the school committee that had them in charge. The people wouldn't go there. So, then, let them be given up. And a school commissioner with whom I argued the case on the way home responded indulgently that some of my notions " were regarded as Utopian," however sincerely held.

Let me see, that was in May. The resolution I speak of had passed the Committee on Care of Buildings on April 18.[1] To-day is the 20th of

---

[1] On the day it was published the newspapers reported the killing in the streets of three children by trucks.

August, and I have just come home from an evening spent on one of those identical school-roofs
under the electric lamps, a veritable fairyland of delight. The music and the song and laughter of
three thousand happy children ring in my ears yet.
It was a long, laborious journey up all the flights of
stairs to that roof, for I am not as young as I was
and sometimes scant of breath; but none sweeter
did I ever take save the one under the wild-rose
hedge I told of in " The Making of an American "
when I went to claim my bride. Ah! brethren,
what are we that we should ever give up, or doubt
the justice of His fight who bade us let the little
ones come unto Him and to clear the briers and
thorns, that choked the path, from their way?

Seven years we hacked away at the briers in that
path. It is so long since the state made it law
that a playground should go with every public
school, five since as secretary of the Small Parks
Committee I pleaded with the Board of Education
to give the roof playground to the neighborhood
after school hours. I remember that the question
was asked who would keep order, and the answer,
" The police will be glad to." I recalled without
trouble the time when they had to establish patrol
posts on the tenement roofs in defence against the
roughs whom the street had trained to rebellion
against law and order. But I was a police reporter;

they were not. They didn't understand. The play-school came; the indoor playgrounds were thrown open evenings under the pressure they brought in their train. And at that point we took a day off, as it were, to congratulate one another on how wondrous smart and progressive we had been. The machinery we had started we let be, to run itself.

It ran into the old rut. The janitor got it in tow, and presently we heard from the "play centres" that "the children didn't avail themselves" of their privileges. On the roof playground the janitor had turned the key. The Committee on Care of Buildings spoke his mind: "They were of little use; too hot in summer and too cold in winter." We were invited to quit our fooling and resume business at the old stand of the three R's, and let it go with that. That was what schools were for. It takes time, you see, to grow an idea, as to grow a colt or a boy, to its full size.

President Burlingham, who in his day drew the bill that made it lawful to use the schools for neighborhood purposes other than the worship of those same three R's, went around with me one night to see what ailed the children who would not play.

In the Mulberry Bend school the janitor had carefully removed the gymnastic apparatus the boys were aching for, and substituted four tables, around which they sat playing cards under the eye of a policeman.

They were "educational" cards, with pictures of Europe and Asia and Africa and America on, but it required only half a minute's observation to tell us that they were gambling — betting on which educational card would turn up next. What the city had provided was a course in scientific gambling with the policeman to see that it was done right. And over at Market and Monroe streets, where they have an acre or more of splendid asphalted floor — such a ball room! — and a matchless yard, the best in the city, twoscore little girls were pitifully cooped up in a corner, being *taught* something, while outside a hundred clamored to get in, making periodic rushes at the door, only to encounter there a janitor's assistant with a big club and a roar like a bull to frighten them away. "Orders," he told us. The yard was dark and dismal. That was the school by the way, whence the report came that they "hadn't availed themselves" of the opportunity to play.

It helped, when that story was told. There is nothing in our day like the facts, and they came out that time. There was the roof-garden on the Educational Alliance Building†with its average of more than five thousand a day, young and old, last summer (a total of 344,424 for the season), in flat contradiction of the claim that the children "wouldn't go up on the roof." Not, surely, if it was only to encoun-

---

†The building, constructed in 1891, is across East Broadway from Seward Park. The Educational Alliance formerly was known as the Hebrew Institute (1889–91). Until 1900, when Yiddish was introduced, its evening classes for adults were offered in English only. In later decades, classes were offered in Spanish and other languages.

ter a janitor with a club there. But a brass band now? There were a few professional shivers at that, but our experience with the one we set playing in the park on Sunday, years ago, came to the rescue. When it had played its last piece to end and there burst forth as with one voice from the mighty throng, " Praise God from whom all blessings flow!" some doubts were set at rest for all time. They were never sensible, but after that they were silly.

So the janitor was bidden bring out his key. Electric lights were strung. " We will save the money somewhere else," said Mayor Low. The experiment was made with five schools, all on the crowded East Side.

I was at dinner with friends at the University Settlement, directly across from which, on the other corner, is one of the great new schools, No. 20, I think. We had got to the salad when through the open window there came a yell of exultation and triumph that made me fairly jump in my chair. Below in the street a mighty mob of children and mothers had been for half an hour besieging the door of the schoolhouse. The yell signalized the opening of it by the policeman in charge. Up the stairs surged the multitude. We could see them racing, climbing, toiling, according to their years, for the goal above where the band was tuning up. One little fellow with a trousers leg and a half,

and a pair of suspenders and an undershirt as his
only other garments, labored up the long flight,
carrying his baby brother on his back. I watched
them go clear up, catching glimpses of them at every
turn, and then I went up after.

I found them in a corner, propped against the
wall, a look of the serenest bliss on their faces as
they drank it all in. It was *their* show at last.
The band was playing "Alabama," and fifteen
hundred boys and girls were dancing, hopping,
prancing to the tune, circling about and about
while they sang and kept time to the music. When
the chorus was reached, every voice was raised to
its shrillest pitch: "Way — down — yonder — in —
the — cornfield." And for once in my life the sug-
gestion of the fields and the woods did not seem
hopelessly out of place in the Tenth Ward crowds.
Baby in its tired mother's lap looked on wide-eyed,
out of the sweep of the human current.

The band ceased playing, and the boys took up
some game, dodging hither and thither in pursuit
of a ball. How they did it will ever be a mystery
to me. There did not seem to be room for another
child, but they managed as if they had it all to
themselves. There was no disorder; no one was
hurt, or even knocked down, unless in the game,
and that *was* the game, so it was as it should be.
Right in the middle of it, the strains of "Sunday

Afternoon," all East Side children's favorite, burst forth, and out of the seeming confusion came rhythmic order as the whole body of children moved, singing, along the floor.

Down below, the deserted street — deserted for once in the day — had grown strangely still. The policeman nodded contentedly: "good business, indeed." This was a kind of roof patrol he could appreciate. Nothing to do; less for to-morrow, for here they were not planning raids on the grocer's stock. They were happy, and when children are happy, they are safe, and so are the rest of us. It is the policeman's philosophy, and it is worth taking serious note of.

A warning blast on a trumpet and the "Star-spangled Banner" floated out over the house-tops. The children ceased dancing; every boy's cap came off, and the chorus swelled loud and clear:

> " — in triumph shall wave
> O'er the land of the free and the home of the brave."

The light shone upon the thousand upturned faces. Scarce one in a hundred of them all that did not bear silent witness to persecution which had driven a whole people over the sea, without home, without flag. And now — my eyes filled with tears. I said it: I am getting old and silly.

It was so at the still bigger school at Hester and

Orchard streets. At the biggest of them all, and the finest, the same No. 177 where the janitor's assistant "shooed" the children away with his club, the once dismal yard had been festooned with electric lamps that turned night into day, and about the band-stand danced nearly three thousand boys and girls to the strains of "Money Musk," glad to be alive and there. A ball-room forsooth! And it is going to be better still; for once the ice has been broken, there are new kinks coming in this dancing programme that is the dear dissipation of the East Side. What is to hinder the girls, when the long winter days come, from inviting in the fellows, and papa

The Fellows and Papa and Mamma shall be invited in yet.

and mamma, for a real dance that shall take the wind
out of the sails of the dance-halls? Nothing in all
the world. Nor even will there be anything to stop
Superintendent Maxwell from taking a turn himself,
as he said he would, or me either, if I haven't
danced in thirty years. I just dare him to try.

The man in charge of the ball-room at No. 177 —
I shall flatly refuse to call it a yard — said that he
didn't believe in any other rule than order, and
nearly took my breath away, for just then I had a
vision of the club in the doorway; but it was only a
vision. The club was not there. As he said it, he
mounted the band-stand and waved the crowd to
order with his speaking-trumpet.

"A young lady has just lost her gold watch on
the floor," he said. "It is here under your feet.
Bring it to me, the one who finds it." There was a
curious movement of the crowd, as if every unit in it
turned once about itself and bowed, and presently a
shout of discovery went up. A little girl with a
poor shawl pinned about her throat came forward
with the watch. The manager waved his trumpet at
me with a bright smile.

"You see it works."

The entire crowd fell in behind him in an ecstatic
cake-walk, expressive of its joy and satisfaction, and
so they went, around and around.

On that very corner, just across the way, a dozen

years ago, I gave a stockbroker a good blowing up for hammering his cellar door full of envious nails to prevent the children using it as a slide. It was all the playground they had.

The "Slide" that was the Children's only Playground once.

On the way home I stopped at the first of all the public schools to acquire a roof playground, to see how they did it there. The janitor had been vanquished, but the pedagogue was in charge, and he had organized the life out of it all. The children sat around listless, and made little or no attempt to dance. A harassed teacher was vainly trying to form the girls into ranks for exercises of some kind.

They held up their hands in desperate endeavor to get her ear, only to have them struck down impatiently, or to be summarily put out if they tried again. They did not want to exercise. They wanted to play. I tried to voice their grievance to the "doctor" who presided.

"Not at all," he said decisively; "there must be system, system!"

"Tommyrot!" said my Chicago friend at my elbow, and I felt like saying "thank you!" I don't know but I did. They have good sense in Chicago. Jane Addams is there.

The doctor resumed his efforts to teach the boys something, having explained to me that downstairs, where they are when it rains, there were seven distinct echoes to bother the band. Two girls "spieled" in the corner, a kind of dancing that is not favored in the playground. There had been none of that at the other places. The policeman eyed the show with a frown.

So there was a fly in our ointment, after all. But for all that, the janitor is downed, his day dead. This of all things at last has been "settled right," and the path cleared for the children's feet, not in New York only, but everywhere and for all time. I, too, am glad to be alive in the time that saw it done.

CHAPTER XV

"NEIGHBOR" THE PASSWORD

TRULY, we live in a wonderful time. Here have I been trying to bring up to date this account of the battle with the slum, and in the doing of it have been compelled, not once, but half a dozen times, to go back and wipe out what I had written because it no longer applied. The ink was not dry on the page that pleaded for the helpless ones who have to leave the hospital before they are fit to take up their battle with the world, so as to make room for others in instant need — one of the saddest of sights that has wrung the heart of the philanthropist these many years — when I read in my paper of the four million dollar gift to build a convalescents' home at once. I would rather be in that man's shoes than be the Czar of all the Russias. I would rather be blessed by the grateful heart of man or woman, who but just now was without hope, than have all the diamonds in the Kimberley mines.† Yes, ours is the greatest of all times. Since I started putting these pages in shape for the printer, the Child Labor Committee and the Tuberculosis Com-

†The city of Kimberley, in South Africa, and the nearby diamond mines had been in the world news in 1900, when the British defenders were besieged by the Boers during the Boer War.

mittee have been formed to put up bars against the slum where it roamed unrestrained; the Tenement House Department has been organized and got under way, and the knell of the double-decker and the twenty-five-foot lot has been sounded. Two hundred tenements are going up to-day under the new law, that are in all respects model buildings, as good as the City and Suburban Home Company's houses, though built for revenue only. All over the greater city the libraries are rising which, when Mr. Carnegie's munificent plan[†] has been worked out to the full, are to make, with the noble central edifice in Bryant Park, the greatest free library system of any day, with a princely fortune to back it.[1] New bridges are spanning our rivers, tunnels are being bored, engineers are blasting a way for the city out of its bonds on crowded Manhattan, devotion and high principle rule once more at the City Hall, Cuba is free, Tammany is out; the boy is coming into his rights; the toughs of Hell's Kitchen have taken to farming on the site of Stryker's Lane, demolished and gone.

And here upon my table lies a letter from the head-worker of the University Settlement, which the

[1] The Astor, Lenox, and Tilden foundations represent a total of some seven millions of dollars. The great central library, erected by the city, is to cost five millions, and the fifty branches for which the city gives the sites and Andrew Carnegie the buildings, $5,200,000. The city's contribution for maintenance will be over half a million yearly.

[†] The original offer made in 1901 by steel-industry millionaire Andrew Carnegie (1835–1919) was to build 65 branch libraries, in all of New York City's boroughs except Richmond (Staten Island). By 1902 it was agreed that Staten Island would get its share of free public lending libraries, but the total was reduced to 50. By the end of 1905, 17 libraries were open.

postman brought half an hour ago, that lets more
daylight in, it seems to me, than all the rest.   He has
been thinking, he writes, of how to yoke the public
school and the social settlement together, and the
conviction that comes to everybody who thinks to
solve problems, has come to him, too, that the way
to do a thing is to do it.   So he proposes, since they
need another house over at the West Side branch,
to acquire it by annexing the public school and
turning " all the force and power that is in the
branch into the bare walls of the school, there to
develop a social spirit and an enthusiasm " among
young and old that shall make of the school truly
the neighborhood house and soul.   And he asks us
all to fall in.

I say it lets daylight in, because we have all felt for
some time that something like this was bound to
come, only how was not clear yet.   Here is this immense need of a tenement house population of more
than two million souls: something to take the place,
as far as anything can, of the home that isn't there, a
place to meet other than the saloon ; a place for the
young to do their courting — there is no room for it
in the tenement, and the street is not the place for it,
yet it has got to be done ; a place to make their elders
feel that they are men and women, something else
than mere rent-paying units.   Why, it was this very
need that gave birth to the social settlement among

us, and we see now that with the old machinery it
does not supply it and never can. " I can reach the
people of just about two blocks about me here,"
said this same head worker of the same settlement
to me an evening or two ago, "and that is all."
But there are hundreds of blocks filled with hungry
minds and souls. A hundred settlements would be
needed where there is one.

The churches could not meet the need. They
ought to and some day they will, when we build
the church down-town and the mission up-town. But
now they can't. There are not enough of them, for
one thing. They do try; for only the other day,
when I went to tell the Methodist ministers of it,
and of how they ought to back up the effort to have
the public school thrown open on Sundays for concerts, lectures, and the like, after the first shock of
surprise they pulled themselves together man-
fully and said that they would do it. They saw
with me that it is a question, not of damaging
the Lord's Day, but of wresting it from the devil,
who has had it all this while over there on the
East Side, and on the West Side too. All along
the swarming streets with no church in sight, but a
saloon on every corner, stand the big schoolhouses
with their spacious halls, empty and silent and grim,
waiting to have the soul breathed into them that
alone can make their teaching effective for good

citizenship. They belong to the people. Why should they not be used by the people Sunday and week-day and day and night, for whatever will serve their ends — if the janitor has a fit?

Now here come the social settlements with their plan of doing it. What claim have they to stand in the gap?

This one, that they are there now, though they do not fill it. The gap has been too much for them. They need the help of those they came to succor quite as much as *they* need them. I have no desire to find fault with any one who wants to help his neighbor. God forbid! I am not even a settlement worker. But when I read, as I did yesterday, a summing up of the meaning of settlements by three or four residents in such houses, and see education, reform politics, local improvements, legislation, characterized as the aim and objects of settlement work, I am afraid somebody is on the wrong track. Those things are good, provided they spring naturally from the intellectual life that moves in and about the settlement house; indeed, unless they do, something has quite decidedly miscarried there. But they are not the object. When I pick up a report of one settlement and another, and find them filled with little essays on the people and their ways and manners, as if the settlement were some kind of a laboratory where they prepare human specimens for inspection and classification, — stick them on pins like bugs and hold them up and twirl them so as to let us have a good look, — then I know that somebody has wandered away off, and that *he knows he has*, for all he is making a brave show trying to persuade himself and us that

A Cooking Lesson in Vacation School: the Best Temperance Sermon.

it was worth the money. No use going into that farther. The fact is that we have all been groping. We saw the need and started to fill it, and in the strange surroundings we lost our bearings and the password. We got to be sociological instead of neighborly. It is not the same thing.

Here is the lost password: "neighbor." That is all

there is to it.   If a settlement isn't the neighbor of
those it would reach, it is nothing at all.   " A place,"
said the sub-warden of Toynbee Hall in the discussion I spoke of, and set it on even keel in an instant,
"a place of good will rather than of good works."
That is it.   We had become strangers, had drifted
apart, and the settlement came to introduce us to
one another again, as it were, to remind us that
we were neighbors.   And because that was the
one thing above all that was wanted, it became an
instant success where it was not converted into
a social experiment station; and even that could
not kill it.   If any one doubts that I have the right
password, let him look for the proof in the organization this past month of a new "coöperative social
settlement," to be carried on "in conjunction and
association with the people in the neighborhood."
Not a new idea at all, only a fresh grip taken on
the old one.   It is sound enough and strong enough
to set itself right if we will only let it.   Only last
week Dr. Elliot of the Hudson Guild over in West
Twenty-sixth Street told me of his boys' and their
fathers' subscribing their savings with the hope of
owning the guild house themselves.   They had
never let go their grip on the idea over there.   They
are of Felix Adler's flock.

But take now the elements as we have them:
this great and terrible longing for neighborliness

where the home feeling is gone with the home; the five hundred school buildings in the metropolis that have already successfully been put to neighborhood use. It was nothing else that Dr. Leipziger did when he began his evening lectures in the schools to grown audiences a dozen years ago, and proudly pointed to a record of twenty-two thousand in attendance for the season. Last winter nearly a million working-men and their wives attended over three thousand lectures.[1] Dr. Leipziger is now the strong advocate of opening the schools on the Sabbath, as a kind of Sunday opening we can all join in. Of course he is; he has seen what it means. These factors, the need, the means, and then the settlement that is there to put the two together, as its own great opportunity — has it not a good claim?

Experimenting with the school? Well, what of it? *They* can stand it. What else have we been doing the last half-dozen years or more, and what splendid results have we not to show for it? It is the spirit that calls every innovation frills, and boasts that we have got the finest schools in the world which blocks the way to progress. It cropped out at a

[1] The first year's record was 186 lectures and 22,149 hearers. Last winter (1901–1902) there were 3172 lectures in over 100 places, and the total attendance was 928,251. This winter there will be 115 centres. It is satisfactory to know that churches and church houses fall in with the plan more and more where there are no schools to serve as halls.

meeting of settlement workers and schoolmen that had for its purpose a better understanding.   In the meeting one gray-haired teacher arose and said that the schools as they are were good enough for his father, and therefore they were good enough for him.   That teacher's place is on the shelf that has been provided now for those who have done good work in a day that is past.   " Vaudeville," sneered the last Tammany mayor,† when the East Side asked for a playground for the children.   " Vaudeville for the masses killed Rome."   The masses responded by killing him politically.   My father was a teacher, and it is because he was a good one and taught me that when growth ceases decay begins, that I am never going to be satisfied, no matter how good the schools get to be.   I want them ever closer to the people's life, because upon that does that very life depend.   Turn back to what I said about the slum tenant and see what it means: in the slum only 4.97 per cent of native parentage.   All but five in a hundred had either come over the sea, or else their parents had.   Nearly half (46.65) were ignorant, illiterate; for the whole city the percentage of illiteracy was only 7.69.   Turn to the reformatory showing: of ten thousand and odd prisoners 66.55 utterly illiterate, or able to read and write only with difficulty.   Do you see how the whole battle with the slum is fought out in and around the public school?   For

†Robert A. Van Wyck (1849–1918), a judge of the City Court (1889–1897), who was found to be involved in the vicious profiteering on ice sold to slum residents that Riis describes on p. 68.

in ignorance selfishness finds its opportunity, and the two together make the slum.

The mere teaching is only a part of it. The school itself is a bigger — the meeting there of rich and poor. Out of the public school comes, must come if we are to last, the real democracy that has our hope in keeping. I wish it were in my power to compel every father to send his boy to the public school; I would do it, and so perchance bring the school up to the top notch where it was lacking. The President of the United States to-day sets a splendid example to us all in letting his boys mingle with those who are to be their fellow-citizens by and by. It is precisely in the sundering of our society into classes that have little in common, *that are no longer neighbors,* that our peril lives. A people cannot work together for the good of the state if they are not on speaking terms. In the gap the slum grows up. That was one reason why I hailed with a shout the proposition of Mr. Schwab, the steel trust millionnaire, to take a regiment of boys down to Staten Island on an excursion every day in summer. Let me see, I haven't told about that, I think. He had bought a large property down there, all beach and lake and field and woodland, and proposed to build a steamer with room for a thousand or two, and then take them down with a band of music on board,

and give them a swim, a romp, and a jolly good
time. As soon as he spoke to me about it, I said:
Yes! and hitch it to the public school somehow;
make it part of the curriculum. No more nature
study out of a barrel! Take the whole school,
teachers and all, and let them do their own gathering
of specimens. So the children shall be under
efficient control, and so the tired teacher shall get
a chance too. But more than all, so it may befall
that the boys themselves shall come to know one another better and that more of them shall get together;
for what boy does not want a jolly good romp,
and why should he not be Mr. Schwab's guest for
the day, if he does count his dollars by millions?

The working plan the Board of Education can be
trusted to provide. I think it will do it gladly, once
it understands. Indeed, why should it not? No
one thinks of surrendering the schools, but simply
of enlisting the young enthusiasm that is looking
for employment, and of a way of turning it to
use, while the board is constantly calling for just
that priceless personal element which money cannot buy and without which the schools will never
reach their highest development. Precedents there
are in plenty. If not, we can make them. New
York is the metropolis. In Toledo the Park
Commissioners take the public school boys sleigh-
riding in winter. Our Park Commissioner is

ploughing up land for them to learn farming and gardening. It is all experimenting, and let us be glad we have got to that, if we do blunder once and again. The laboratory study, the bug business, we shall get rid of, and we shall get rid of some antediluvian ways that hamper our educational development yet. We shall find a way to make the schools centres of distribution in our library system as its projectors have hoped. Just now it cannot be done, because it takes about a year for a book to pass the ten or twelve different kinds of censorship our sectarian zeal has erected about the school. We shall have the assembly halls thrown open, not only for Dr. Leipziger's lectures and Sunday concerts (already one permit has been granted for the latter), but for trades-union meetings, and for political meetings, if I have my way. Until we consider our politics quite good enough to be made welcome in the school, they won't be good enough for it. The day we do let them in, the saloon will lose its grip, and not much before. When the fathers and mothers meet under the school roof as in their neighborhood house, and the children have their games, their clubs, and their dances there — when the school, in short, takes the place in the life of the people in the crowded quarters which the saloon now monopolizes, there will no longer be a saloon question in politics; and that day the slum is beaten.

Such a Ball-room!

Very likely I shall not find many to agree with
me on this question of political meetings. Non-
partisan let them be then. So we shall more readily
find our way out of the delusion that national politics have any place in municipal elections or affairs,
a notion that has delayed the day of decency too
long. We shall grow, along with the schools, and
by and by our party politics will be clean enough
to sit in the school seats too. And oh! by the way,
as to those seats, is there any special virtue in the
"dead-line" of straight rows that have come down
to us from the time of the Egyptians or farther back
still? No. I would not lay impious hand on any

hallowed tradition, educational or otherwise. But
is it that? And why is it? It would be so much
easier to make the school the people's hall and the
boys' club, if those seats could be moved around in
human fashion; they might come naturally into human shape in the doing of it. But, as I said, I
wouldn't for the world — not for the world. Only,
why is the dead-line hallowed?

I am willing to leave it to the Board. We are singularly fortunate in having just now a mayor who
will listen, a Board of Education that will act, and a
superintendent of school buildings who can and
will build schools to meet neighborhood needs — if
we will make them plain. The last time I dropped
into his office I found him busy, between tiffs with
contractors, sketching an underground story for the
schoolhouse, like the great hall of the Cooper Institute, that should at the same time serve the purpose
of an assembly hall, and put the roof garden one
story nearer the street. That was his answer to
the cry of elevators. "We do not need municipal
boys' club houses," said Mayor Low†in vetoing the
bill to build them last winter, "we have the schools."
True! Then let us have them used, and if the class-
room is not the best kind of place for them, the experience of the settlements will show us what kind
is. They carry on no end of such clubs. And let
the Board of Education trustily leave the rest to

†Seth Low (1850–1916), elected in 1901, served 1902–1903.

Superintendent Snyder, who knows.   Isn't it enough to make a man believe the millennium has come, to find that there is at last some one who knows? Not necessarily all at once.

In a copy of *Charities* which just now came in (did I not say that it goes that way all the time?) I read that the Chicago Small Parks Commission has recommended nine neighborhood parks at a cost of a million dollars, — wise City of the Winds! we waited till we had to pay a million for each park, — but that the playgrounds had been left to the Board of Education, which body was "not certain whether school funds may be spent for playgrounds apart from buildings."   However, they are going to provide seventy-five school yards big enough to romp in, and the other trouble will be got over.   In Boston they are planning neighborhood entertainment as a proper function of the school.   Here we shall find for both school and settlement their proper places with one swoop.   The kindergarten, manual training, and the cooking school, all experiments in their day, cried out as fads by some, have brought common sense in their train.   When it rules the public school in our cities — I said it before — we can put off our armor; the battle with the slum will be over.

Teaching the Girls to Swim: Part of the Public School Course.

CHAPTER XVI

REFORM BY HUMANE TOUCH

I HAVE sketched in outline the gains achieved in the metropolis since its conscience awoke. Now, in closing this account, I am reminded of the story of an old Irishman who died here a couple of years ago. Patrick Mullen was an honest blacksmith. He made guns for a living. He made them so well that one with his name on it was worth a good deal more than the market price of guns. Other makers went to him with offers of money for the use of his stamp; but they never went twice. When sometimes a gun of very superior make was brought to him to finish, he would stamp it P. Mullen, never Patrick Mullen. Only to that which he himself had wrought did he give his honest name without reserve. When he died, judges and bishops and other great men crowded to his modest home by the East River, and wrote letters to the newspapers telling how proud they had been to call him friend. Yet he was, and remained to the end, plain Patrick Mullen, blacksmith and gun-maker.

In his life he supplied the answer to the sigh of

dreamers in all days: when will the millennium
come? It will come when every man is a Patrick
Mullen at his own trade; not merely a P. Mullen,
but a Patrick Mullen. The millennium of municipal politics, when there shall be no slum to fight,
will come when every citizen does his whole duty
as a citizen, not before. As long as he "despises
politics," and deputizes another to do it for him,
whether that other wears the stamp of a Croker or
of a Platt,[†]— it matters little which, — we shall
have the slum, and be put periodically to the trouble
and the shame of draining it in the public sight. A
citizen's duty is one thing that cannot be farmed
out safely; and the slum is not limited by the rookeries of Mulberry or Ludlow streets. It has long
roots that feed on the selfishness and dulness of
Fifth Avenue quite as greedily as on the squalor
of the Sixth Ward. The two are not nearly so far
apart as they look.

I am not saying this because it is anything new,
but because we have had, within the memory of us
all, an illustration of its truth in municipal politics. Waring and Roosevelt were the Patrick Mul-
lens of the reform administration which Tammany
replaced with her insolent platform, "To hell with
‚reform!" It was not an ideal administration, but
it can be said of it, at least, that it was up to the
times it served. It made compromises with spoils

†Richard Croker, the last Tammany boss, controlled the Democratic
Party in New York City, 1886–1901. Thomas Platt, a U.S. Senator
(1897–1909), was the Republican Party boss of New York State from the
mid-1880s.

politics, and they were wretched failures. It took Waring and Roosevelt on the other plan, on which they insisted, of divorcing politics from the public business, and they let in more light than even my small parks over on the East Side. For they showed us where we stood and what was the matter

Athletic Meets in Crotona Park.

with us. We believed in Waring when he demonstrated the success of his plan for cleaning the streets; not before. When Roosevelt announced his programme, of enforcing the excise law because it *was* law, a howl arose that would have frightened a less resolute man from his purpose. But he went right on doing the duty he was sworn to do. And when, at the end of three months of clamor and abuse, we saw the spectacle of the saloon keepers formally resolving to help the police instead of hindering them; of the prison ward in Bellevue Hospital standing empty for three days at a time, an astonishing and unprecedented thing, which the warden could only attribute to the "prompt closing of the saloon at one A.M."; and of the police force recovering its lost self-respect, — we had found out more and greater things than whether the excise law was a good or a bad law. We understood what Roosevelt meant when he insisted upon the "primary virtues" of honesty and courage in the conduct of public business. For the want of them in us, half the laws that touched our daily lives had became dead letters or vehicles of blackmail and oppression. It was worth something to have that lesson taught us in that way; to find out that simple, straightforward, honest dealing as between man and man is after all effective in politics as in gun-making. Perhaps we have not mastered the lesson yet. But we have not discharged the teacher, either.

Courage, indeed! There were times during that stormy spell when it seemed as if we had grown wholly and hopelessly flabby as a people. All the outcry against the programme of order did not come from the lawless and the disorderly, by any means. Ordinarily decent, conservative citizens joined in counselling moderation and virtual compromise with the law-breakers — it was nothing else — to "avoid trouble." The old love of fair play had been whittled down by the jack-knife of all-pervading expediency to an anæmic desire to "hold the scales even," which is a favorite modern device of the devil for paralyzing action in men. You cannot hold the scales even in a moral issue. It inevitably results in the triumph of evil, which asks nothing better than the even chance to which it is not entitled. When the trouble in the Police Board had reached a point where it seemed impossible not to understand that Roosevelt and his side were fighting a cold and treacherous conspiracy against the cause of good government, we had the spectacle of a Christian Endeavor Society inviting the man who had hatched the plot, the bitter and relentless enemy whom the mayor had summoned to resign, and afterward did his best to remove as a fatal obstacle to reform, — inviting this man to come before it and speak of Christian citizenship! It was a sight to make the bosses hug themselves with glee. For Christian citizenship is their nightmare, and nothing is so cheering to them as evidence that those who profess it have no sense.

Apart from the moral bearings of it, what this

question of enforcement of law means in the life of the poor was illustrated by testimony given before the Police Board under oath. A captain was on trial for allowing the policy swindle to go unchecked in his precinct. Policy is a kind of penny lottery, with alleged daily drawings which never take place. The whole thing is a pestilent fraud, which is allowed to exist only because it pays heavy blackmail to the police and the politicians. Expert witnesses testified that eight policy shops in the Twenty-first Ward, which they had visited, did a business averaging about thirty-two dollars a day each. The Twenty-first is a poor Irish tenement ward. The policy sharks were getting two hundred and fifty dollars or more a day of the hard-earned wages of those poor people, in sums of from one and two cents to a quarter, without making any return for it. The thing would seem incredible were it not too sadly familiar. The saloon keeper got his share of what was left, and rewarded his customer by posing as the "friend of the poor man" whenever his business was under scrutiny; I have yet in my office the record of a single week during the hottest of the fight between Roosevelt and the saloons, as showing of what kind that friendship is. It embraces the destruction of eight homes by the demon of drunkenness; the suicide of four wives, the murder of two others by drunken husbands, the killing of a policeman in the street, and the torture of an aged woman by her rascal son, who "used to be a good boy till he took to liquor, when he became a perfect devil." In that rôle he finally beat her to death for giving shelter to some evicted fellow-tenants who else would have had to sleep in the street. Nice friendly turn, wasn't it?

And yet there was something to be said for the saloon keeper. He gave the man the refuge from his tenement which he needed. I say needed, purposely. There has been a good deal of talk in our day about the saloon as a social necessity. About all there is to that is that the saloon is there, and the necessity too. Man is a social animal, whether he lives in a tenement or in a palace. But the palace has resources; the tenement has not. It is a good place to get away from at all times. The saloon is cheery and bright, and never far away. The man craving human companionship finds it there. He finds, too, in the saloon keeper one who understands his wants much better than the reformer who talks civil service in the meetings. "Civil service" to him and his kind means yet a contrivance for keeping them out of a job. The saloon keeper knows the boss, if he is not himself the boss or his lieutenant, and can steer him to the man who will spend all day at the City Hall, if need be, to get a

job for a friend, and all night pulling wires to keep
him in it, if trouble is brewing.   Mr. Beecher used
to say, when pleading for bright hymn tunes, that
he didn't want the devil to have the monopoly of all
the good music in the world.   The saloon has had
the monopoly up to date of all the cheer in the
tenements.   If its owner has made it pan out to his
own advantage and the boss's, we at least have no
just cause of complaint.   We let him have the field
all to himself.

It is good to know that the day is coming when
he will have a rival.   Model saloons may never be
more than a dream in New York, but even now the
first of a number of "social halls" is being planned
by Miss Lillian Wald of the Nurses' Settlement and
her co-workers that shall give the East Side the
chance to eat and dance and make merry without
the stigma of the bar upon it all.   The first of the
buildings will be opened within a year.

As to this boss, of whom we hear so much, what
manner of man is he?   That depends on how you
look at him.   I have one in mind, a district boss,
whom you would accept instantly as a type if I
were to mention his name, which I shall not do for
a reason which I fear will shock you: he and I are
friends.   In his private capacity I have real regard
for him.   As a politician and a boss I have none at
all.   I am aware that this is taking low ground in a

discussion of this kind, but perhaps the reader will
better understand the relations of his " district " to
him, if I let him into mine. There is no political
bond between us, of either district or party, just
the reverse. It is purely personal. He was once
a police justice, — at that time he kept a saloon, —
and I have known few with more common sense,
which happens to be the one quality especially
needed in that office. Up to the point where politics came in I could depend upon him entirely.
At that point he let me know bluntly that he was
in the habit of running his district to suit himself.
The way he did it brought him under the just accu-
sation of being guilty of every kind of rascality
known to politics. When next our paths would
cross each other, it would very likely be on some
errand of mercy, to which his feet were always
swift. I recall the distress of a dear and gentle lady
at whose table I once took his part. She could not
believe that there was any good in him; what he
did must be done for effect. Some time after that
she wrote, asking me to look after an East Side
family that was in great trouble. It was during the
severe cold spell of the winter of 1898, and there
was need of haste. I went over at once; but although I had lost no time, I found my friend the
boss ahead of me. It was a real pleasure to me to
be able to report to my correspondent that he had

seen to their comfort, and to add that it was unpolitical charity altogether.   The family was that of a
Jewish widow with a lot of little children.   He is a
Roman Catholic.   There was not even a potential
vote in the house, the children being all girls.
They were not in his district, to boot; and as for
effect, he was rather shamefaced at my catching him
at it.   I do not believe that a soul has ever heard of
the case from him to this day.

My friend is a Tammany boss, and I shall not be
accused of partiality for him on that account.   During that same cold spell a politician of the other
camp came into my office and gave me a hundred
dollars to spend as I saw fit among the poor.   His
district was miles up-town, and he was most unwill-
ing to disclose his identity, stipulating in the end
that no one but I should know where the money
came from.   He was not seeking notoriety.   The
plight of the suffering had appealed to him, and he
wanted to help where he could, that was all.

Now, I have not the least desire to glorify the
boss in this.   He is not glorious to me.   He is
simply human.   Often enough he is a coarse and
brutal fellow, in his morals as in his politics.   Again,
he may have some very engaging personal traits
that bind his friends to him with the closest of ties.
The poor man sees the friend, the charity, the
power that is able and ready to help him in need;

is it any wonder that he overlooks the source of this power, this plenty, — that he forgets the robbery in the robber who is "good to the poor"? Anyhow, if anybody got robbed, it was "the rich." With the present ethical standards of the slum, it is easy to construct a scheme of social justice out of it that is very comforting all round, even to the boss himself, though he is in need of no sympathy or excuse. "Politics," he will tell me in his philosophic moods, "is a game for profit. The city foots the bills." Patriotism means to him working for the ticket that shall bring more profit.

"I regard," he says, lighting his cigar, "a repeater as a shade off a murderer, but you are obliged to admit that in my trade he is a necessary evil." I am not obliged to do anything of the kind, but I can understand his way of looking at it. He simply has no political conscience. He has gratitude, loyalty to a friend, — that is part of his stock in trade, — fighting blood, plenty of it, all the good qualities of the savage; nothing more. And a savage he is, politically, with no soul above the dross. He would not rob a neighbor for the world; but he will steal from the city — though he does not call it by that name — without a tremor, and count it a good mark. When I tell him that, he waves his hand toward Wall Street as representative of the business community, and toward the office of his neighbor, the padrone, as representative of the railroads, and says with a laugh, "Don't they all do it?"

The boss believes in himself. It is one of his strong points. And he has experience to back him. In the fall of 1894 we shook off boss rule in New York, and set up housekeeping for ourselves. We kept it up three years, and then went back to the old style. I should judge that we did it because we were tired of too much virtue. Perhaps we were not built to hold such a lot at once. Besides, it is much easier to be ruled than to rule. That fall, after the election, when I was concerned about what would become of my small parks, of the Health Department in which I took such just pride, and of a dozen other things, I received one unvarying reply to my anxious question, or rather two. If it was the Health Department, I was told: "Go to Platt. He is the only man who can do it. He is a sensible man, and will see that it is protected." If small parks, it was: "Go to Croker. He will not allow the work to be stopped." A playgrounds bill was to be presented in the legislature, and everybody advised: "Go to Platt. He won't object, it is popular." And so on. My advisers were not politicians. They were business men, but recently honestly interested in reform. I was talking one day, with a gentleman of very wide reputation as a philanthropist, about the unhappy lot of the old fire-

engine horses, — which, after lives of toil that
deserve a better fate, are sold for a song to drag
out a weary existence hauling some huckster's cart
around, — and wishing that they might be pen-
sioned off to live out their years on a farm, with
enough to eat and a chance to roll in the grass. He
was much interested, and promptly gave me this
advice: " I tell you what you do. You go and see
Croker. He likes horses." No wonder the boss
believes in himself. He would be less than human
if he did not. And he is very human.

I had voted on the day of the Greater New York
election,[†]— the Tammany election, as we learned to
call it afterward, — in my home out in the Borough
of Queens, and went over to the depot to catch the
train for the city. On the platform were half a
dozen of my neighbors, all business men, all
"friends of reform." Some of them were just down
from breakfast. One I remember as introducing a
resolution, in a meeting we had held, about the dis-
courtesy of local politicians. He looked surprised
when reminded that it was election day. " Why, is
it to-day?" he said. " They didn't send any carriage," said another regretfully. " I don't see what's
the use," said the third; " the roads are just as bad
as when we began talking about it." (We had been
trying to mend them.) The fourth yawned and said:
" I don't care. I have my business to attend to."

†The election of November 1897, in which Seth Low was defeated by
the corrupt Tammany candidate, Robert A. Van Wyck, who became
mayor for a four-year term.

And they took the train, which meant that they lost their votes. The Tammany captain was busy hauling his voters by the cart-load to the polling place. Over there stood a reform candidate who had been defeated in the primary, and puffed out his chest. "The politicians are afraid of me," he said. They slapped him on the back, as they went by, and told him that he was a devil of a fellow.

So Tammany came back. And four long years we swore at it. But I am afraid we swore at the wrong fellow. The real Tammany is not the conscienceless rascal that plunders our treasury and fattens on our substance. That one is a mere counterfeit. It is the voter who waits for a carriage to take him to the polls; the man who "doesn't see what's the use"; the business man who says "business is business," and has no time to waste on voting; the citizen who "will wait to see how the cat jumps, because he doesn't want to throw his vote away"; the cowardly American who "doesn't want to antagonize" anybody; the fool who "washes his hands of politics." These are the real Tammany, the men after the boss's own heart. For every one whose vote he buys, there are two of these who give him theirs for nothing. We shall get rid of him when these withdraw their support, when they become citizens of the Patrick Mullen stamp, as faithful at the polling place as he was at the forge; not before.

There is as much work for reform at the top as at the bottom. The man in the slum votes according to his light, and the boss holds the candle. But the boss is in no real sense a leader. He follows instead, always as far behind the moral sentiment of the community as he thinks is safe. He has heard it said that a community will not be any better than its citizens, and that it will be just as good as they are, and he applies the saying to himself. He is no worse a boss than the town deserves. I can conceive of his taking credit to himself as some kind of a moral instrument by which the virtue of the community may be graded, though that is most unlikely. He does not bother himself with the morals of anything. But right here is his Achilles heel. The man has no conscience. He cannot tell the signs of it in others. It always comes upon him unawares. Reform to him simply means the "outs" fighting to get in. The real thing he will always underestimate. Witness Richard Croker in the last election offering Bishop Potter, after his crushing letter to the mayor, to join him in purifying the city, and, when politely refused, setting up an "inquiry" of his own. The conclusion is irresistible that he thought the bishop either a fool or a politician playing for points. Such a man

is not the power he seems. He is formidable only
in proportion to the amount of shaking it takes to
rouse the community's conscience.

The boss is like the measles, a distemper of a
self-governing people's infancy. When we shall
have come of age politically, he will have no terrors for us. Meanwhile, being charged with the
business of governing, which we left to him because we were too busy making money, he follows
the track laid out for him, and makes the business
pan out all that is in it. He fights when we want
to discharge him. Of course he does ; no man
likes to give up a good job. He will fight or bargain, as he sees his way clear. He will give us
small parks, play piers, new schools, anything we
ask, to keep his place, while trying to find out " the
price " of this conscience which he does not understand. Even to the half of his kingdom he will
give, to be " in " on the new deal. He has done
it before, and there is no reason that he can see
why it should not be done again. And he will
appeal to the people whom he is plundering to
trust him because they know him.

Odd as it sounds, this is where he has his real
hold. I have shown why this is so. To the poor
people of his district the boss is a friend in need.
He is one of them. He does not want to reform
them ; far from it. No doubt it is very ungrateful

of them, but the poor people have no desire to be reformed. They do not think they need to be. They consider their moral standards quite as high as those of the rich, and resent being told that they are mistaken. The reformer comes to them from another world to tell them these things, and goes his way. The boss lives among them. He helped John to a job on the pipes in their hard winter, and got Mike on the force. They know him as a good neighbor, and trust him to their harm. He drags their standard ever farther down. The question for those who are trying to help them is how to make them transfer their allegiance, and trust their real friends instead.

It ought not be a difficult question to answer. Any teacher could do it. He knows, if he knows anything, that the way to get and keep the children's confidence is to trust them, and let them know that they are trusted. They will almost always come up to the demand thus made upon them. Preaching to them does little good; preaching at them still less. Men, whether rich or poor, are much like children. The good in them is just as good, and the bad, in view of their enlarged opportunities for mischief, not so much worse, all considered. A vigorous optimism, a stout belief in one's fellow-man, is better equipment in a campaign for civic virtue than stacks of tracts and

arguments, economic and moral. There is good
bottom, even in the slum, for that kind of an
anchor to get a grip on. Some years ago I went
to see a boxing match there had been much
talk about. The hall was jammed with a rough
and noisy crowd, hotly intent upon its favorite.
His opponent, who hailed, I think, from somewhere
in Delaware, was greeted with hostile demonstra-
tions as a "foreigner." But as the battle wore on,
and he was seen to be fair and manly, while the
New Yorker struck one foul blow after another,
the attitude of the crowd changed rapidly from
enthusiastic approval of the favorite to scorn and
contempt; and in the last round, when he knocked
the Delawarean over with a foul blow, the audience
rose in a body and yelled to have the fight given
to the "foreigner," until my blood tingled with
pride. For the decision would leave it practically
without a cent. It had staked all it had on the
New Yorker. "He is a good man," I heard on all
sides, while the once favorite sneaked away without
a friend. "Good" meant fair and manly to that
crowd. I thought, as I went to the office the next
morning, that it ought to be easy to appeal to such
a people with measures that were fair and just, if
we could only get on common ground. But the
only hint I got from my reform paper was an edi-
torial denunciation of the brutality of boxing, on

the same page that had an enthusiastic review of the
college football season. I do not suppose it did
any harm, for the paper was probably not read by
one of the men it had set out to reform. But suppose it had been, how much would it have appealed
to them? Exactly the qualities of robust manli-
ness which football is supposed to encourage in
college students had been evoked by the trial of
strength and skill which they had witnessed. As
to the brutality, they knew that fifty young men are
maimed or killed at football to one who fares ill
in a boxing match. Would it seem to them common sense, or cant and humbug?

That is what it comes down to in the end: common sense and common honesty. Common sense
to steer us clear of the "sociology" reef that would
make our cause ridiculous, on Fifth Avenue and in
East Broadway. I have no quarrel with the man
who would do things by system and in order; but
the man who would reduce men and women and
children to mere items in his infallible system and
classify and sub-classify them until they are as dried
up as his theories, that man I will fight till I die.
One throb of a human heart is worth a whole book
of his stuff. Common honesty to keep us afloat at
all. If we worship as success mere money-getting,
closing our eyes to the means, let us at least say it
like the man who told me to-day that "after all, one

has to admire Bill Devery; he's got the dough."
Devery was Tammany's police chief. The man is
entitled to his opinion, but if it gets hitched to the
reform cart by mistake, the load is going to be
spilled. It has been, more than once.

A saving sense of humor might have avoided
some of those pitfalls. I am seriously of the
opinion that a professional humorist ought to be
attached to every reform movement, to keep it from
making itself ridiculous by either too great solemnity
or too much conceit. As it is, the enemy sometimes employs him with effect. Failing the adoption of that plan, I would recommend a decree of
banishment against photographers, press-clippings
men, and the rest of the congratulatory staff. Why
should the fact that a citizen has done a citizen's
duty deserve to be celebrated in print and picture,
as if something extraordinary had happened? The
smoke of battle had not cleared away after the
victory of reform in the fall of 1894, before the citizens' committee and all the little sub-committees
rushed pell-mell to the photographer's to get themselves on record as the men who did it. The spectacle might have inspired in the humorist the
advice to get two sets made, while they were about
it, one to serve by and by as an exhibit of the men
who didn't; and, as the event proved, he would have
been right.

But it is easy to find fault, and on that tack we get no farther. Those men did a great work, and they did it well. They built from the bottom and they built the foundation broad and strong. Good schools, better homes, and a chance for the boy are good bricks to build with in such a structure as we are rearing. They last. Just now we are laying another course; more than one, I hope. But even if it were different, we need not despair. Let the enemy come back once more, it will not be to stay. It may be that, like Moses and his followers, we of the present day shall see the promised land only from afar and with the eye of faith, because of our sins; that to a younger and sturdier to-morrow it shall be given to blaze the path of civic righteousness that was our dream. I like to think that it is so, and that that is the meaning of the coming of men like Roosevelt and Waring at this time with their simple appeal to the reason of honest men. Unless I greatly err in reading the signs of the times, it is indeed so, and the day of the boss and of the slum is drawing to an end. Our faith has felt the new impulse; rather, I should say, it has given it. The social movements, and that which we call politics, are but a reflection of what the people honestly believe, a chart of their aims and aspirations. Charity in our day no longer means alms, but justice. The social settlements are sub-

stituting vital touch for the machine charity that
reaped a crop of hate and beggary.   Charity organization — "conscience born of love" some one has
well called it — is substituting its methods in high
and low places for the senseless old ways.   Its
champions are oftener found standing with organized
labor for legislation to correct the people's wrongs,
and when the two stand together nothing can resist
them.   Through its teaching we are learning that
our responsibility as citizens for a law does not cease
with its enactment, but rather begins there.   We
are growing, in other words, to the stature of real
citizenship.   We are emerging from the kind of barbarism that dragged children to the jail and thrust
them in among hardened criminals there, and that
sat by helpless and saw the foundlings die in the
infant hospital at the rate — really there was no rate;
they practically all died, every one that was not immediately removed to a home and a mother.   For
four years now a joint committee of the State Charities' Aid Association and the Association for Improving the Condition of the Poor has taken them
off the city's hands and adopted them out, and in
every hundred now eighty-nine live and grow up!
After all, not even a Jersey cow can take the place
of a mother with a baby.   And we are building a
children's court that shall put an end to the other
outrage, for boys taken there are let off on pro-

bation, to give them the chance under a different
teaching from the slum's, which it denied them till
now.

We have learned that we cannot pass off checks
for human sympathy in settlement of our brotherhood arrears. The Church, which once stood by

Flag-drill in the " King's Garden." The Playground at the Jacob A.
Riis House.

indifferent, or uncomprehending, is hastening to
enter the life of the people. I have told of how, in
the memory of men yet living, one church, moving
uptown away from the crowd, left its old Mulberry
Street home to be converted into tenements that
justly earned the name of " dens of death " in the

Health Department's records, while another became
the foulest lodging house in an unclean city, and of
how it was a church corporation that owned the
worst underground dive down-town in those bad old
days, and turned a deaf ear to all remonstrances.
The Church was "angling for souls." But souls in
this world live in bodies endowed with reason. The
results of that kind of fishing were empty pews and
cold hearts, and the conscience-stricken cry that
went up, "What shall we do to lay hold of this
great multitude that has slipped from us?"

The years have passed and brought the answer.
To-day we see churches of every denomination uniting in a systematic canvass of the city to get at the
facts of the people's life of which they had ceased to
be a part, pleading for parks, playgrounds, kindergartens, libraries, clubs, and better homes. There
is a new and hearty sound to the word "brother"
that is full of hope. The cry has been answered.
The gap in the social body, between rich and
poor, is no longer widening. We are certainly
coming closer together. A dozen years ago, when
the King's Daughters lighted a Christmas tree in
Gotham Court, the children ran screaming from
Santa Claus as from a "bogey·man." Here lately
the boys in the Hebrew Institute's schools nearly
broke the bank laying in supplies to do him honor.
I do not mean that the Jews are deserting to join

the Christian Church. They are doing that which is better, — they are embracing its spirit; and they and we are the better for it.

"The more I know of the Other Half," writes a friend to me, "the more I feel the great gulf that is fixed between us, and the more profoundly I grieve that this is the best that Christian civilization has as yet been able to do toward a true social system." Let my friend take heart. She herself has been busy in my sight all these years binding up the wounds. If that be the most a Christian civilization has been able to do for the neighbor till now, who shall say that it is not also the greatest? "This do and thou shalt live," said the Lord of him who showed mercy. That was the mark of the brotherhood. No, the gulf is not widening. It is only that we have taken soundings and know it, and in the doing of it we have come to know one another. The rest we may confidently leave with Him who knows it all.

God knows we waited long enough; and how close we were to one another all the while without knowing it! Two or three years ago at Christmas a clergyman, who lives out of town and has a houseful of children, asked me if I could not find for them a poor family in the city with children of about the same ages, whom they might visit and befriend. He worked every day in the office of a foreign mission in Fifth Avenue, and knew little of the life that

moved about him in the city. I picked out a
Hungarian widow in an East Side tenement, whose
brave struggle to keep her little flock together had
enlisted my sympathy and strong admiration. She
was a cleaner in an office building; not until all the
arrangements had been made did it occur to me to
ask where. Then it turned out that she was scrub-
bing floors in the missionary society's house, right
at my friend's door. They had passed one another
every day, each in need of the other, and each as
far from the other as if oceans separated them
instead of a doorstep four inches wide.

Looking back over the years that lie behind
with their work, and forward to those that are
coming, I see only cause for hope. As I write
these last lines in a far-distant land, in the city of
my birth, the children are playing under my window, and calling to one another with glad cries
in my sweet mother-tongue, even as we did in the
long ago. Life and the world are before them,
bright with the promise of morning. So to me
seem the skies at home. Not lightly do I say it,
for I have known the toil of rough-hewing it on
the pioneer line that turns men's hair gray; but I
have seen also the reward of the toil. New York
is the youngest of the world's great cities, barely
yet out of knickerbockers. It may be that our
century will yet see it as the greatest of them all.

The task that is set it, the problem it has to solve and which it may not shirk, is the problem of civilization, of human progress, of a people's fitness for self-government, that is on trial among us. We shall solve it by the world-old formula of human sympathy, of humane touch. Somewhere in these pages I have told of the woman in Chicago who accounted herself the happiest woman alive because she had at last obtained a playground for her poor neighbors' children. " I have lived here for years," she said to me, "and struggled with principalities and powers, and have made up my mind that the most and the best I can do is to live right here with my people and smile with them, — keep smiling; weep when I must, but smile as long as I possibly can." And the tears shone in her gentle old eyes as she said it. When we have learned to smile and weep with the poor, we shall have mastered our problem. Then the slum will have lost its grip and the boss his job.

Until then, while they are in possession, our business is to hold taut and take in slack right along, never letting go for a moment.

And now, having shown you the dark side of the city, which, after all, I love, with its great memories, its high courage, and its bright skies, as I love the little Danish town where my cradle stood, let me, before I close this account of the struggle with evil, show you also its good heart by telling you "the unnecessary story of Mrs. Ben Wah and her parrot." Perchance it may help you to grasp better the meaning of the Battle with the Slum. It is for such as she and for such as "Jim," whose story I told before, that we are fighting.

CHAPTER XVII

THE UNNECESSARY STORY OF MRS. BEN WAH AND HER
PARROT

Mrs. Ben Wah was dying. Word came up from
the district office of the Charity Organization Society to tell me of it. Would I come and see her
before I went away? Mrs. Ben Wah was an old
charge of mine, the French Canadian widow of an
Iroquois Indian, whom, years before, I had un-
earthed in a Hudson Street tenement. I was
just then making ready for a voyage across the
ocean to the old home to see my own mother, and
the thought of the aged woman who laid away her
children long ago by the cold camp-fires of her tribe
in Canadian forests was a call not to be resisted. I
went at once.

The signs of illness were there in a notice tacked
up on the wall, warning everybody to keep away
when her attic should be still, until her friends
could come from the charity office. It was a notion
she had, Mrs. McCutcheon, the district visitor, explained, that would not let her rest till her " paper "
was made out. For her, born in the wilderness,
death had no such terror as prying eyes.

"Them police fellows," she said, with the least touch of resentment in her gentle voice, "they might take my things and sell them to buy cigars to smoke." I suspect it was the cigar that grated harshly. It was ever to her a vulgar slur on her beloved pipe. In truth, the mere idea of Mrs. Ben

Mrs. Ben Wah.

Wah smoking a cigar rouses in me impatient resentment. Without her pipe she was not herself. I see her yet, stuffing it with approving forefinger, on the Christmas day when I had found her with tobacco pouch empty, and pocket to boot, and nodding the quaint comment from her corner, "It's no disgrace to be poor, but it's sometimes very inconvenient."

There was something in the little attic room that spoke of the coming change louder than the warning paper. A half-finished mat, with its bundle of rags put carefully aside; the thirsty potato-vine on the fire-escape, which reached appealingly from its soap-box toward the window, as if in wondering search for the hands that had tended it so faithfully, — bore silent testimony that Mrs. Ben Wah's work-day was over at last. It had been a long day — how long no one may ever know. "The winter of the big snow," or "the year when deer was scarce" on the Gatineau, is not as good a guide to time-reckoning in the towns as in the woods, and Mrs. Ben Wah knew no other. Her thoughts dwelt among the memories of the past as she sat slowly nodding her turbaned head, idle for once. The very head-dress, arranged and smoothed with unusual care, was "notice," proceeding from a primitive human impulse. Before the great mystery she "was ashamed and covered her head."

The charity visitor told me what I had half guessed. Beyond the fact that she was tired and had made up her mind to die, nothing ailed Mrs. Ben Wah. But at her age, the doctor had said, it was enough; she would have her way. In faith, she was failing day by day. All that could be done was to make her last days as easy as might be. I talked to her of my travels, of the great salt water upon which I should journey many days; but her thoughts were in the lonely woods, and she did not understand. I told her of beautiful France, the language of which she spoke with a singularly sweet accent, and asked her if there was not something I might bring back to her to make her happy. As I talked on, a reminiscent smile came into her eyes and lingered there. It was evidently something that pleased her. By slow degrees we dragged the bashful confession out of her that there was yet one wish she had in this life.

Once upon a time, long, long ago, when, as a young woman, she had gone about peddling beads, she had seen a bird, such a splendid bird, big and green and beautiful, with a red turban, and that could talk. Talk! As she recalled the glorious apparition, she became quite her old self again, and reached for her neglected pipe with trembling hands. If she could ever see that bird again — but she guessed it was long since gone. She was a young woman then, and now she was old, so old. She settled back in her chair, and let the half-lighted pipe go out.

"Poor old soul!" said Mrs. McCutcheon, patting the wrinkled hand in her lap. Her lips framed the word "parrot" across the room to me, and I nodded back. When we went out together it was settled between us that Mrs. Ben Wah was to be doctored according to her own prescription, if it broke the rules of every school of medicine.

I went straight back to the office and wrote in my newspaper that Mrs. Ben Wah was sick and needed a parrot, a green one with a red tuft, and that she must have it right away. I told of her lonely life,

and of how, on a Christmas Eve, years ago, I had
first met her at the door of the Charity Organization Society, laboring up the stairs with a big bundle
done up in blue cheese-cloth, which she left in the
office with the message that it was for those who
were poorer than she.   They were opening it when
I came in.   It contained a lot of little garments of
blanket stuff, as they used to make them for the
pappooses among her people in the far North.   It
was the very next day that I found her in her attic,
penniless and without even the comfort of her pipe.
Like the widow of old, she had cast her mite into
the treasury, even all she had.

All this I told in my paper, and how she whose
whole life had been kindness to others was now in
need — in need of a companion to share her lonely
life, of something with a voice, which would not
come in and go away again, and leave her.   And I
begged that any one who had a green parrot with a
red tuft would send it in at once.

New York is a good town to live in.   It has a
heart.   It no sooner knew that Mrs. Ben Wah wanted
a parrot than it hustled about to supply one at once.
The morning mail brought stacks of letters, with
offers of money to buy a parrot.   They came from
lawyers, business men, and bank presidents, men
who pore over dry ledgers and drive sharp bargains
on 'Change, and are never supposed to give a thought

to lonely widows pining away in poor attics.   While
they were being sorted, a poor little tramp song-bird
flew in through the open window of the Charities
Building in great haste, apparently in search of Mrs.
McCutcheon's room.   Its feathers were ruffled and
its bangs awry, as if it had not had time to make its
morning toilet, it had come in such haste to see if
it would do.   Though it could not talk, it might at
least sing to the sick old woman — sing of the silent
forests with the silver lakes deep in their bosom,
where the young bucks trailed the moose and the
panther, and where she listened at the lodge door
for their coming; and the song might bring back
the smile to her wan lips.   But though it was nearly
green and had a tousled top, it was not a parrot,
and it would not do.   The young women who
write in the big books in the office caught it and
put it in a cage to sing to them instead.   In the
midst of the commotion came the parrot itself, big
and green, in a " stunning " cage.   It was an ami-
able bird, despite its splendid get-up, and cocked
its crimson head one side to have it scratched
through the bars, and held up one claw, as if to
shake hands.

How to get it to Mrs. Ben Wah's without the
shock killing her was the problem that next presented itself.   Mrs. McCutcheon solved it by doing
the cage up carefully in newspapers and taking it

along herself. All the way down the bird passed muffled comments on the Metropolitan Railway service and on its captivity, to the considerable embarrassment of its keeper; but they reached the Beach Street tenement and Mrs. Ben Wah's attic at last. There Mrs. McCutcheon stowed it carefully away in a corner, while she busied herself about her aged friend.

She was working slowly down through an address which she had designed to break the thing gently and by degrees, when the parrot, extending a feeler on its own hook, said " K-r-r-a-a ! " behind its paper screen.

Mrs. Ben Wah sat up straight and looked fixedly at the corner. Seeing the big bundle there, she went over and peered into it. She caught a quick breath and stared, wide-eyed.

" Where you get that bird ? " she demanded of Mrs. McCutcheon, faintly.

" Oh, that is Mr. Riis's bird," said that lady, sparring for time; " a friend gave it to him — "

" Where you take him ? " Mrs. Ben Wah gasped, her hand pressed against her feeble old heart.

Her friend saw, and gave right up.

" I am not going to take it anywhere," she said. " I brought it for you. This is to be its home, and you are to be its mother, grandma, and its friend. You are to be always together from now on —

always, and have a good time." With that she tore the paper from the cage.

The parrot, after all, made the speech of the occasion. He considered the garret; the potato-field on the fire-escape, through which the sunlight came in, making a cheerful streak on the floor; Mrs. Ben Wah and her turban; and his late carrier: then he climbed upon his stick, turned a somersault, and said, "Here we are," or words to that effect. Thereupon he held his head over to be scratched by Mrs. Ben Wah in token of a compact of friendship then and there made.

Joy, after all, does not kill. Mrs. Ben Wah wept long and silently, big, happy tears of gratitude. Then she wiped them away, and went about her household cares as of old. The prescription had worked. The next day the "notice" vanished from the wall of the room, where there were now two voices for one.

I came back from Europe to find my old friend with a lighter step and a lighter heart than in many a day. The parrot had learned to speak Canadian French to the extent of demanding his crackers and water in the lingo of the *habitant*. Whether he will yet stretch his linguistic acquirements to the learning of Iroquois I shall not say. It is at least possible. The two are inseparable. The last time I went to see them, no one answered my knock on the door-jamb. I raised the curtain that serves for a door, and looked in. Mrs. Ben Wah was asleep upon the bed. Perched upon her shoulder was the parrot, no longer constrained by the bars of a cage, with his head tucked snugly in her neck, asleep too. So I left them, and so I like to remember them always, comrades true.

It happened that when I was in Chicago last spring I told their story to a friend, a woman. "Oh, write it!" she said. "You must!" And when I asked why, she replied, with feminine logic: "Because it is so unnecessary. The barrel of flour doesn't stick out all over it."

Now I have done as she bade me. Perhaps she was right. Women know these things best. Like my own city, they have hearts, and will understand the unnecessary story of Mrs. Ben Wah and her parrot.

INDEX

451

A CATALOG OF SELECTED
DOVER BOOKS
IN ALL FIELDS OF INTEREST

A CATALOG OF SELECTED DOVER
BOOKS IN ALL FIELDS OF INTEREST

CONCERNING THE SPIRITUAL IN ART, Wassily Kandinsky. Pioneering work by father of abstract art. Thoughts on color theory, nature of art. Analysis of earlier masters. 12 illustrations. 80pp. of text. 5⅜ x 8½.   23411-8 Pa. $3.95

ANIMALS: 1,419 Copyright-Free Illustrations of Mammals, Birds, Fish, Insects, etc., Jim Harter (ed.). Clear wood engravings present, in extremely lifelike poses, over 1,000 species of animals. One of the most extensive pictorial sourcebooks of its kind. Captions. Index. 284pp. 9 x 12.   23766-4 Pa. $12.95

CELTIC ART: The Methods of Construction, George Bain. Simple geometric techniques for making Celtic interlacements, spirals, Kells-type initials, animals, humans, etc. Over 500 illustrations. 160pp. 9 x 12. (USO)   22923-8 Pa. $9.95

AN ATLAS OF ANATOMY FOR ARTISTS, Fritz Schider. Most thorough reference work on art anatomy in the world. Hundreds of illustrations, including selections from works by Vesalius, Leonardo, Goya, Ingres, Michelangelo, others. 593 illustrations. 192pp. 7⅛ x 10¼.   20241-0 Pa. $9.95

CELTIC HAND STROKE-BY-STROKE (Irish Half-Uncial from "The Book of Kells"): An Arthur Baker Calligraphy Manual, Arthur Baker. Complete guide to creating each letter of the alphabet in distinctive Celtic manner. Covers hand position, strokes, pens, inks, paper, more. Illustrated. 48pp. 8¼ x 11.   24336-2 Pa. $3.95

EASY ORIGAMI, John Montroll. Charming collection of 32 projects (hat, cup, pelican, piano, swan, many more) specially designed for the novice origami hobbyist. Clearly illustrated easy-to-follow instructions insure that even beginning papercrafters will achieve successful results. 48pp. 8¼ x 11.   27298-2 Pa. $3.50

THE COMPLETE BOOK OF BIRDHOUSE CONSTRUCTION FOR WOODWORKERS, Scott D. Campbell. Detailed instructions, illustrations, tables. Also data on bird habitat and instinct patterns. Bibliography. 3 tables. 63 illustrations in 15 figures. 48pp. 5¼ x 8½.   24407-5 Pa. $2.50

BLOOMINGDALE'S ILLUSTRATED 1886 CATALOG: Fashions, Dry Goods and Housewares, Bloomingdale Brothers. Famed merchants' extremely rare catalog depicting about 1,700 products: clothing, housewares, firearms, dry goods, jewelry, more. Invaluable for dating, identifying vintage items. Also, copyright-free graphics for artists, designers. Co-published with Henry Ford Museum & Greenfield Village. 160pp. 8¼ x 11.   25780-0 Pa. $10.95

HISTORIC COSTUME IN PICTURES, Braun & Schneider. Over 1,450 costumed figures in clearly detailed engravings—from dawn of civilization to end of 19th century. Captions. Many folk costumes. 256pp. 8⅜ x 11¾.   23150-X Pa. $12.95

CATALOG OF DOVER BOOKS

STICKLEY CRAFTSMAN FURNITURE CATALOGS, Gustav Stickley and L. & J. G. Stickley. Beautiful, functional furniture in two authentic catalogs from 1910. 594 illustrations, including 277 photos, show settles, rockers, armchairs, reclining chairs, bookcases, desks, tables. 183pp. 6½ x 9¼. 23838-5 Pa. $9.95

AMERICAN LOCOMOTIVES IN HISTORIC PHOTOGRAPHS: 1858 to 1949, Ron Ziel (ed.). A rare collection of 126 meticulously detailed official photographs, called "builder portraits," of American locomotives that majestically chronicle the rise of steam locomotive power in America. Introduction. Detailed captions. xi + 129pp. 9 x 12. 27393-8 Pa. $12.95

AMERICA'S LIGHTHOUSES: An Illustrated History, Francis Ross Holland, Jr. Delightfully written, profusely illustrated fact-filled survey of over 200 American lighthouses since 1716. History, anecdotes, technological advances, more. 240pp. 8 x 10¾. 25576-X Pa. $12.95

TOWARDS A NEW ARCHITECTURE, Le Corbusier. Pioneering manifesto by founder of "International School." Technical and aesthetic theories, views of industry, economics, relation of form to function, "mass-production split" and much more. Profusely illustrated. 320pp. 6⅛ x 9¼. (USO) 25023-7 Pa. $9.95

HOW THE OTHER HALF LIVES, Jacob Riis. Famous journalistic record, exposing poverty and degradation of New York slums around 1900, by major social reformer. 100 striking and influential photographs. 233pp. 10 x 7⅞. 22012-5 Pa. $10.95

FRUIT KEY AND TWIG KEY TO TREES AND SHRUBS, William M. Harlow. One of the handiest and most widely used identification aids. Fruit key covers 120 deciduous and evergreen species; twig key 160 deciduous species. Easily used. Over 300 photographs. 126pp. 5⅜ x 8½. 20511-8 Pa. $3.95

COMMON BIRD SONGS, Dr. Donald J. Borror. Songs of 60 most common U.S. birds: robins, sparrows, cardinals, bluejays, finches, more–arranged in order of increasing complexity. Up to 9 variations of songs of each species. Cassette and manual 99911-4 $8.95

ORCHIDS AS HOUSE PLANTS, Rebecca Tyson Northen. Grow cattleyas and many other kinds of orchids–in a window, in a case, or under artificial light. 63 illustrations. 148pp. 5⅜ x 8½. 23261-1 Pa. $4.95

MONSTER MAZES, Dave Phillips. Masterful mazes at four levels of difficulty. Avoid deadly perils and evil creatures to find magical treasures. Solutions for all 32 exciting illustrated puzzles. 48pp. 8¼ x 11. 26005-4 Pa. $2.95

MOZART'S DON GIOVANNI (DOVER OPERA LIBRETTO SERIES), Wolfgang Amadeus Mozart. Introduced and translated by Ellen H. Bleiler. Standard Italian libretto, with complete English translation. Convenient and thoroughly portable–an ideal companion for reading along with a recording or the performance itself. Introduction. List of characters. Plot summary. 121pp. 5¼ x 8½. 24944-1 Pa. $2.95

TECHNICAL MANUAL AND DICTIONARY OF CLASSICAL BALLET, Gail Grant. Defines, explains, comments on steps, movements, poses and concepts. 15-page pictorial section. Basic book for student, viewer. 127pp. 5⅜ x 8½. 21843-0 Pa. $4.95

BRASS INSTRUMENTS: Their History and Development, Anthony Baines. Authoritative, updated survey of the evolution of trumpets, trombones, bugles, cornets, French horns, tubas and other brass wind instruments. Over 140 illustrations and 48 music examples. Corrected and updated by author. New preface. Bibliography. 320pp. 5⅜ x 8½. 27574-4 Pa. $9.95

HOLLYWOOD GLAMOR PORTRAITS, John Kobal (ed.). 145 photos from 1926-49. Harlow, Gable, Bogart, Bacall; 94 stars in all. Full background on photographers, technical aspects. 160pp. 8⅜ x 11¼. 23352-9 Pa. $12.95

MAX AND MORITZ, Wilhelm Busch. Great humor classic in both German and English. Also 10 other works: "Cat and Mouse," "Plisch and Plumm," etc. 216pp. 5⅜ x 8½. 20181-3 Pa. $6.95

THE RAVEN AND OTHER FAVORITE POEMS, Edgar Allan Poe. Over 40 of the author's most memorable poems: "The Bells," "Ulalume," "Israfel," "To Helen," "The Conqueror Worm," "Eldorado," "Annabel Lee," many more. Alphabetic lists of titles and first lines. 64pp. 5³⁄₁₆ x 8¼. 26685-0 Pa. $1.00

PERSONAL MEMOIRS OF U. S. GRANT, Ulysses Simpson Grant. Intelligent, deeply moving firsthand account of Civil War campaigns, considered by many the finest military memoirs ever written. Includes letters, historic photographs, maps and more. 528pp. 6⅛ x 9¼. 28587-1 Pa. $11.95

AMULETS AND SUPERSTITIONS, E. A. Wallis Budge. Comprehensive discourse on origin, powers of amulets in many ancient cultures: Arab, Persian Babylonian, Assyrian, Egyptian, Gnostic, Hebrew, Phoenician, Syriac, etc. Covers cross, swastika, crucifix, seals, rings, stones, etc. 584pp. 5⅜ x 8½. 23573-4 Pa. $12.95

RUSSIAN STORIES/PYCCKNE PACCKA3bl: A Dual-Language Book, edited by Gleb Struve. Twelve tales by such masters as Chekhov, Tolstoy, Dostoevsky, Pushkin, others. Excellent word-for-word English translations on facing pages, plus teaching and study aids, Russian/English vocabulary, biographical/critical introductions, more. 416pp. 5⅜ x 8½. 26244-8 Pa. $8.95

PHILADELPHIA THEN AND NOW: 60 Sites Photographed in the Past and Present, Kenneth Finkel and Susan Oyama. Rare photographs of City Hall, Logan Square, Independence Hall, Betsy Ross House, other landmarks juxtaposed with contemporary views. Captures changing face of historic city. Introduction. Captions. 128pp. 8¼ x 11. 25790-8 Pa. $9.95

AIA ARCHITECTURAL GUIDE TO NASSAU AND SUFFOLK COUNTIES, LONG ISLAND, The American Institute of Architects, Long Island Chapter, and the Society for the Preservation of Long Island Antiquities. Comprehensive, well-researched and generously illustrated volume brings to life over three centuries of Long Island's great architectural heritage. More than 240 photographs with authoritative, extensively detailed captions. 176pp. 8¼ x 11. 26946-9 Pa. $14.95

NORTH AMERICAN INDIAN LIFE: Customs and Traditions of 23 Tribes, Elsie Clews Parsons (ed.). 27 fictionalized essays by noted anthropologists examine religion, customs, government, additional facets of life among the Winnebago, Crow, Zuni, Eskimo, other tribes. 480pp. 6⅛ x 9¼. 27377-6 Pa. $10.95

FRANK LLOYD WRIGHT'S HOLLYHOCK HOUSE, Donald Hoffmann. Lavishly illustrated, carefully documented study of one of Wright's most controversial residential designs. Over 120 photographs, floor plans, elevations, etc. Detailed perceptive text by noted Wright scholar. Index. 128pp. 9¼ x 10¾. 27133-1 Pa. $11.95

THE MALE AND FEMALE FIGURE IN MOTION: 60 Classic Photographic Sequences, Eadweard Muybridge. 60 true-action photographs of men and women walking, running, climbing, bending, turning, etc., reproduced from rare 19th-century masterpiece. vi + 121pp. 9 x 12. 24745-7 Pa. $10.95

1001 QUESTIONS ANSWERED ABOUT THE SEASHORE, N. J. Berrill and Jacquelyn Berrill. Queries answered about dolphins, sea snails, sponges, starfish, fishes, shore birds, many others. Covers appearance, breeding, growth, feeding, much more. 305pp. 5¼ x 8¼. 23366-9 Pa. $8.95

GUIDE TO OWL WATCHING IN NORTH AMERICA, Donald S. Heintzelman. Superb guide offers complete data and descriptions of 19 species: barn owl, screech owl, snowy owl, many more. Expert coverage of owl-watching equipment, conservation, migrations and invasions, etc. Guide to observing sites. 84 illustrations. xiii + 193pp. 5⅜ x 8½. 27344-X Pa. $8.95

MEDICINAL AND OTHER USES OF NORTH AMERICAN PLANTS: A Historical Survey with Special Reference to the Eastern Indian Tribes, Charlotte Erichsen-Brown. Chronological historical citations document 500 years of usage of plants, trees, shrubs native to eastern Canada, northeastern U.S. Also complete identifying information. 343 illustrations. 544pp. 6½ x 9¼. 25951-X Pa. $12.95

STORYBOOK MAZES, Dave Phillips. 23 stories and mazes on two-page spreads: Wizard of Oz, Treasure Island, Robin Hood, etc. Solutions. 64pp. 8¼ x 11. 23628-5 Pa. $2.95

NEGRO FOLK MUSIC, U.S.A., Harold Courlander. Noted folklorist's scholarly yet readable analysis of rich and varied musical tradition. Includes authentic versions of over 40 folk songs. Valuable bibliography and discography. xi + 324pp. 5⅜ x 8½. 27350-4 Pa. $9.95

MOVIE-STAR PORTRAITS OF THE FORTIES, John Kobal (ed.). 163 glamor, studio photos of 106 stars of the 1940s: Rita Hayworth, Ava Gardner, Marlon Brando, Clark Gable, many more. 176pp. 8⅜ x 11¼. 23546-7 Pa. $12.95

BENCHLEY LOST AND FOUND, Robert Benchley. Finest humor from early 30s, about pet peeves, child psychologists, post office and others. Mostly unavailable elsewhere. 73 illustrations by Peter Arno and others. 183pp. 5⅜ x 8½. 22410-4 Pa. $6.95

YEKL and THE IMPORTED BRIDEGROOM AND OTHER STORIES OF YIDDISH NEW YORK, Abraham Cahan. Film Hester Street based on Yekl (1896). Novel, other stories among first about Jewish immigrants on N.Y.'s East Side. 240pp. 5⅜ x 8½. 22427-9 Pa. $6.95

SELECTED POEMS, Walt Whitman. Generous sampling from *Leaves of Grass*. Twenty-four poems include "I Hear America Singing," "Song of the Open Road," "I Sing the Body Electric," "When Lilacs Last in the Dooryard Bloom'd," "O Captain! My Captain!"–all reprinted from an authoritative edition. Lists of titles and first lines. 128pp. 5$\frac{3}{16}$ x 8¼. 26878-0 Pa. $1.00

THE BEST TALES OF HOFFMANN, E. T. A. Hoffmann. 10 of Hoffmann's most important stories: "Nutcracker and the King of Mice," "The Golden Flowerpot," etc. 458pp. 5⅜ x 8½.   21793-0 Pa. $9.95

FROM FETISH TO GOD IN ANCIENT EGYPT, E. A. Wallis Budge. Rich detailed survey of Egyptian conception of "God" and gods, magic, cult of animals, Osiris, more. Also, superb English translations of hymns and legends. 240 illustrations. 545pp. 5⅜ x 8½.   25803-3 Pa. $13.95

FRENCH STORIES/CONTES FRANÇAIS: A Dual-Language Book, Wallace Fowlie. Ten stories by French masters, Voltaire to Camus: "Micromegas" by Voltaire; "The Atheist's Mass" by Balzac; "Minuet" by de Maupassant; "The Guest" by Camus, six more. Excellent English translations on facing pages. Also French-English vocabulary list, exercises, more. 352pp. 5⅜ x 8½.   26443-2 Pa. $8.95

CHICAGO AT THE TURN OF THE CENTURY IN PHOTOGRAPHS: 122 Historic Views from the Collections of the Chicago Historical Society, Larry A. Viskochil. Rare large-format prints offer detailed views of City Hall, State Street, the Loop, Hull House, Union Station, many other landmarks, circa 1904-1913. Introduction. Captions. Maps. 144pp. 9⅜ x 12¼.   24656-6 Pa. $12.95

OLD BROOKLYN IN EARLY PHOTOGRAPHS, 1865-1929, William Lee Younger. Luna Park, Gravesend race track, construction of Grand Army Plaza, moving of Hotel Brighton, etc. 157 previously unpublished photographs. 165pp. 8⅞ x 11¾.
23587-4 Pa. $13.95

THE MYTHS OF THE NORTH AMERICAN INDIANS, Lewis Spence. Rich anthology of the myths and legends of the Algonquins, Iroquois, Pawnees and Sioux, prefaced by an extensive historical and ethnological commentary. 36 illustrations. 480pp. 5⅜ x 8½.   25967-6 Pa. $8.95

AN ENCYCLOPEDIA OF BATTLES: Accounts of Over 1,560 Battles from 1479 B.C. to the Present, David Eggenberger. Essential details of every major battle in recorded history from the first battle of Megiddo in 1479 B.C. to Grenada in 1984. List of Battle Maps. New Appendix covering the years 1967-1984. Index. 99 illustrations. 544pp. 6½ x 9¼.   24913-1 Pa. $14.95

SAILING ALONE AROUND THE WORLD, Captain Joshua Slocum. First man to sail around the world, alone, in small boat. One of great feats of seamanship told in delightful manner. 67 illustrations. 294pp. 5⅜ x 8½.   20326-3 Pa. $5.95

ANARCHISM AND OTHER ESSAYS, Emma Goldman. Powerful, penetrating, prophetic essays on direct action, role of minorities, prison reform, puritan hypocrisy, violence, etc. 271pp. 5⅜ x 8½.   22484-8 Pa. $6.95

MYTHS OF THE HINDUS AND BUDDHISTS, Ananda K. Coomaraswamy and Sister Nivedita. Great stories of the epics; deeds of Krishna, Shiva, taken from puranas, Vedas, folk tales; etc. 32 illustrations. 400pp. 5⅜ x 8½.   21759-0 Pa. $10.95

BEYOND PSYCHOLOGY, Otto Rank. Fear of death, desire of immortality, nature of sexuality, social organization, creativity, according to Rankian system. 291pp. 5⅜ x 8½.
20485-5 Pa. $8.95

A THEOLOGICO-POLITICAL TREATISE, Benedict Spinoza. Also contains unfinished Political Treatise. Great classic on religious liberty, theory of government on common consent. R. Elwes translation. Total of 421pp. 5⅜ x 8½. 20249-6 Pa. $9.95

MY BONDAGE AND MY FREEDOM, Frederick Douglass. Born a slave, Douglass became outspoken force in antislavery movement. The best of Douglass' autobiographies. Graphic description of slave life. 464pp. 5⅜ x 8½. 22457-0 Pa. $8.95

FOLLOWING THE EQUATOR: A Journey Around the World, Mark Twain. Fascinating humorous account of 1897 voyage to Hawaii, Australia, India, New Zealand, etc. Ironic, bemused reports on peoples, customs, climate, flora and fauna, politics, much more. 197 illustrations. 720pp. 5⅜ x 8½. 26113-1 Pa. $15.95

THE PEOPLE CALLED SHAKERS, Edward D. Andrews. Definitive study of Shakers: origins, beliefs, practices, dances, social organization, furniture and crafts, etc. 33 illustrations. 351pp. 5⅜ x 8½. 21081-2 Pa. $8.95

THE MYTHS OF GREECE AND ROME, H. A. Guerber. A classic of mythology, generously illustrated, long prized for its simple, graphic, accurate retelling of the principal myths of Greece and Rome, and for its commentary on their origins and significance. With 64 illustrations by Michelangelo, Raphael, Titian, Rubens, Canova, Bernini and others. 480pp. 5⅜ x 8½. 27584-1 Pa. $9.95

PSYCHOLOGY OF MUSIC, Carl E. Seashore. Classic work discusses music as a medium from psychological viewpoint. Clear treatment of physical acoustics, auditory apparatus, sound perception, development of musical skills, nature of musical feeling, host of other topics. 88 figures. 408pp. 5⅜ x 8½. 21851-1 Pa. $10.95

THE PHILOSOPHY OF HISTORY, Georg W. Hegel. Great classic of Western thought develops concept that history is not chance but rational process, the evolution of freedom. 457pp. 5⅜ x 8½. 20112-0 Pa. $9.95

THE BOOK OF TEA, Kakuzo Okakura. Minor classic of the Orient: entertaining, charming explanation, interpretation of traditional Japanese culture in terms of tea ceremony. 94pp. 5⅜ x 8½. 20070-1 Pa. $3.95

LIFE IN ANCIENT EGYPT, Adolf Erman. Fullest, most thorough, detailed older account with much not in more recent books, domestic life, religion, magic, medicine, commerce, much more. Many illustrations reproduce tomb paintings, carvings, hieroglyphs, etc. 597pp. 5⅜ x 8½. 22632-8 Pa. $11.95

SUNDIALS, Their Theory and Construction, Albert Waugh. Far and away the best, most thorough coverage of ideas, mathematics concerned, types, construction, adjusting anywhere. Simple, nontechnical treatment allows even children to build several of these dials. Over 100 illustrations. 230pp. 5⅜ x 8½. 22947-5 Pa. $7.95

DYNAMICS OF FLUIDS IN POROUS MEDIA, Jacob Bear. For advanced students of ground water hydrology, soil mechanics and physics, drainage and irrigation engineering, and more. 335 illustrations. Exercises, with answers. 784pp. 6⅛ x 9¼. 65675-6 Pa. $19.95

SONGS OF EXPERIENCE: Facsimile Reproduction with 26 Plates in Full Color, William Blake. 26 full-color plates from a rare 1826 edition. Includes "TheTyger," "London," "Holy Thursday," and other poems. Printed text of poems. 48pp. 5¼ x 7. 24636-1 Pa. $4.95

OLD-TIME VIGNETTES IN FULL COLOR, Carol Belanger Grafton (ed.). Over 390 charming, often sentimental illustrations, selected from archives of Victorian graphics—pretty women posing, children playing, food, flowers, kittens and puppies, smiling cherubs, birds and butterflies, much more. All copyright-free. 48pp. 9¼ x 12¼. 27269-9 Pa. $7.95

PERSPECTIVE FOR ARTISTS, Rex Vicat Cole. Depth, perspective of sky and sea, shadows, much more, not usually covered. 391 diagrams, 81 reproductions of drawings and paintings. 279pp. 5⅜ x 8½. 22487-2 Pa. $7.95

DRAWING THE LIVING FIGURE, Joseph Sheppard. Innovative approach to artistic anatomy focuses on specifics of surface anatomy, rather than muscles and bones. Over 170 drawings of live models in front, back and side views, and in widely varying poses. Accompanying diagrams. 177 illustrations. Introduction. Index. 144pp. 8⅜ x11¼. 26723-7 Pa. $8.95

GOTHIC AND OLD ENGLISH ALPHABETS: 100 Complete Fonts, Dan X. Solo. Add power, elegance to posters, signs, other graphics with 100 stunning copyright-free alphabets: Blackstone, Dolbey, Germania, 97 more–including many lower-case, numerals, punctuation marks. 104pp. 8⅛ x 11. 24695-7 Pa. $8.95

HOW TO DO BEADWORK, Mary White. Fundamental book on craft from simple projects to five-bead chains and woven works. 106 illustrations. 142pp. 5⅜ x 8. 20697-1 Pa. $4.95

THE BOOK OF WOOD CARVING, Charles Marshall Sayers. Finest book for beginners discusses fundamentals and offers 34 designs. "Absolutely first rate . . . well thought out and well executed."–E. J. Tangerman. 118pp. 7¾ x 10⅝. 23654-4 Pa. $6.95

ILLUSTRATED CATALOG OF CIVIL WAR MILITARY GOODS: Union Army Weapons, Insignia, Uniform Accessories, and Other Equipment, Schuyler, Hartley, and Graham. Rare, profusely illustrated 1846 catalog includes Union Army uniform and dress regulations, arms and ammunition, coats, insignia, flags, swords, rifles, etc. 226 illustrations. 160pp. 9 x 12. 24939-5 Pa. $10.95

WOMEN'S FASHIONS OF THE EARLY 1900s: An Unabridged Republication of "New York Fashions, 1909," National Cloak & Suit Co. Rare catalog of mail-order fashions documents women's and children's clothing styles shortly after the turn of the century. Captions offer full descriptions, prices. Invaluable resource for fashion, costume historians. Approximately 725 illustrations. 128pp. 8⅜ x 11¼. 27276-1 Pa. $11.95

THE 1912 AND 1915 GUSTAV STICKLEY FURNITURE CATALOGS, Gustav Stickley. With over 200 detailed illustrations and descriptions, these two catalogs are essential reading and reference materials and identification guides for Stickley furniture. Captions cite materials, dimensions and prices. 112pp. 6½ x 9¼. 26676-1 Pa. $9.95

EARLY AMERICAN LOCOMOTIVES, John H. White, Jr. Finest locomotive engravings from early 19th century: historical (1804–74), main-line (after 1870), special, foreign, etc. 147 plates. 142pp. 11⅜ x 8¼. 22772-3 Pa. $10.95

THE TALL SHIPS OF TODAY IN PHOTOGRAPHS, Frank O. Braynard. Lavishly illustrated tribute to nearly 100 majestic contemporary sailing vessels: Amerigo Vespucci, Clearwater, Constitution, Eagle, Mayflower, Sea Cloud, Victory, many more. Authoritative captions provide statistics, background on each ship. 190 black-and-white photographs and illustrations. Introduction. 128pp. 8⅞ x 11¾. 27163-3 Pa. $13.95

EARLY NINETEENTH-CENTURY CRAFTS AND TRADES, Peter Stockham (ed.). Extremely rare 1807 volume describes to youngsters the crafts and trades of the day: brickmaker, weaver, dressmaker, bookbinder, ropemaker, saddler, many more. Quaint prose, charming illustrations for each craft. 20 black-and-white line illustrations. 192pp. 4⅝ x 6. 27293-1 Pa. $4.95

VICTORIAN FASHIONS AND COSTUMES FROM HARPER'S BAZAR, 1867–1898, Stella Blum (ed.). Day costumes, evening wear, sports clothes, shoes, hats, other accessories in over 1,000 detailed engravings. 320pp. 9⅜ x 12¼. 22990-4 Pa. $14.95

GUSTAV STICKLEY, THE CRAFTSMAN, Mary Ann Smith. Superb study surveys broad scope of Stickley's achievement, especially in architecture. Design philosophy, rise and fall of the Craftsman empire, descriptions and floor plans for many Craftsman houses, more. 86 black-and-white halftones. 31 line illustrations. Introduction 208pp. 6½ x 9¼. 27210-9 Pa. $9.95

THE LONG ISLAND RAIL ROAD IN EARLY PHOTOGRAPHS, Ron Ziel. Over 220 rare photos, informative text document origin (1844) and development of rail service on Long Island. Vintage views of early trains, locomotives, stations, passengers, crews, much more. Captions. 8⅞ x 11¾. 26301-0 Pa. $13.95

THE BOOK OF OLD SHIPS: From Egyptian Galleys to Clipper Ships, Henry B. Culver. Superb, authoritative history of sailing vessels, with 80 magnificent line illustrations. Galley, bark, caravel, longship, whaler, many more. Detailed, informative text on each vessel by noted naval historian. Introduction. 256pp. 5⅜ x 8½. 27332-6 Pa. $7.95

TEN BOOKS ON ARCHITECTURE, Vitruvius. The most important book ever written on architecture. Early Roman aesthetics, technology, classical orders, site selection, all other aspects. Morgan translation. 331pp. 5⅜ x 8½. 20645-9 Pa. $8.95

THE HUMAN FIGURE IN MOTION, Eadweard Muybridge. More than 4,500 stopped-action photos, in action series, showing undraped men, women, children jumping, lying down, throwing, sitting, wrestling, carrying, etc. 390pp. 7⅞ x 10⅝. 20204-6 Clothbd. $25.95

TREES OF THE EASTERN AND CENTRAL UNITED STATES AND CANADA, William M. Harlow. Best one-volume guide to 140 trees. Full descriptions, woodlore, range, etc. Over 600 illustrations. Handy size. 288pp. 4½ x 6⅜. 20395-6 Pa. $6.95

SONGS OF WESTERN BIRDS, Dr. Donald J. Borror. Complete song and call repertoire of 60 western species, including flycatchers, juncoes, cactus wrens, many more–includes fully illustrated booklet. Cassette and manual 99913-0 $8.95

GROWING AND USING HERBS AND SPICES, Milo Miloradovich. Versatile handbook provides all the information needed for cultivation and use of all the herbs and spices available in North America. 4 illustrations. Index. Glossary. 236pp. 5⅜ x 8½. 25058-X Pa. $6.95

BIG BOOK OF MAZES AND LABYRINTHS, Walter Shepherd. 50 mazes and labyrinths in all–classical, solid, ripple, and more–in one great volume. Perfect inexpensive puzzler for clever youngsters. Full solutions. 112pp. 8⅛ x 11. 22951-3 Pa. $4.95

PIANO TUNING, J. Cree Fischer. Clearest, best book for beginner, amateur. Simple repairs, raising dropped notes, tuning by easy method of flattened fifths. No previous skills needed. 4 illustrations. 201pp. 5⅜ x 8½. 23267-0 Pa. $6.95

A SOURCE BOOK IN THEATRICAL HISTORY, A. M. Nagler. Contemporary observers on acting, directing, make-up, costuming, stage props, machinery, scene design, from Ancient Greece to Chekhov. 611pp. 5⅜ x 8½. 20515-0 Pa. $12.95

THE COMPLETE NONSENSE OF EDWARD LEAR, Edward Lear. All nonsense limericks, zany alphabets, Owl and Pussycat, songs, nonsense botany, etc., illustrated by Lear. Total of 320pp. 5⅜ x 8½. (USO) 20167-8 Pa. $6.95

VICTORIAN PARLOUR POETRY: An Annotated Anthology, Michael R. Turner. 117 gems by Longfellow, Tennyson, Browning, many lesser-known poets. "The Village Blacksmith," "Curfew Must Not Ring Tonight," "Only a Baby Small," dozens more, often difficult to find elsewhere. Index of poets, titles, first lines. xxiii + 325pp. 5⅝ x 8¼. 27044-0 Pa. $8.95

DUBLINERS, James Joyce. Fifteen stories offer vivid, tightly focused observations of the lives of Dublin's poorer classes. At least one, "The Dead," is considered a masterpiece. Reprinted complete and unabridged from standard edition. 160pp. 5$\frac{3}{16}$ x 8¼. 26870-5 Pa. $1.00

THE HAUNTED MONASTERY and THE CHINESE MAZE MURDERS, Robert van Gulik. Two full novels by van Gulik, set in 7th-century China, continue adventures of Judge Dee and his companions. An evil Taoist monastery, seemingly supernatural events; overgrown topiary maze hides strange crimes. 27 illustrations. 328pp. 5⅜ x 8½. 23502-5 Pa. $8.95

THE BOOK OF THE SACRED MAGIC OF ABRAMELIN THE MAGE, translated by S. MacGregor Mathers. Medieval manuscript of ceremonial magic. Basic document in Aleister Crowley, Golden Dawn groups. 268pp. 5⅜ x 8½. 23211-5 Pa. $8.95

NEW RUSSIAN-ENGLISH AND ENGLISH-RUSSIAN DICTIONARY, M. A. O'Brien. This is a remarkably handy Russian dictionary, containing a surprising amount of information, including over 70,000 entries. 366pp. 4½ x 6⅛. 20208-9 Pa. $9.95

HISTORIC HOMES OF THE AMERICAN PRESIDENTS, Second, Revised Edition, Irvin Haas. A traveler's guide to American Presidential homes, most open to the public, depicting and describing homes occupied by every American President from George Washington to George Bush. With visiting hours, admission charges, travel routes. 175 photographs. Index. 160pp. 8¼ x 11. 26751-2 Pa. $11.95

NEW YORK IN THE FORTIES, Andreas Feininger. 162 brilliant photographs by the well-known photographer, formerly with *Life* magazine. Commuters, shoppers, Times Square at night, much else from city at its peak. Captions by John von Hartz. 181pp. 9¼ x 10¾. 23585-8 Pa. $12.95

INDIAN SIGN LANGUAGE, William Tomkins. Over 525 signs developed by Sioux and other tribes. Written instructions and diagrams. Also 290 pictographs. 111pp. 6⅛ x 9¼. 22029-X Pa. $3.95

ANATOMY: A Complete Guide for Artists, Joseph Sheppard. A master of figure drawing shows artists how to render human anatomy convincingly. Over 460 illustrations. 224pp. 8⅜ x 11¼. 27279-6 Pa. $10.95

MEDIEVAL CALLIGRAPHY: Its History and Technique, Marc Drogin. Spirited history, comprehensive instruction manual covers 13 styles (ca. 4th century thru 15th). Excellent photographs; directions for duplicating medieval techniques with modern tools. 224pp. 8⅜ x 11¼. 26142-5 Pa. $12.95

DRIED FLOWERS: How to Prepare Them, Sarah Whitlock and Martha Rankin. Complete instructions on how to use silica gel, meal and borax, perlite aggregate, sand and borax, glycerine and water to create attractive permanent flower arrangements. 12 illustrations. 32pp. 5⅜ x 8½. 21802-3 Pa. $1.00

EASY-TO-MAKE BIRD FEEDERS FOR WOODWORKERS, Scott D. Campbell. Detailed, simple-to-use guide for designing, constructing, caring for and using feeders. Text, illustrations for 12 classic and contemporary designs. 96pp. 5⅜ x 8½. 25847-5 Pa. $2.95

SCOTTISH WONDER TALES FROM MYTH AND LEGEND, Donald A. Mackenzie. 16 lively tales tell of giants rumbling down mountainsides, of a magic wand that turns stone pillars into warriors, of gods and goddesses, evil hags, powerful forces and more. 240pp. 5⅜ x 8½. 29677-6 Pa. $6.95

THE HISTORY OF UNDERCLOTHES, C. Willett Cunnington and Phyllis Cunnington. Fascinating, well-documented survey covering six centuries of English undergarments, enhanced with over 100 illustrations: 12th-century laced-up bodice, footed long drawers (1795), 19th-century bustles, 19th-century corsets for men, Victorian "bust improvers," much more. 272pp. 5⅜ x 8¼. 27124-2 Pa. $9.95

ARTS AND CRAFTS FURNITURE: The Complete Brooks Catalog of 1912, Brooks Manufacturing Co. Photos and detailed descriptions of more than 150 now very collectible furniture designs from the Arts and Crafts movement depict davenports, settees, buffets, desks, tables, chairs, bedsteads, dressers and more, all built of solid, quarter-sawed oak. Invaluable for students and enthusiasts of antiques, Americana and the decorative arts. 80pp. 6½ x 9¼. 27471-3 Pa. $8.95

HOW WE INVENTED THE AIRPLANE: An Illustrated History, Orville Wright. Fascinating firsthand account covers early experiments, construction of planes and motors, first flights, much more. Introduction and commentary by Fred C. Kelly. 76 photographs. 96pp. 8¼ x 11. 25662-6 Pa. $8.95

THE ARTS OF THE SAILOR: Knotting, Splicing and Ropework, Hervey Garrett Smith. Indispensable shipboard reference covers tools, basic knots and useful hitches; handsewing and canvas work, more. Over 100 illustrations. Delightful reading for sea lovers. 256pp. 5⅜ x 8½. 26440-8 Pa. $7.95

FRANK LLOYD WRIGHT'S FALLINGWATER: The House and Its History, Second, Revised Edition, Donald Hoffmann. A total revision—both in text and illustrations—of the standard document on Fallingwater, the boldest, most personal architectural statement of Wright's mature years, updated with valuable new material from the recently opened Frank Lloyd Wright Archives. "Fascinating"—*The New York Times*. 116 illustrations. 128pp. 9¼ x 10¾. 27430-6 Pa. $11.95

PHOTOGRAPHIC SKETCHBOOK OF THE CIVIL WAR, Alexander Gardner. 100 photos taken on field during the Civil War. Famous shots of Manassas Harper's Ferry, Lincoln, Richmond, slave pens, etc. 244pp. 10⅝ x 8¼. 22731-6 Pa. $9.95

FIVE ACRES AND INDEPENDENCE, Maurice G. Kains. Great back-to-the-land classic explains basics of self-sufficient farming. The one book to get. 95 illustrations. 397pp. 5⅜ x 8½. 20974-1 Pa. $7.95

SONGS OF EASTERN BIRDS, Dr. Donald J. Borror. Songs and calls of 60 species most common to eastern U.S.: warblers, woodpeckers, flycatchers, thrushes, larks, many more in high-quality recording. Cassette and manual 99912-2 $9.95

A MODERN HERBAL, Margaret Grieve. Much the fullest, most exact, most useful compilation of herbal material. Gigantic alphabetical encyclopedia, from aconite to zedoary, gives botanical information, medical properties, folklore, economic uses, much else. Indispensable to serious reader. 161 illustrations. 888pp. 6½ x 9¼. 2-vol. set. (USO) Vol. I: 22798-7 Pa. $9.95
Vol. II: 22799-5 Pa. $9.95

HIDDEN TREASURE MAZE BOOK, Dave Phillips. Solve 34 challenging mazes accompanied by heroic tales of adventure. Evil dragons, people-eating plants, blood-thirsty giants, many more dangerous adversaries lurk at every twist and turn. 34 mazes, stories, solutions. 48pp. 8¼ x 11. 24566-7 Pa. $2.95

LETTERS OF W. A. MOZART, Wolfgang A. Mozart. Remarkable letters show bawdy wit, humor, imagination, musical insights, contemporary musical world; includes some letters from Leopold Mozart. 276pp. 5⅜ x 8½. 22859-2 Pa. $7.95

BASIC PRINCIPLES OF CLASSICAL BALLET, Agrippina Vaganova. Great Russian theoretician, teacher explains methods for teaching classical ballet. 118 illustrations. 175pp. 5⅜ x 8½. 22036-2 Pa. $5.95

THE JUMPING FROG, Mark Twain. Revenge edition. The original story of The Celebrated Jumping Frog of Calaveras County, a hapless French translation, and Twain's hilarious "retranslation" from the French. 12 illustrations. 66pp. 5⅜ x 8½. 22686-7 Pa. $3.95

BEST REMEMBERED POEMS, Martin Gardner (ed.). The 126 poems in this superb collection of 19th- and 20th-century British and American verse range from Shelley's "To a Skylark" to the impassioned "Renascence" of Edna St. Vincent Millay and to Edward Lear's whimsical "The Owl and the Pussycat." 224pp. 5⅜ x 8½. 27165-X Pa. $4.95

COMPLETE SONNETS, William Shakespeare. Over 150 exquisite poems deal with love, friendship, the tyranny of time, beauty's evanescence, death and other themes in language of remarkable power, precision and beauty. Glossary of archaic terms. 80pp. 5³⁄₁₆ x 8¼. 26686-9 Pa. $1.00

BODIES IN A BOOKSHOP, R. T. Campbell. Challenging mystery of blackmail and murder with ingenious plot and superbly drawn characters. In the best tradition of British suspense fiction. 192pp. 5⅜ x 8½. 24720-1 Pa. $6.95

THE INFLUENCE OF SEA POWER UPON HISTORY, 1660–1783, A. T. Mahan. Influential classic of naval history and tactics still used as text in war colleges. First paperback edition. 4 maps. 24 battle plans. 640pp. 5⅜ x 8½. 25509-3 Pa. $12.95

THE STORY OF THE TITANIC AS TOLD BY ITS SURVIVORS, Jack Winocour (ed.). What it was really like. Panic, despair, shocking inefficiency, and a little heroism. More thrilling than any fictional account. 26 illustrations. 320pp. 5⅜ x 8½. 20610-6 Pa. $8.95

FAIRY AND FOLK TALES OF THE IRISH PEASANTRY, William Butler Yeats (ed.). Treasury of 64 tales from the twilight world of Celtic myth and legend: "The Soul Cages," "The Kildare Pooka," "King O'Toole and his Goose," many more. Introduction and Notes by W. B. Yeats. 352pp. 5⅜ x 8½. 26941-8 Pa. $8.95

BUDDHIST MAHAYANA TEXTS, E. B. Cowell and Others (eds.). Superb, accurate translations of basic documents in Mahayana Buddhism, highly important in history of religions. The Buddha-karita of Asvaghosha, Larger Sukhavativyuha, more. 448pp. 5⅜ x 8½. 25552-2 Pa. $12.95

ONE TWO THREE . . . INFINITY: Facts and Speculations of Science, George Gamow. Great physicist's fascinating, readable overview of contemporary science: number theory, relativity, fourth dimension, entropy, genes, atomic structure, much more. 128 illustrations. Index. 352pp. 5⅜ x 8½. 25664-2 Pa. $8.95

ENGINEERING IN HISTORY, Richard Shelton Kirby, et al. Broad, nontechnical survey of history's major technological advances: birth of Greek science, industrial revolution, electricity and applied science, 20th-century automation, much more. 181 illustrations. ". . . excellent . . ."–*Isis*. Bibliography. vii + 530pp. 5⅜ x 8¼. 26412-2 Pa. $14.95

DALÍ ON MODERN ART: The Cuckolds of Antiquated Modern Art, Salvador Dalí. Influential painter skewers modern art and its practitioners. Outrageous evaluations of Picasso, Cézanne, Turner, more. 15 renderings of paintings discussed. 44 calligraphic decorations by Dalí. 96pp. 5⅜ x 8½. (USO) 29220-7 Pa. $4.95

ANTIQUE PLAYING CARDS: A Pictorial History, Henry René D'Allemagne. Over 900 elaborate, decorative images from rare playing cards (14th–20th centuries): Bacchus, death, dancing dogs, hunting scenes, royal coats of arms, players cheating, much more. 96pp. 9¼ x 12¼. 29265-7 Pa. $11.95

MAKING FURNITURE MASTERPIECES: 30 Projects with Measured Drawings, Franklin H. Gottshall. Step-by-step instructions, illustrations for constructing handsome, useful pieces, among them a Sheraton desk, Chippendale chair, Spanish desk, Queen Anne table and a William and Mary dressing mirror. 224pp. 8⅛ x 11¼. 29338-6 Pa. $13.95

THE FOSSIL BOOK: A Record of Prehistoric Life, Patricia V. Rich et al. Profusely illustrated definitive guide covers everything from single-celled organisms and dinosaurs to birds and mammals and the interplay between climate and man. Over 1,500 illustrations. 760pp. 7½ x 10⅛. 29371-8 Pa. $29.95

Prices subject to change without notice.

Available at your book dealer or write for free catalog to Dept. GI, Dover Publications, Inc., 31 East 2nd St., Mineola, N.Y. 11501. Dover publishes more than 500 books each year on science, elementary and advanced mathematics, biology, music, art, literary history, social sciences and other areas.

AUTOBIOGRAPHY: The Story of My Experiments with Truth, Mohandas K. Gandhi. Boyhood, legal studies, purification, the growth of the Satyagraha (nonviolent protest) movement. Critical, inspiring work of the man responsible for the freedom of India. 480pp. 5⅜ x 8½. (USO)   24593-4 Pa. $8.95

CELTIC MYTHS AND LEGENDS, T. W. Rolleston. Masterful retelling of Irish and Welsh stories and tales. Cuchulain, King Arthur, Deirdre, the Grail, many more. First paperback edition. 58 full-page illustrations. 512pp. 5⅜ x 8½.   26507-2 Pa. $9.95

THE PRINCIPLES OF PSYCHOLOGY, William James. Famous long course complete, unabridged. Stream of thought, time perception, memory, experimental methods; great work decades ahead of its time. 94 figures. 1,391pp. 5⅜ x 8½. 2-vol. set.
Vol. I: 20381-6 Pa. $12.95
Vol. II: 20382-4 Pa. $12.95

THE WORLD AS WILL AND REPRESENTATION, Arthur Schopenhauer. Definitive English translation of Schopenhauer's life work, correcting more than 1,000 errors, omissions in earlier translations. Translated by E. F. J. Payne. Total of 1,269pp. 5⅜ x 8½. 2-vol. set.
Vol. 1: 21761-2 Pa. $11.95
Vol. 2: 21762-0 Pa. $12.95

MAGIC AND MYSTERY IN TIBET, Madame Alexandra David-Neel. Experiences among lamas, magicians, sages, sorcerers, Bonpa wizards. A true psychic discovery. 32 illustrations. 321pp. 5⅜ x 8½. (USO)   22682-4 Pa. $8.95

THE EGYPTIAN BOOK OF THE DEAD, E. A. Wallis Budge. Complete reproduction of Ani's papyrus, finest ever found. Full hieroglyphic text, interlinear transliteration, word-for-word translation, smooth translation. 533pp. 6½ x 9¼.
21866-X Pa. $10.95

MATHEMATICS FOR THE NONMATHEMATICIAN, Morris Kline. Detailed, college-level treatment of mathematics in cultural and historical context, with numerous exercises. Recommended Reading Lists. Tables. Numerous figures. 641pp. 5⅜ x 8½.
24823-2 Pa. $11.95

THEORY OF WING SECTIONS: Including a Summary of Airfoil Data, Ira H. Abbott and A. E. von Doenhoff. Concise compilation of subsonic aerodynamic characteristics of NACA wing sections, plus description of theory. 350pp. of tables. 693pp. 5⅜ x 8½.   60586-8 Pa. $14.95

THE RIME OF THE ANCIENT MARINER, Gustave Doré, S. T. Coleridge. Doré's finest work; 34 plates capture moods, subtleties of poem. Flawless full-size reproductions printed on facing pages with authoritative text of poem. "Beautiful. Simply beautiful."—*Publisher's Weekly.* 77pp. 9¼ x 12.   22305-1 Pa. $6.95

NORTH AMERICAN INDIAN DESIGNS FOR ARTISTS AND CRAFTSPEOPLE, Eva Wilson. Over 360 authentic copyright-free designs adapted from Navajo blankets, Hopi pottery, Sioux buffalo hides, more. Geometrics, symbolic figures, plant and animal motifs, etc. 128pp. 8⅜ x 11. (EUK)   25341-4 Pa. $8.95

SCULPTURE: Principles and Practice, Louis Slobodkin. Step-by-step approach to clay, plaster, metals, stone; classical and modern. 253 drawings, photos. 255pp. 8⅛ x 11.
22960-2 Pa. $11.95

THE WIT AND HUMOR OF OSCAR WILDE, Alvin Redman (ed.). More than 1,000 ripostes, paradoxes, wisecracks: Work is the curse of the drinking classes; I can resist everything except temptation; etc. 258pp. 5⅜ x 8½.   20602-5 Pa. $5.95

SHAKESPEARE LEXICON AND QUOTATION DICTIONARY, Alexander Schmidt. Full definitions, locations, shades of meaning in every word in plays and poems. More than 50,000 exact quotations. 1,485pp. 6½ x 9¼. 2-vol. set.
Vol. 1: 22726-X Pa. $16.95
Vol. 2: 22727-8 Pa. $16.95

SELECTED POEMS, Emily Dickinson. Over 100 best-known, best-loved poems by one of America's foremost poets, reprinted from authoritative early editions. No comparable edition at this price. Index of first lines. 64pp. 5³⁄₁₆ x 8¼.
26466-1 Pa. $1.00

CELEBRATED CASES OF JUDGE DEE (DEE GOONG AN), translated by Robert van Gulik. Authentic 18th-century Chinese detective novel; Dee and associates solve three interlocked cases. Led to van Gulik's own stories with same characters. Extensive introduction. 9 illustrations. 237pp. 5⅜ x 8½.   23337-5 Pa. $6.95

THE MALLEUS MALEFICARUM OF KRAMER AND SPRENGER, translated by Montague Summers. Full text of most important witchhunter's "bible," used by both Catholics and Protestants. 278pp. 6⅝ x 10.   22802-9 Pa. $12.95

SPANISH STORIES/CUENTOS ESPAÑOLES: A Dual-Language Book, Angel Flores (ed.). Unique format offers 13 great stories in Spanish by Cervantes, Borges, others. Faithful English translations on facing pages. 352pp. 5⅜ x 8½.
25399-6 Pa. $8.95

THE CHICAGO WORLD'S FAIR OF 1893: A Photographic Record, Stanley Appelbaum (ed.). 128 rare photos show 200 buildings, Beaux-Arts architecture, Midway, original Ferris Wheel, Edison's kinetoscope, more. Architectural emphasis; full text. 116pp. 8¼ x 11.   23990-X Pa. $9.95

OLD QUEENS, N.Y., IN EARLY PHOTOGRAPHS, Vincent F. Seyfried and William Asadorian. Over 160 rare photographs of Maspeth, Jamaica, Jackson Heights, and other areas. Vintage views of DeWitt Clinton mansion, 1939 World's Fair and more. Captions. 192pp. 8⅞ x 11.   26358-4 Pa. $12.95

CAPTURED BY THE INDIANS: 15 Firsthand Accounts, 1750-1870, Frederick Drimmer. Astounding true historical accounts of grisly torture, bloody conflicts, relentless pursuits, miraculous escapes and more, by people who lived to tell the tale. 384pp. 5⅜ x 8½.   24901-8 Pa. $8.95

THE WORLD'S GREAT SPEECHES, Lewis Copeland and Lawrence W. Lamm (eds.). Vast collection of 278 speeches of Greeks to 1970. Powerful and effective models; unique look at history. 842pp. 5⅜ x 8½.   20468-5 Pa. $14.95

THE BOOK OF THE SWORD, Sir Richard F. Burton. Great Victorian scholar/adventurer's eloquent, erudite history of the "queen of weapons"—from prehistory to early Roman Empire. Evolution and development of early swords, variations (sabre, broadsword, cutlass, scimitar, etc.), much more. 336pp. 6⅛ x 9¼.
25434-8 Pa. $9.95